STRANGE & MYSTERIOUS ANOMALIES

MYTHS, CONSPIRACIES, DISCREPANCIES AND OUT OF PLACE OBJECTS

"The most beautiful thing we can experience is the mysterious. It is the source of all true art and science."

Albert Einstein

IAN ROSS VAYRO

Joshua Books
JoshuaBooks.com

All correspondence to the publisher
Joshua Books
PO Box 1668
Buddina 4575
Queensland Australia

First Printed 2008

Category: Hidden Mysteries: Paranormal: Title: Author

ISBN 978 0 9804551 8 2

Cover Picture: The cover picture depicts a rare phenomenon called 'Fire Rainbow' - the rarest of all naturally occurring atmospheric phenomena. This picture was captured in August 2007 on the Idaho/Washington border and the event lasted about an hour. For Fire Rainbow to occur, clouds have to be Cirrus and up at least 20,000 feet holding just the right amount of ice crystals and the sun lightning them at an angle of precisely 58 degrees.
This creates the stunning effect shown here.

"Man's ignorance ain't cause he ain't ever learned nutten;
It's cause he learned too many things that jes' ain't so."

Henry Wheeler Shaw's character Uncle Josh Billings.

Did you notice as a youngster, as I did, that when friends got together at parties or functions, the conversation often turned to things esoteric and mysterious, from re-hashing urban myths to the old colonial ghost stories. In these re-tellings, it was not always necessary to let the truth get in the way of a good story and actually, an entertaining storyteller was always the centre of attention at a bush barbeque or other event. Since ancient times man has struggled to understand the abnormalities that plagued his universe. He sought order in his life and dependability in the structure of his beliefs. A miraculous dimension of angels and demons was sometimes employed to explain the things that could not be otherwise explained, to help find stability and meaning to this life. In time, the drawing mystery of ghost stories moved on to the Yowie, UFO's, Crop Circles and other mysteries until today these are again being replaced with 'conspiracy theory' tales such as who shot JFK in 1963, the fate of Princess Diana in 1997 or what happened at the WTC on 9/11, 2001.

I have long held an interest in the mysterious and am pleased to now research some of these anomalies and record a fascinating new compendium of mystifying, thrilling and entertaining stories from Australia and abroad. Some of these chapters involve my personal experiences, some have explanations, some do not, but all are there to bemuse and fascinate the reader. Many stories revolve around Bible theology because I am, after all, a theological archaeologist with daily involvement in this area, but there's lots of other stuff as well. This book takes the form of short chapters, pretty much unrelated to one another, and I hope readers find this format entertaining but also enlightening reading. Let these selected stories take you on a journey into the amazing, the mysterious and the unexplained.

"Truth is so hard to tell, it sometimes needs fiction to make it plausible."

Sir Francis Bacon

What would possess an artist of the early 1500s to paint the Christ babe playing with a toy helicopter?

Baby Jesus with Helicopter!

In these European paintings, *'The Virgin and Child in a Landscape'*, attributed to Dutch painter Jan Provoost (1491-1529) and the French work *'Madonna & Child'* from 1460, one can clearly see baby Jesus playing with a cord-spun helicopter. In the work of Provoost, the extensive and detailed background landscape is typical of the Netherlands painting style of the timeframe. Experts say both paintings are genuine and date from the late 1400s. The concept of the spinning propeller top (helicopter) supposedly dates from the later 16th century and is thought to be Chinese in origin. I have no idea what these paintings might be trying to convey. Just possibly the blades of the helicopter were perceived as a cross and it became a devotional toy. If this is not the case, then we would need to ascertain why the artists chose to include the helicopter toy in their work and where they became acquainted with this concept. Why they would then backdate this device to the time of Christ in their paintings is a complete mystery.

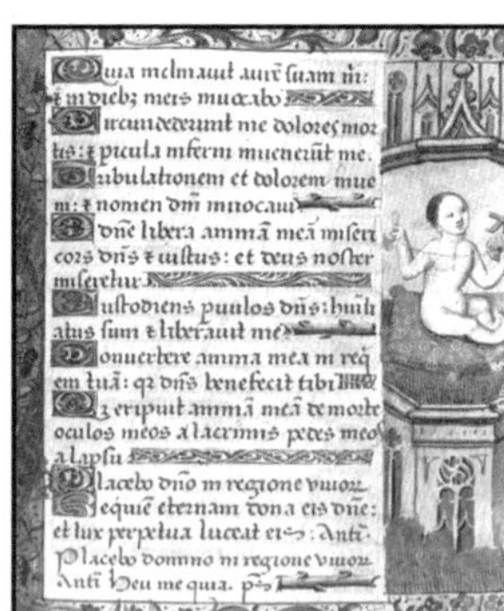

French painting 'Madonna and Child' from the year 1460, depicts the Madonna and child, but again shows baby Jesus playing with a helicopter toy. Amazingly, the concept of the Christ babe playing with a cord spun helicopter toy, is repeated on this intricate, Bible page. Glorification of Christ through such a toy is not an idea that comes naturally to a modern mind ...

This book is dedicated to Rene

"We must not allow ourselves to become like the system we oppose. We cannot afford to use methods of which we will be ashamed when we look back, when we say, ... we shouldn't have done that."

Desmond Tutu (1931-)

CONTENTS

CHAPTER ONE

OLD AUSTRALIAN YARNS

'If ever you come across anyone who claims to have spent time on the Speewah or met Crooked Mick, listen to them with deep respect, for they will be a prodigious liar.'

Bill Wannan

Crooked Mick of the Speewah

Australian stories of Crooked Mick and the sheep station called the Speewah first came to public notice in the *Australian Worker* in the early 1920s, when a writer named Julian Stuart commenced finally putting the verbal traditions in print. Stuart was a former shearer who had been involved in the 1891 Shearers' Strike and he documented the fireside yarns that had been very popular in the shearing sheds in those troubled times. In the Australian 'bush' the pioneers had to make their own entertainment and a good yarn spinner was always welcome at any camp. Many Australian bushmen have mastered the art of 'pulling your leg', which means telling a ridiculous story with a straight face, pretending to be deadly serious as if every part was completely true. An entertaining bushman can tell a crimson lie with more fluency than the average person can tell the truth casually and they would boast about the size of the stations they had worked on, exaggerate the number and size of the sheep they shore and the crook tucker and the tough conditions they had endured.

Storytellers found it hilarious to exaggerate these things out of all proportion and hence, *'Crooked Mick'* on *'The Speewah'* became an Australian mythical icon and was often used in bragging competitions. His exaggerated exploits also served to very effectively counter skites and boasters. Whatever the boaster had done, Crooked Mick would somehow have done it bigger and better. Hey! Mick was the very best at everything he undertook; he was the best shearer, the best fencer, the best tracker, he could ride anything with hair and broke in horses before breakfast. He would jump bulls over fences and once roped a whole herd of cattle with one rope. He was so strong they said he had used Ayers Rock to stone the crows. When Mick was born, it took a whole squadron of giant storks flapping like mad, to deliver the baby to his parents. He cut his teeth on an ironbark stump and grew so fast that after two weeks he had to wear his dad's clothes. His father tried to retard his growth by ring-barking both his legs. This didn't work, but it did give him a bit of a limp - hence the name *Crooked Mick!*

America too, had a mythical frontier hero called Paul Bunyan, and writer Daniel Hoffman suggested: *'The exploits of a national hero – particularly of mythical personage – are always clues to the character of the people who celebrate him. He embodies their ideals of personal conduct, their ethical code, their goals; although super-human, he is created in the image of human aspirations, and his preternatural strength helps men to ward off human fears.'* (1) This, of course, is also true of the Australian Speewah stories where work ethic was paramount and every man had hidden aspirations to be a 'ringer' and gain widespread respect and acclaim. In Australian folklore yarns, however, there was an additional entertainment element of sardonic humour and the inbuilt instrument to put down 'greenhorns' or boasters. Perhaps to a greater degree than their American cousins, they also needed to reduce the potency of bush hardships encountered daily. This created a sort of bravado that reduced their tolerance to amateurs and newcomers to the bush. This was later reflected in the adaptability and resourcefulness of the Australian digger of World Wars I and II. To playfully tease or 'send up' a greenhorn visitor with elaborate local tales was considered first-rate sport for Aussie bushmen. In the absence of a foil or target for these tales, the yarn spinner would grossly down play the incredibly harsh bush landscape, by attributing much worse conditions being the norm on the Speewah where, of course, he had worked and likely his father before him.

'You blanks call this hot!' he would say, *'When we wuz on the Speewah it*

was so hot, the billies would melt, the stockmen had to wear asbestos hats and the chooks laid hard boiled eggs." Thus would commence the story, as the yarn spinner explained to his receptive audience that, in the northern part of the Speewah, it could get so hot, that freezing point had to be re-set to 99 degrees. The droughts were so severe that the inhabitants considered themselves lucky when they could put water in their tea again. It was the complete opposite on the south side though. There it was so cold that the horses had to be defrosted each morning before you could put their saddles on, and at times words would freeze as they came out of your mouth, so your mate had to thaw them by the campfire before he could hear what you had said. The last flood was so bad that all the fish drowned and the dogs were kept busy herding the sheep into the upper branches of the taller trees. After the flood subsided, the mud was a bit of a problem. Riding around the sheep one day, Mick spied a decent looking felt hat lying on the ground and stooped to retrieve it. *'Hang on mate'*, came an Aussie drawl, *'I've still got the chin strap on'*. Mick strained harder with no luck, when the voice spoke again, *'It's no use, I carn't get me feet out of the bloody stirrups.'*

Crooked Mick was a big man and his clothes had to be made out of wool bales. It took a monstrous big bullock hide to make him a pair of boots. He ate two sheep each meal, three if they were weaners, about a bushel of potatoes, plus three loaves of bread, a tin of plum jam, two dozen eggs washed down with a couple of quarts of tea. Following his meal, Mick used small trees for toothpicks. It was said that the Speewah lay west of the sunset, out where the crows fly backwards, to keep the dust out of their eyes so they could see where they'd been. Dust storms were so thick on the Speewah that you could walk over them. Once they even built a new shearing shed on one. Many stories specifically focused on conveying to the listener the enormous size of the Speewah. When the boss sent a man to close the front gate to the station, he had to take a month's rations and a jackeroo who went to bring the horses in from the house paddock was gone for a week. One day a wiry old man on horseback came into the Speewah asking to re-stock his rations. He was as tough as a Mallee root and explained that he was the son of the young boundary rider they had sent out to check the boundary fence a while back. He asked, *'How's the war going?'*. The cook was aghast and told him the war had been over for many years. *'Who won?'* drawled the old man quietly. *'Well ... we did'*, stated the cook shaking his head. *'Great!'* exclaimed to old timer, *'Queen Victoria will be pleased, she never did like them Boers!'*

Since shearers compiled many of the original tales, it was said that the sheep on the Speewah station were the biggest in Australia. In fact, it usually took three good men using step ladders just to shear one. A good fleece would fill a wool bale. Crooked Mick, though, was a helluva shearer and the ringer at every shed. He worked so hard and fast that he kept a roustabout busy putting ice cubes in a bucket to cool down his shears. At times the roustie couldn't keep up and the water boiled, so Mick would make a quick cuppa and get right back to work again. Unfortunately, though, when Mick was at top speed, he could be just a tad rough, with bits of sheep – blood, skin and ears, flying in every direction! One morning the boss came down and seeing the rough shearing, screamed at Mick, *'You're bloody well fired!'* Mick was shearing so fast that before he could stop he'd shorn another fifteen sheep! [(2)] The shearing shed on the Speewah was so long the boss on the board did his inspections on a motor bike and often he couldn't cover the length in a day. Any cagey shearer he sacked would just step over the other side and start work again. Feeding all the men could be a bit of a challenge though. When the cook made a billy of tea for the thirsty shearers, he had to row out in a boat to dump in a chest of tea and a couple of bags of sugar. He used a circular saw to cut up the brownie. When Mick wasn't shearing he'd help out the fencers, cutting brigalow posts with an axe in each hand to get more done. When digging postholes he had the crowbar in one hand and the shovel in the other to save a bit of time. In a month he'd wear a shovel down to the nail hole and wear out a crowbar till it looked like a darning needle. He had learned bush skills from the black trackers. The native bloke he learned from could track a sand-fly across Sturt's Stony Desert and Mick wasn't far behind him. Tracking sheep across the dry ground was not even a challenge.

The biggest flock of Galahs ever recorded in Australia, was on the Speewah in the 1930s when the drought broke. They were startled by a loud thunderclap and took flight. The galahs were so thick that not a drop of rain hit the parched ground for two days. Mick's nephew, a lad of 12 had never seen rain before and promptly fainted at the sight. Mick had to throw two shovelfuls of dust over him to bring him round. The galahs had been giving the harvest a bit of a caning, and the boss asked Crooked Mick to do something about it. Mick located a large tree where the birds would roost each night and coated the limbs and branches with a strong batch of bird lime (a sort of glue). Well, it worked like a charm, and next morning the birds were all firmly stuck to the tree. Mick was creeping up on them, when he trod on a twig from one of the broken branches. It made a loud snapping noise like a shotgun and alarmed the flock. They all tried to take off at once, and pulled the tree up by the roots. Within minutes, it was about half a mile high with a slight lean to the left and heading south.

Truthful Lewis was a Speewah stockman and since he would never tell a lie we can be sure all the stories here are true. Truthful told about the time three prospectors had an accident when their dynamite safe blew up, burning them badly and spilling all their guts out. They couldn't wait for the Flying Doctor so a message was sent to Mick who was killing sheep for the cookhouse at the time. Mick had to act quickly; he wrapped the fresh sheep skins around the worst of the burns, inserted the sheep's guts and sewed each of the men up with a bag needle and twine. *'But surely they couldn't have lived!'* asked one of the mob. *'Course they lived'*, said Truthful, *'at shearing time, we got a good clip off all three and if yer wanna know, one lambed next spring'.*

Mick's best mate was Big Bill, who made his fortune on the Broken Hill goldfields cutting up mining shafts and selling them in the rough country, as post holes. The red-headed, Bluey the Cook was sometimes assisted by Big Bill's sister, a sweet girl called Gentle Annie who baked sponge cakes so light they had to be chained down so they didn't float away. The blokes loved Annie and wanted her to permanently replace Greasy George, the cooks slushy who had been dispensing indigestion for a season or two. He was a man so greasy that when you tried to look at him square on, your eyes slipped off. To give him his due though, Greasy tried hard to vary the men's diet away from mutton every meal and experimented with galahs, since these birds were so readily available. He shot a few and tried to roast them, boil them, grill them, fry them, marinade them and even bake them in a pie, but they always came out too tough to eat. He asked the old campaigner, Bluey the Cook, if he knew a recipe for galah. *'Yer cun pick from two'* said Bluey knowingly. *'The first one, yer place the galah and a large stone in a pot and boil it until the stone goes soft; then throw away the galah and eat the stone. The other way is to work on the galah with a hoof rasp from the farrier and then make soup out of the shavings.'*

Crooked Mick himself was considered a bit of a gourmet chef and the bush folk would ride for a week just to sample one of his pies. (3) This cuisine created a bit of an enigma because the Speewah had both the *best* and the *worst* tucker in the country. A bushman in a rough camp would exclaim, *'You blokes call this crook tucker? When we wuz drovin' on the Speewah, the chops was so bad they wuz, fair dinkum - crawling!'*

'Crawling?' someone would question.

'Yeah crawling; we had to tie them up at night so they didn't take the track. If we ever forgot to tie them up, they'd go on the wallaby and we'd have to send the dogs to round them up'.

The station bullocky, Slab-face Joe, drove a team so long that he communicated with the Aboriginal lad who rode the lead bullock, by telephone. One day he got a wrong number, (an Indian telemarketer, I think) ... and the team went 6 miles out of their way. There was another woman on the Speewah called Prickly Pear Polly who was a notoriously plain woman with a foul temper. She looked like a ladder with a dress on and had nagged three husbands to death. There were days a man took his life in his hands if he even opened his mouth near her. When she hit hard times after the death of her last husband, one of the local cockys called Alby, gave her a job as a scarecrow in an attempt to save his crop. A few days later a neighbor asked him, *'Alby, how's Polly going? Is she scaring them cockatoos at all?' 'Good Lord, is she scaring 'em?'* echoed Alby, *'I've got birds bringing back corn they stole six months back'.*

There were also giant rabbits on the Speewah, as large as sheep, and they were thick on the ground. You had to pull a few out of the burrows to get the ferrets in, and knock them out of the way with a stick, just to set your traps. The crows were like condors and the kangaroos said to be as tall as elephants. The emus laid eggs so large that men blew them and used the shells for line huts. *'If the centipedes are as big as snakes out here'*, a new chum Jackeroo asked Mick one morning, *'then how big are the snakes?'* Mick tilted his hat forward and scratched the back of his head a bit, considering the question. *'Don't rightly know,'* he said at last, *'I spotted the tail of one in the bush the other morning*

early… and had to ride until smoko looking for the sharp end.' Another time Mick came face to face with a giant Speewah boar. *'He was coming straight at me'*, Mick recalled the next day, *'I fired the last bullet I had but it didn't stop him. I ran a little way down the track 'til I reached a tree. It had a good-sized branch about twenty feet up. I made a mighty jump for it … and missed!'*
'Well what happened then', asked one of the listeners when Mick paused.
'I caught it on the way back down, didn't I', explained Mick.

One time Mick decided to get together a football team and have a Shearers verses Roustabouts match. If it was successful, he would pick a combined team and challenge the adjoining stations to a match. His boys were tough enough but just couldn't get their heads around the rules. Training sessions against each other were like a controlled brawl with the ball and the scoring, just incidental. Mick could see that this tactic wasn't going to work so to promote more discipline, he lined up some 44 gallon oil drums to represent the other team so his shearers could get stuck into training. At half time the drums were leading 12 – Nil, so they gave the idea away altogether and went to the pub. My word! They could drink beer out there, just to clear the dust out of their throats, you understand. The local pub served it in buckets and a dozen largies was just a sociable drink at Mick's place. His visitors had to ride their horse's home; they were usually too drunk to walk!

The Speewah mozzies were a decent size too. They were known to lift the covers off the beds to bite the unfortunate sleepers. Sometimes, they would steal dogs and would even get in a group and cart off a horse when they were really hungry! One of Mick's visitors had heard these tales and was totally petrified. Just on dusk, he heard the whining approach and ducked inside a water tank, pulling a hatch cover over to protect himself. There was total panic inside the tank, when he heard the mossies discussing whether to eat him there, or take him home. When mossie barbs started to penetrate the tank, he quickly bent them over with his boots, congratulating himself for trapping the angry insects by the stinger. Before long though, the tank was airborne and headed west giving the scared visitor the flight of his life. I know the size of these mossies is true from my Air Force days because during a particularly bad wind storm late one Friday evening, three Speewah mosquitoes landed at the Darwin R.A.A.F. base. The Duty Crew aircraft refuelers were a bit tired after a tough week but they got thirty thousand litres of Avgas into them before they realised what was happening.

Now this next bit is quite serious and important to remember for those considering a visit to Australia. Foreigners and city dwellers may not be aware of the very dangerous Australian 'Drop Bears'. Fair dinkum, mate, those things are well worth avoiding and last year alone, at least four Pommie backpackers were taken by Drop Bears. Even Crooked Mick reckoned there was little chance of escaping the big ones on the Speewah if they landed on you. Now, Crooked Mick had the laziest dog in Australia but it saved him once from a Drop Bear. The Bear dropped on the unfortunate dog but as there was no reaction at all it must have assumed the dog was already dead. With a stump-splitting oath, Crooked Mick pulled his knife and was on it, but Mick only ever did it once and the end result wasn't worth eating. Anyway, back to Mick's lazy dog ...the moment Crooked Mick would whistle to *'Get round behind!'* the dog froze and was actually pronounced dead on more than one occasion by station vets! One season a plover made its nest on his back and was able to raise the chicks before that dog bothered to shake itself!

The mythical Speewah was so ingrained in Australian folklore that many unsuccessful attempts have been made to locate this mysterious, larger than life community. Its boundaries have never really been satisfactorily defined and it seems the Speewah can be anywhere that the storyteller wants it to be. Tales have it situated anywhere from Cape York to the Otways, from Brisbane to Broome. Perhaps its location is deliberately kept ambiguous since, when questioned, people from different regions of Australia will give a different direction, from the never-never land to somewhere further out. The men from the Darling Ranges said it was 'back o' Bourke' and the men of Bourke said it was 'way out west'. Some said it was situated so far west that the sun there sets in the east. The men of the west pointed to Queensland and the Queenslanders told you it was way beyond the black stump, just a bit past Woop Woop.

Far North Queensland actually boasts a real Speewah about 10 kilometres west of Cairns - a few kilometres south of Kuranda. This was the home of the Veivers boys and they were tough men too. An old timer called Mac once lived there and told me some stories about this mob. One of these Speewah boys was bitten on the finger by a snake, so he grabbed his gun, blew the finger off wrapped a hanky around it and went back to work. Another time the boys came into Comino's Café in Kuranda and Jack Veivers ordered a large steak with a dozen eggs. Not to be outdone, his brother ordered two steaks and two dozen eggs. They sat down and ate the lot, to the amazement of the Camino Café cook. A portion of land owned by an old retired drover named Jim Dillon, south-west of Wyndham, in the north of Western Australia was also named after the mythical land and this property still appears on today's maps as 'The Speewah'. There are also supposed Speewah locations in Victoria (actually it wouldn't fit) and on the New South Wales/South Australian border.

In modern times, these wonderful old yarns have all but disappeared for the younger generation. Today's heroes are no longer hard working, hard riding men with a tough work ethic and a desire to excel. With so many other options for entertainment readily available, gone is the classic bush storyteller and even the actual requirement for the larger than life Crooked Mick and the Speewah. Unfortunately, these old Australian legends are in danger of becoming lost forever. [4] Nevertheless, those who still remember must concede: They were tough men on the Speewah!

CHAPTER TWO

OUT OF PLACE OBJECTS

'... after you have eliminated the impossible, what remains, no matter how improbable, must be the truth.'

Sherlock Holmes

What This Section is Not

John Williams was out hiking on a date best know to himself, in a location that is not disclosed and supposedly discovered the rock pictured below. He stated on the web:

> ***"My Rock's material is solid natural quartz and feldspar granite (very little observed mica; I am not a Geologist) - not an accretion, concretion or pumice - does not contain any resins, cements, glues, limestone, mortar, or other non-granite binding agents - is very hard, is estimated to be at least 100,000 years old, and has embedded in it an electrical-like component (I assume to be a connector of some sort) ... For fear of ridicule and Government and skeptics harassment and possible persecution of my family and I, to rip-off or destroy my Rock and discredit me, and also to give me the time to try to find some manmade explanation for it, I quietly and secretly held on to it for several years ... Only last year, after I had exhausted my efforts to find a modern man made duplicate of my Rock or its component, did I decide to get it professionally and objectively evaluated, and took the risks of exposing it to the public for that purpose."***

An obvious fake using an old rock and a rectifier vacuum tube.

This has to be absolute rubbish! With all due respect to John Williams, who just possibly could have been duped himself by this obvious fraud, I can duplicate this easily myself. Just take a selected rock preferably 100 thousand years old, core drill it with a rock drill and tap in an old four pin vacuum tube base, possibly a rectifier valve from the appearance. You can see the obvious core drilling in the photo and if you look carefully you can even locate the diamond shaped brand on the base of the vacuum tube. In addition William's verbalization is nonsensical. He kept it a secret because 'they' might steal his rock and victimize him and his family but several years later it's quite OK to reveal it, so here it is. The time in the interim was supposedly used to *'search for a man-made duplicate'*. Are you kidding me! This is a very earthly artefact and an obvious fraud and this is not what this chapter is about. Certainly, we can all be fooled but I have tried hard to eliminate all such spurious items and to present only the genuinely strange and mysterious objects that have been found over time. There are an abundance of these and no need whatever to resort to deliberately fraudulent items.

Creatures Locked in Coal & Stone

There have been quite a number of reports of frogs, toads and more than one lizard found inside rocks and lumps of coal - most still living in a hibernated state but quickly revived once exposed to the air. This is of course quite impossible but these creatures have been found with the stone appearing to be an exact mould of their bodies with even the texture of the skin imprinted on the rock or coal. This has to mean that somehow the rock or coal solidified around the hibernating creature. Coal was supposedly formed before the time of the dinosaurs, hundreds of millions of years ago in the Carboniferous Period of the Paleozoic Era.

Many stories from Africa tell of mud solidifying around hapless crocodiles who are not freed until the next monsoon rains but we would believe that their hibernation would be something like 6 months and probably no more than 1 year. Frogs are known to hibernate in mud for months at a time but we would think there is absolutely no logical way a frog or toad could hibernate long enough for coal or rock to form around them. The creature would then have to survive for millennia without food or water to be released in our current era. We would all think that this is quite impossible but the problem is that however improbable, it has happened repeatedly!

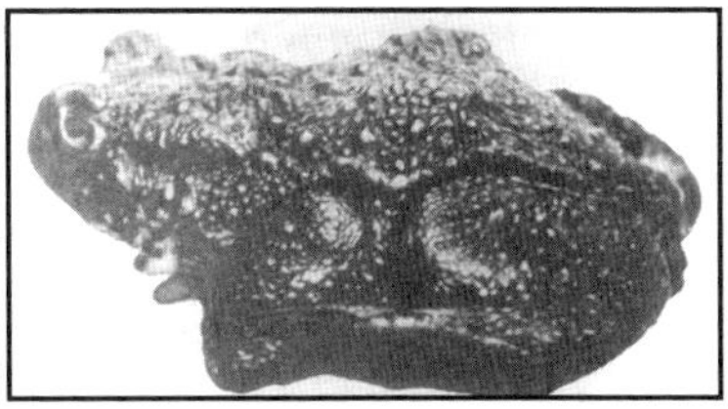

The live toad that surprised Mr. Rugby.

Imagine for a moment you had loaded a lump of coal into your fireplace, when the piece broke open and out hopped a live toad.

This happened to Mr. W. J. Clarke of Rugby, Warwickshire, England in 1901.[(5)] The toad's mouth had grown over and after no nourishment for 5 weeks on release, it died. Another similar event was reported in the U.K. in 1865 when workmen were excavating for the Hartlepool waterworks and freed a living toad from a block of limestone. This event was covered by the two local newspapers and other papers across the country. The *Leeds Mercury* reported that the toad has suffered no ill-effects and was living in the possession of Mr. S. Horner, president of the Natural History Society. Although it had some problems breathing on release and was making little barking noises through its nostrils, it was now, *'in as lively a state as when found'*. The *Hartlepool Free Press* and the *Stockton and Hartlepool Mercury* both reported that on 7th April 1865, this live toad had been discovered by workmen digging twenty-five feet (nearly eight metres) below ground level. The following is one of those reports:

> ***"We have often heard of frogs being found at fabulous depths in petrified cells of solid rock; but until yesterday (Thursday) have had no really well authenticated case brought before us. Yesterday forenoon a quarryman named William Ashmore who has been for some years in the service of Mr. James Yeal, of Hartlepool, while at work in the Dyke-House quarry, near West Hartlepool, brought to light and liberty the little wonder. It is apparently a full-grown toad.***
>
> ***The block from which it was released was a huge irregular mass recently dislodged from the magnesium limestone stratum which is now being quarried for ordinary building purposes, and the particular fracture which liberated his toadship was made at a point upwards of eight feet from any spring water vein, twelve feet from the upper surface of the stratum, and some twenty five feet from the upper surface of the soil. The toad, when first released, was of a pale colour, and not readily distinguishable from the stone from which a lucky stroke of the hammer set him free, and the place in***

> ***which he had lain was no larger than his body and presented the appearance of being an exact cast of it.***
> ***There was no trace near of any recent fissure, or other means of communicating with the open air. Very shortly after the toad was out, his colour got darker and darker, until the prevailing [shade] was of fine olive brown; the eyes opened, the pupils clear and bright, with a circumference of golden bistre of peculiar beauty; the nostrils got to work freely, as if re-testing the long-excluded atmosphere. The creature emitted frequent and loud sounds ... In the charge of his captor, he has since paid a visit to the Mercury office, and, we are given to understand, is likely to follow up his scientific tour and probably close his earthly career among the treasures of the District Natural History Society."*** (6)

Now this report suggests that the readers had 'often' heard of frogs being released from petrified cells of solid rock in that Durham -Yorkshire region and in fact, three reports of similar events in 1833, 1835 and 1849 are contained in the '*Local Records of Northumberland and Durham, 1833 to 1866*', edited by T. Fordyce. Whilst it seems there are a number of reports from this coal bearing region of the U.K., further reports come from other parts of Europe, America and South Africa. It is interesting that many of the discoveries were during the 19th century and this probably coincides with digging of coal mines and railway cuttings being done by hand at that time. Heavy digging is done by mechanical diggers today, with no one close enough to the coal or rock face to observe if an animal of this size should emerge.

A first hand report in the magazine '*The Unexplained*', by M. Laver of Horndean, Hampshire, told of wartime quarrying operations in Algeria in 1943 in which he was involved. This group were quarrying stone to make roads and to fill in bomb craters. M. Laver tells of finding a lizard and a large toad both very much alive after rock was cracked open with explosives. Amazingly the animals were released from rock 6 metres from the surface and again there were no cracks, fissures or inlets leading to the cavity. (7)

I wonder if many people ever considered a strange Bible anomaly in Genesis 1 : 28 '*And God blessed them, and said unto them, be fruitful, and multiply, and replenish the earth...*' It doesn't say '*populate*' the Earth; it says '*replenish*' as if this is not the first time around. Manmade objects and even human remains have been found in coal and rock - in places where they plainly should not be. This indicates we may be replenishing the Earth and certainly gives us something to think about. It would also seem that our early ancestors knew more about the sciences, about nature and about the universe, than our conventional academia believes they should have.

- In 1853, a horned lizard found alive in solid rock was sent to the Smithsonian Institute in Washington by Judge Houghton of New Mexico but once released the reptile only lived for two days. [8]
- Geologist, Dr. Edward D. Clarke, mentioned in a lecture at Cambridge University that he had discovered some unusual newts amongst fossils in a chalk quarry at a depth of 270 feet. To his absolute amazement, three of the 'fossilized' newts laid out on a sheet of paper in the sun began to move. In time, two died but the third was so lively that Dr. Clarke placed it in a pond where it immediately swam away. According to Dr. Clarke the rejuvenated newts belonged to an apparently extinct species unknown to science. [9]
- A fossilized human skull was found in coal that was sold in Germany in the mid -1800s.
- A jawbone of a child was found in coal in Tuscany in 1958.
- In 1812, on the Caribbean island of Guadeloupe, a human skeleton was found, lacking the head and feet, inside very ancient and extremely hard limestone, which was part of a formation over a mile in length.
- In 1876, a human skull was found in the *'2 million year old'* Pliocene strata. It was certified as completely mineralized and is now known as the *'Caveras skull'*. Dozens of stone mortars, bowls, and other man made artefacts were found near this skull, 130 feet below ground level.
- A group of ancient human skulls were found in Castinedolo, Italy, and these *'Castinedolo skulls'* along with the *'Caveras Skull'* (above), are considered among the most ancient human skulls yet found. Way outside what Darwinists would expect, these are all perfectly human with no apelike attributes at all.
- Perhaps the geological books will need to be re-written regarding the formation of rock since the discovery of the two *'Moab Skeletons'*. These were found in cretaceous rock (supposedly dated at 100 million

years old) in Moab, Utah, about 15 feet below the surface. Both skeletons were definitely human and appeared ancient but it would be impossible to accept a similar age to the rock strata. They had been undisturbed till they were found but when tested for age, they were apparently only a few thousand years old. [10]

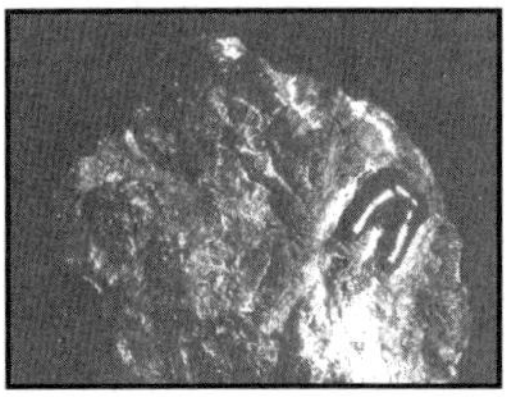

A tooth in a lump of Coal from the Bearcreek Mine.

- Two human molars were found in Bearcreek Mine, Montana in 1926 by Dr. J.C.F. Siegfriedt.
- A human leg was found by a West Virginia coal miner firmly enveloped in a seam of coal. The leg must have been very ancient as it had been almost entirely turned to coal.
- In 1891, a lady in Illinois found a gold chain in a chunk of coal which broke open leaving two lumps joined by the chain, firmly embedded in each. There was absolutely no sign of fraud.
- A small steel cube was found in a block of coal in Austria in1885, its purpose or origins entirely unknown.
- A woman found a child's spoon in coal in 1937.

This exquisitely worked vessel was hurled from a bed of rock during blasting.

- A very elaborate engraved vessel made of an unknown metal alloy with silver inlays was found in solid rock in Dorchester, Massachusetts in 1851 during blasting. The vessel was depicted in Scientific American 7:298 on 5th Jun 1852 with the only opinion to its manufacture expressed by the editor that perhaps it had been made by the Biblical metallurgist, Tubal-Cain. The artifact's current whereabouts is now unknown.
- The mold of a metal screw was found in a chunk of feldspar in1851.

Just as baffling is the case of an iron pot found in a block of coal. According to an affidavit made by Frank J. Kenwood: *"While I was working in the Municipal*

Electric Plant in Thomas, Oklahoma, in 1912, I came upon a solid chunk of coal which was too large to use. I broke it with a sledge hammer. This iron pot fell from the center, leaving the impression or mold of the pot in the piece of coal...I traced the source of the coal and found that it came from the Wilburton, Oklahoma, Mine'. According to Robert O. Fay of the Oklahoma Geological Survey, the coal in the Wilburton mine is about 312 million years old. (11)

The Chinese *Lanzhou Morning News* of 26th June 2002 featured the following news item about another screw thread, dispatched by reporters Bao Feng and HaiZhu Tian: *"Coinciding with our recent inspiring series reports on a visit to the 'E.T. relics', an uncommon stone from a collector in Lanzhou drew enormous attention from many experts and collectors. The stone is imbedded with a screw-threaded metal bar and is suspected of being from outer space ... Mr. Zhilin Wang found this stone on a field research trip to the Mazong Mountain area located on the border of Gansu and Xijiang provinces. The pear-shaped stone is extremely hard and has a mysterious black color. It is about 8 x 7 cm and weighs 466 grams. The most surprising part of the stone is the imbedded 6 cm cone-shaped metal bar which bears clear screw threads. This mysterious stone attracted enormous attention from many geologists and collectors. More than 10 geologists and global physicists from the National Land Resources Bureau of Gansu Province, Colored Metal Survey Bureau of Gansu Province, the Institute of Geology and Minerals Research of China Academy, Lanzhou Branch, and the School of Resources and Environment of Lanzhou College gathered to study the origin of this mysterious stone."* (12)

- An intricately carved and inlaid metal bowl was found in solid rock in1852.
- An iron nail was found in rock in a Peruvian mine by Spanish conquistadors in 1572.
- On 22nd June 1844, this curious report appeared in the *London Times*: *"A few days ago, as some workmen were employed in quarrying a rock close to the Tweed about a quarter of a mile below Rutherford-mill, a gold thread was discovered embedded in the stone at a depth of eight feet."* Dr. A. W. Medd of the *British Geological Survey* wrote in 1985 that this stone is of Early Carboniferous age between 320 and 360 million years old. We might ask; Just who dropped this gold thread

in the ancient fern forests in a distant time when the most advanced life forms on the planet were supposedly amphibians and insects?

- A communication from Sir David Brewster in 1845, described how a nail had been found in a block of stone from Kingoodie Quarry, in the north of Britain. The stone block in which the nail was found was nine inches thick. The quarry had been worked for about twenty years and consisted of alternate layers of hard stone and a substance called 'till'. The point of the nail, quite eaten with rust, projected from the stone into a layer of till. The rest of the nail lay along the surface of the stone with just an inch from the head actually embedded in the stone.
- The *London Times*, December 1851 reported: *"Hiram De Witt, of Springfield, Mass. dropped a piece of auriferous quartz about the size of a man's fist. It split open and there was found inside a cut-iron nail, slightly corroded and the size of a six-penny nail. It was entirely straight and had a perfect head."*
- In Whiteside County, Illinois, two copper artefacts, a hook and a ring, were brought up during the drilling of a well from a sand stratum 120 feet deep. The stratum was dated at 150,000 years old.
- While digging a cellar under his property in 1936, a resident of Plateau City (near Grand Junction, Colorado, USA) discovered a floor at a depth of 3 metres (ten feet) that consisted of tiles set in mortar. The tiles were apparently dated at between 20,000 and 80,000 years old and lay in a 25 million year old Miocene geological stratum. [13]
- What would appear to be a spark plug was located in 1961 by Mike Mikesell of Olancha, California, when he ruined a diamond saw blade cutting open a geode. The geode had been collected by Mike along with Wally Lane and Virginia Maxey, his partners in *'L M & V Rockhounds Gem and Gift Shop'.* The site was in the Coso Mountains, six miles northeast of Olancha overlooking the dry bed of Owens Lake. In 1963 the item was displayed in the Eastern California Museum in Independence, California and was later offered for sale.

The inordinate amount of digging carried out during the California gold rush of the mid 1800s yielded many out of place objects. These findings were mostly uncovered from gold-bearing rock or gravel:

- A prehistoric mining shaft, more than 210 feet below the surface carved from solid rock was found.
- An ancient mortar for grinding gold ore was found at a depth of 300 feet in a mining tunnel.
- The plainly impossible discovery of a human skull was found at a depth of 130 feet under five beds of lava and tufa.
- Ancient bones of camels, rhinoceroses, hippopotami, horses, and other animals were also found in California. (14)

As if to beggar belief, man-made markings have been discovered on petrified wood. We would reasonably assume that petrified wood would need to be quite ancient, yet somehow discoveries have been found where humans have worked the wood prior to its solidification. Hand-worked petrified wood was found in India that had quite obviously been shaped prior to fossilization. Several petrified pieces had been hacked with a cutting tool. The wood was dated to the Pliocene Epoch, before humans were supposed to have lived.

- At a site near Paris, France, fossilized rhinoceros bones had human cutting marks on them which appeared to be record keeping. No rhinos have been in Europe in recorded history and the fossilized bones would have to be very ancient.
- Another rhino bone, cut by a sharp tool, was found in Ireland. (15)

Out of Place Objects

A number of ancient copper alloy coins were found 114 feet below the surface at Lawn Ridge, 20 miles north of Peoria, Illinois in August 1870 with no explanation how they possibly could have got there. Three men were drilling an artesian well when, from a depth of over a hundred feet, the pump brought up a metal coin to the surface. One of the workmen, Jacob W. Moffat, from Chillicothe, discovered the first 'coin' in the drill residue. A noted scholar of the time, Professor Alexander Winchell, reported in his book, *'Sparks From a Geologist's Hammer'*, that he received a detailed statement dated 4th December 1871 concerning the layers encountered at various depths during the drilling process. Another eye-witness, W. H. Wilmot confirmed that this helped to precisely identify the depths from which the metal coins were uncovered.

The coins (or medallions) were remarkably uniform in thickness, perfectly round and the edges appeared to have been stamped or cut. Researcher William E. Dubois of the Smithsonian Institute, presented his investigation to the American Philosophical Society, and was convinced that the edges showed *'evidence of the machine shop'.* Both sides of the medallion were marked with artwork and hieroglyphs, but these had apparently not been metal-engraved or stamped but rather, the figures had somehow been etched in acid, to a remarkable degree of intricacy. Dubois concluded that one coin in particular could only have been made in a modern machine shop. Noting its uniform thickness, he said the coin must have *"passed through a rolling mill, and if the ancient Indians had such a contrivance, it must have been pre-historic."* (16) The Illinois State Geological Survey estimates the deposits at 114 feet deep were formed *"sometime between 200,000 and 400,000 years ago."*

The discoverer, Moffat, reported to the Smithsonian that other anomalous objects had been found whilst drilling in nearby Whiteside County, Illinois. At a depth of 120 feet, workmen discovered, *"a large copper ring or ferrule, similar to those used on ship spars at the present time... They also found something fashioned like a boat-hook."* Moffat concluded that: *"There are numerous instances of relics found at lesser depths. A spear-shaped hatchet, made of iron, was found embedded in clay at 40 feet, and stone pipes and pottery have been unearthed at depths varying from 10 to 50 feet in several localities."*

A hammer was found in Germany, encased in, (according to geologists) *'100 million year old rock'*, which has formed around it. What makes this more amazing is that the hammer was made from an alloy of iron which is fairly new technology yet it is encased in rock at least a few thousand years old. The handle had become very hard petrified crystal with an intact structure and the find simply cannot be explained.

Antikythera Mechanism

Mystery still surrounds a device salvaged from an ancient Roman shipwreck by a Greek sponge diver named Elias Stadiatis, who reported the find in April of 1900. On 17th May 1901, archaeologist Valerios Stais was shown what appeared to be an encrusted piece of rock recovered from the site by Stadiatis and noted that it had a bronze gear wheel embedded in it. Further examination revealed that the artefact was a heavily encrusted and corroded bronze mechanism of 37 gear wheels, dials, clock-like hands and a wooden and bronze casing bearing ancient Greek inscriptions. It was now in three main parts with dozens of smaller fragments.

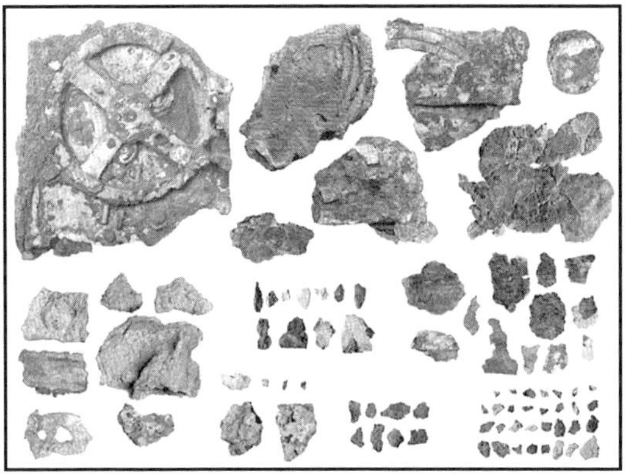

The Antikythera Mechanism salvaged from a Roman ship wrecked in 85 B.C.E.

The recovered device has astounded scientists since subsequent investigation in 2006, have dated the device, with a fair degree of certainty, to times B.C.E. This is further confirmed by the fact that the Roman ship sank in 65 B.C.E. en route from the Greek island of Rhodes to Rome. Now known as the Antikythera mechanism, its uncannily accurate planetary gear system is now known to be part of an ancient mechanical calculator designed to compute astronomical positions and likely used in ancient times as a very precise navigational aid. In addition, the device utilizes a differential gear, which was previously believed to have been invented in the 16th century. The level of miniaturization and complexity of its parts is comparable to that of the most intricate 18th-century clocks.

The case was inscribed with a text of over 3,000 Greek characters that describe how to set up the instrument and how to utilize it for celestial observations and calculations. For these it utilizes the Sun and the planets such as Aphrodite (Venus) and Hermes (Mercury). It could also predict any alignment of planets and eclipses and could even re-create the irregular orbit of the Moon. The erratic motion of the Earth's moon, was observed by the astronomer *Hipparchus of Rhodes* in the 2nd century B.C.E. and it could be speculated that he may have been consulted or involved in the machine's construction. [17]

Professor Michael Edmunds, a physicist at Cardiff University U.K. who along with Tony Freeth, led the study of the mechanism, stated: *"This device is just extraordinary, the only thing of its kind. The design is beautiful, the astronomy is exactly right. The way the mechanics are designed just makes your jaw drop.*

Whoever has done this has done it extremely carefully … in terms of historic and scarcity value, I have to regard this mechanism as being more valuable than the Mona Lisa." The device now rests in the National Archaeological Museum of Athens, accompanied by a working reconstruction made and offered to the museum by Derek de Solla Price. How this technology was available in times B.C.E. is simply astounding.

Stone Balls

In the 1930s hundreds of stone balls came to light in the Diquis Delta of Costa Rica. They ranged in size from a few centimetres to over two metres in diameter and were more than 300 in number. The stones are made of granodiorite, a hard igneous stone, and weigh up to 16 tons. Today, many have been removed to decorate official buildings, hospitals and schools. One is in the museum of the National Geographic Society in Washington, D.C. and another is displayed in a courtyard near the Peabody Museum of Archaeology and Ethnography at Harvard University in Cambridge, Massachusetts. (18) Dr. Samuel Lothrop and his wife investigated these artefacts in the 1940s. The objects are unequivocally man made chipped and sanded from boulders and their purpose is entirely unknown. It is believed the stone was quarried at the mouth of the Diquis River, about 30 miles from their discovery point.

Painstaking hours were spent creating these amazing stone artifacts.

Without the chipped remnants and other artefacts, it is virtually impossible to date these objects and no technique exists for determining when they were shaped. Some were found above human graves. Perhaps they were items of worship and it was religious fervor that drove man to work with such patient precision, all day long in the hot sun, creating these amazing spherical balls for some special purpose … we simply don't know.

The Nazca monkey.

Nazca Lines

Located on a high arid plateau that stretches more than 80 kilometers between the towns of Nazca and Palpa on the *Pampas de Jumana* in Peru are found a series of geoglyphs depicting creatures such as a spaceman, a stylized monkey, spider, hummingbird, fish, shark, a particularly unusual llama and others. There are hundreds of individual figures, ranging in complexity from simple lines to ornate figures. They are believed to have been created by the Nazca culture between 200 B.C.E. and 700 A.D. by turning over or removing the iron oxide coated pebbles that litter the surface.

The Nazca drawings cannot be recognized as coherent figures except from the air so we have to question their purpose. Since it is presumed the Nazca people could never have seen their work from a high vantage point, there has been much speculation on the builders' motivation. Until recently we had no idea how, working from the ground, anybody could execute these figures in such perfect proportion; however, Joe Nickell of the University of Kentucky, has now reproduced, without aerial supervision, identical figures using the technology he believes was available to the Nazca Indians of that timeframe.

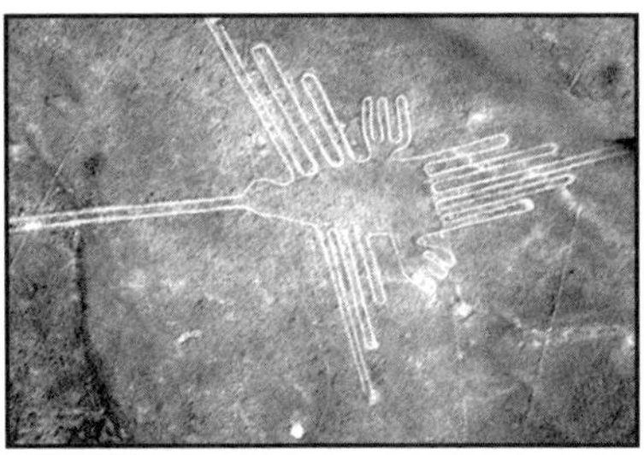

The Nazca hummingbird.

The spider depicted in the Nazca patterns has an extended leg that at first was thought to be artistic license within the drawing. The stylized spider is now thought to represent a member of the rare genus *Ricinulei*, which is only found in the most remote and inaccessible parts of the Amazon Jungle. With these creatures, one leg is noticeably longer, as it is a protrusible tube, and at its tip is the spider's reproductive organ, normally only visible with the aid of a microscope. Again we can but wonder, how, when, where and most particularly why would the primitive people venture into this desert wasteland and expel so much effort in capturing their depictions of nature that we can view all these years later. We simply have no idea!

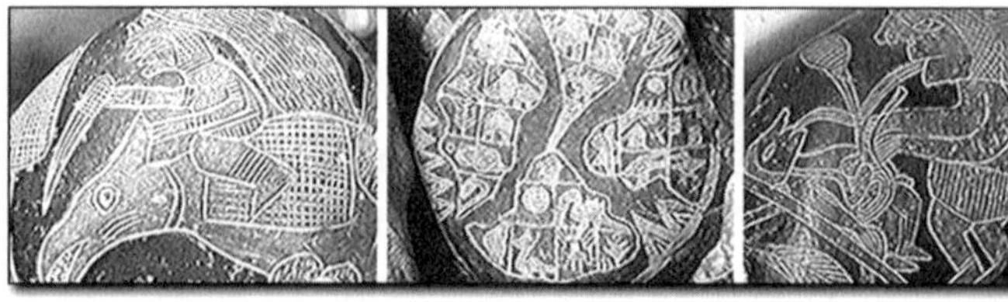

Impossible depictions on ancient carved stones.

The Ica Stones

In the 1960's, during flooding in a small town near the Nazca lines in Peru, the usually narrow Ica River eroded away its banks. As the water receded, hundreds of carved stones were revealed, with others deposited on the river bank. It is believed the stones were grouped in subterranean chambers. The local physician, Dr. Javier Cabrera noticed on one of the stones, a particular image of an extinct species of fish and sought out more of the stones. A local farmer provided him with dozens and dozens of the carved stones but it is not known if he found a cache on his farm or collected them from the river cutting. Over time the doctor collected a 'library'- of these stone enigmas.

Images on the Ica Stones show impossible depictions such as a human figure flying on the back of a Pteranodon, an astronomer viewing a comet through a telescope, a heart transplant operation and other advanced medical practices such as Caesarian surgery and blood transfusions, men hunting dinosaurs, an amazing global map showing the continents and several other activities that as yet, are not understood. Another appears to be the blueprint for the Nazca lines with the same images carved on the stone.

The sheer quantity of amazing Ica stones tender them unexplainable.

It is usual procedure, when seemingly impossible finds like this are made, for scientists to yell, "Fake!" The supposition of fraud, however, should be based on something more substantial than the need to be rid of unconventional evidence. Nevertheless, these stones are not just anomalies, they seem plainly impossible; yet around the world various archeological finds are continually being unearthed that do not fit into the conventional time-scale of pre-history. The fact that some of these carved stones were originally found centuries ago helps support their authenticity. A few of the stones were first seen and recorded by Father Simon, a Jesuit missionary who accompanied Pizarro to Ica in 1525 and it is recorded that a number of carved stones were taken back to Spain from South America in the 16th century. The proof that the stones are not a hoax, says Dr. Cabrera, is in their vast number. There are plainly too many stones for a single man, or even a collective of hoaxers to produce. Dr. Cabrera claims that the locals have now unearthed close to 50,000 stones and that they showed him a cave where there are another 100,000. Members of the scientific community have apparently decided that it would not look good on a resume to be involved with such an anomalous find and have not even attempted to date the stones. Meanwhile a large collection is housed in a warehouse in Ica, simply gathering dust.

So are the stones authentic? Can the preposterous be made plausible? These are actually not the first finds that depict dinosaurs and humans together but we must consider this concept highly unlikely. These artefacts simply defy conventional archeology. Depictions of intricate surgery and astrological instruments from ancient times are likewise considered highly improbable if not entirely impossible. That very negative though, could become a positive for the validity. If the stones are fakes, how could those known to have been located in the 1500s possibly depict heart transplants and Caesarian sections which were unheard of at that time. Nevertheless, with no scientific investigation attempted, no scientific dating in place and no record of the civilization who apparently carved the stones put forward, a reasonable person would probably have to conclude at this time that somehow the stones are a hoax.

Mystery Skulls

Another seemingly impossible find sits in London's Museum of Natural History and would appear to defy all conventional archeology and all common sense. The Kabwe skull (often known as 'Broken Hill Man' after the name of a nearby town) is supposedly a Paleolithic skull dated between 150,000 and 250,000 years old. It was excavated 17th June 1921 by a Swiss miner, Tom Zwiglaar, in a limestone cave in modern Zambia. This was the first early human fossil to be discovered in Africa and was sent to Arthur Smith Woodward

(1864-1944), who gave it the new species name *Homo rhodesiensis* (Rhodesian Man).

It is widely reported that this skull shows all the signs of a bullet hole on its left side. Opposite the hole, the cranium is said to be shattered, and reconstruction of the fragments by ballistics experts, indicates conclusively that the skull was smashed from the inside out, from the bullet wound. This is not entirely true because whatever caused the hole did not kill the man. The edges of the lesion have started to heal, so whatever caused the hole was not the cause of death and not many people survive a bullet in the brain. We must therefore conclude that the wound may be pathological, rather than a traumatic lesion. The healing of the skull bone makes it equally clear that someone could not have found an old skull and taken a pot shot at it with a rifle. If we can believe the evidence presented, the hole has been in the skull since antiquity and the cranial damage could not have been caused by an arrow or other weapon. The fact that the skull was excavated from a depth of 60 feet of mostly lead rock only deepens the mystery.

Many other abnormalities exist concerning human skulls. We have all likely heard of groups binding the head so the skulls grow long and pointed. Mutations and diseases can also account for deformed skull shapes but others simply will not fit into any known category. The discrepancy in size and shape among collections of skulls leads some to believe they are looking at the remains of a different species of man or in fact an alien being. Although various brain abnormalities have been cited to account for apparently deformed skulls, in the absence of specific diagnostic information, the finders often believe they have the skull of a 'star-man'. Who knows, possibly they do!

The Sumerians and Egyptians recorded that the Sky-Gods (Watchers) were not entirely immortal. Although these Gods had extreme longevity, the scribes reported, that these beings aged and died and were buried in special cemeteries set aside for them. The Egyptians recorded that these Gods came from *'Ta-Ur'* which means something like *'far off land'*. The Bible had this to say; *Jeremiah 4 : 16 "Make ye mention to the nations; behold, publish against Jerusalem, that Watchers come from a far country, and give out their voice against the cities of Judah."*

Crystal Skulls

Quartz masks were relatively common in various parts of the ancient world. A rare extraordinary, life sized, crystal 'skull' was, however, discovered in Belize (then British Honduras) in 1927 by the explorer F. A. (Mike) Mitchell-Hedges. He named it the *'Skull of Doom'*, and according to his 1954 book, *'Danger My Ally'*, the process of grinding down the solid rock crystal would have taken 150 years continuous work over a number of generations. He also suggests the chief priest of the Maya utilized the *Skull of Doom* for enforcement of law and order; and if a tribe member was sentenced to death with the skull; death invariably followed. We know that Australian Aborigines did something similar with 'bone pointing' and 'song chants'.

The artefact was found beneath the altar of an ancient Mayan Temple in the City of Lubaantum, by the daughter of Mitchell-Hedges on her 17th birthday. This causes critics to believe that the skull could have been 'planted' by her father during his excavations, as a surprise for her. This actually poses more questions than it answers and in no way addresses or discounts the amazing complexity of the crystal skull or how it was made. Myths from ancient times about stone softening substances and laser cutting tools are not so easily discounted when artefacts such as the *Skull of Doom* are encountered. Some criticism can be leveled at Mitchell-Hedges and his dating of the artefact to the Maya of 1600 B.C.E. a time thought to be well before the Maya were around. In addition the existence of the skull was not referenced until 1931 and we would question the reason for this. Arthur C. Clarke used an image of this bravura skull as a logo for his *'Mysterious World'* television series.

The British Museum holds another magnificent Crystal Skull, bought through the New York based jewelers, Tiffany & Company, in 1897. It was thought to be smuggled out of Mexico by a mercenary soldier but skeptics claim it was manufactured in Europe for which there appears to be no evidence except a desire to discredit the find.

The Mayan culture believed the creation of the world was by 'New Fire' and there was a requirement to repeat this process for each new era. It has been reasonably alleged that the skulls just may have been used in that ritual. It is factual that the sun's rays can be focused through the crystal skull and can be utilized to actually start a fire. Correctly positioned at midday, it would have been fairly easy for a Sharman to predict exactly when strategically placed tinder would catch fire. Religious reverence would have been directed towards an icon that could start the New Fire to usher in each new age, and the skulls would have been seen to possess God-like powers.

Wall of Polished Blocks

A firsthand account first published in Brad Steigers *'World's Before Our Own'* stated: *"In the year 1928, I, Atlas Almon Mathis, was working in coal mine No. 5, located two miles north of Heavener, Oklahoma. This was a shaft mine, and they told us it was two miles deep. The mine was so deep that they let us down in an elevator . . . They pumped air down to us, it was so deep."* After one particular blasting the miners came across what appeared to be some concrete blocks. Here is how Mathis himself described that incident: *"These blocks were 12-inch cubes and were so smooth and polished on the outside that all six sides could serve as mirrors. Yet they were full of gravel, because I chipped one of them with my pick, and it was plain gravel-concrete inside."*

Mathis continued; *"As I started to timber up the area, it caved in and I barely escaped. When I came back after the cave-in, a solid wall of these polished blocks was left exposed. About 100 to 150 yards farther down our air core, another miner struck this same wall, or one very similar."* The coal in the mine was probably carboniferous which, according to standard dating methods, would mean that the wall was at least 286 million years old. After this discovery, the mining company officials pulled the men out of the mine and forbade them to speak about what they had found. In a strange twist of fate the men were then sent to the Wilburton mine (mentioned previously). According to Mathis the miners there spoke of having found; *"a solid block of silver in the shape of a barrel ... with the prints of the barrel staves on it."* [(19)] Needless to say the valuable artefact 'disappeared' and was never subjected to evaluation.

Footprints We Leave Behind

'The American Journal of Science' reported that huge footprints, of a giant human wearing sandals, were found in 1882, during quarrying operations in a layer of sandstone in the yard of the State Prison, near Carson City, Nevada. The prints were from 18-20 inches long and about 8 inches wide. [(20)] This was

an amazing discovery but paled into insignificance compared to the following. It is thought perhaps man still holds memories from the time of the dinosaurs that we find reflected in our myths about dragons and monsters? It is plainly impossible that man has lived on the Earth for hundreds of millions of years since the time of the dinosaurs but some of these finds have no other tenable explanation. The only other explanation is equally implausible, that we are not the first tenants of this planet.

On 8th October 1922, *The New York Sunday American* ran a prominent feature by Dr. W. H. Ballou, who disclosed the following: *"...while he was prospecting for fossils in Nevada, John T. Reid, a distinguished mining engineer and geologist, stopped suddenly and looked down in utter bewilderment at a rock near his feet."* What Reid had actually stumbled on appeared to be a fossilized footprint. According to Ballou it was: *"apparently, a shoe sole which had turned into stone . . .there was the outline of at least two-thirds of it , and around this outline ran a well defined sewn thread which had, attached the welt to the sole. Further on there was another line of sewing".* He went on to describe, *"... an indentation, exactly such as would have been made by the bone of the heel rubbing upon and wearing down, the material of which the sole had been made."*

Reid took the fossil to New York where it was examined by a number of eminent scientists who agreed the find defied everything they had been taught. Their conclusions were unanimous: in effect, *"it was the most remarkable natural imitation of an artificial object they had ever seen."* The scientists were also agreed that the rock formation was Triassic in origin whilst Dr. W. D. Mathew of *The American Museum of Natural History* declared it a remarkable imitation, *"an absolute freak of nature."* The fact that the artefact was so far outside archaeological orthodoxy, it was apparent that no member of the established academy was going to risk his reputation and position by stating otherwise. Reid persisted and stated: *"I next got hold of a micro-photographer and an analytical chemist ... The micro-photo magnifications are twenty times larger than the specimen itself, showing the minutest detail of thread twist and warp, proving conclusively that the shoe sole is not a resemblance, but is strictly the handiwork of man. Even to the naked eye the threads can be seen distinctly. I will add that at least two geologists have admitted (privately) that the shoe sole is valid, a genuine fossilization in Triassic rocks."*(21) No matter how radical this artefact sounds, it is supported by another find that is equally baffling.

The Squashed Trilobite

In June 1968 William J. Meister an amateur fossil collector, discovered at Antelope Spring, 43 miles west of Delta, Utah, what appears to be the track of a human wearing a sandal. What is truly amazing about this discovery, however, is that the sandal print had crushed a living trilobite. Now trilobites were around 300-600 million years ago so any explanation at all within our current conventionally accepted ideas, is plainly impossible. Meister was accompanied by his wife and two daughters, and Mr. Francis Shape with his wife and two daughters. What sandal wearing biped could have crushed a trilobite hundreds of millions of years ago? The other alternate is just as obscure. Trilobites were small marine invertebrates, the ancestor of crabs and shrimps that became extinct some 280 million years ago. So ...what was a live trilobite doing, standing around waiting to be crushed by what is quite apparently a sandal wearing biped, apparently from the modern era?

Meister took the rock bearing the print to Dr. Melvin Cook, Professor of Metallurgy at the University of Utah, who directed him to the University Geology Department. He also alerted the local newspaper, *The Desert News,* and the artefact received worldwide coverage. In a subsequent news conference the Curator of the University of Utah's *Museum of Earth Science* stated: *There were no men 600 million years ago. Neither were there monkeys or bears or ground sloths to make pseudo-human tracks. What 'man-thing' could possibly have been walking about on this planet before vertebrates evolved?'* [(22)] There are simply no answers to explain finds like this and they can only make us wonder!

Atlantis

The legendary island of Atlantis is claimed to have existed in the Atlantic Ocean far to the west of the Pillars of Heracles (Hercules) known today as the Straits of Gibraltar. The story was mentioned by Plato about 350 B.C.E. when he described the island and its destruction in his dialogues, *'Timaeus'* and *'Kritias'*. All of the men mentioned in the dialogues, except for Timaeus, are known to have actually existed in ancient Greece, and records of their lives and deeds have been located in other writings from the time. Ancient Greek historical records tell us a man called Kritias was the son of Dropides and great-grandfather of the Kritias of the Dialogues. This Kritias was said to be the great-grandfather of Plato.

There is much written about Atlantis today including considerable channeled material and a lot of supposition. It becomes difficult to remember that the only 'real' evidence we have regarding Atlantis is the few lines of hearsay penned by Plato, who claimed that the story was told to the Greek statesman Solon of Athens, in 600 B.C.E. by the Egyptian Priests and relayed to him via the characters he mentions. At the time Solon was considered to be the wisest man in the world. Plato's own disciple and student, Aristotle, was the first of many critics who claimed that Atlantis was an invention that came from the fertile mind of Plato, to augment his dream of a 'perfect society'. Since then various Atlantis sites have been promulgated, each with its own believers and devotees, but the reality is we have insufficient evidence to categorically postulate any location. Even if we locate an underwater City, regardless of its location, it does not necessarily mean we have found Atlantis.

We should also question why a hundred and fifty years later, Herodotus of Halicarnassus (ca. 484 BC – ca. 425 BC), the Greek *'Father of History'* appears to have heard nothing about the mythical island. Herodotus spent many months in Egypt, in deep discourse with the priests, and yet made no mention whatever of Atlantis in his work. Herodotus did write about a mountain, Mount Atlas, which he located at the westernmost part of Africa, a place he believed to be the western edge of the world. Mount Atlas, he claimed, was *"a peak so high that its top was never seen"*, inhabited by a vegetarian race who *"see no dreams in their sleep"*. This, of course, is a fallacy and no such mountain exists in that location. Even if it did exist this could not be construed to refer to Atlantis. The passion to prove Atlantis as factual has led many researchers to folly. Herodotus also stated that Sardinia was the largest known island in the world whereas Plato described Atlantis as a *huge* island making any chance of Herodotus referring to Atlantis, whimsical at best.

Some believe it is possible that a Mayan manuscript just could change all that. The pictograms on this ancient document are exceedingly clear but the meanings are still obscure. An eminent ethnographer, Brasseur de Bourbourge, claimed back in 1869 that he had deciphered the script and it tells of the

This Mayan document was claimed to record the annihilation of two entire countries.

annihilation of two entire countries, some millennia before. They were rocked by earth tremors and suddenly disappeared in the night along with the 64 million inhabitants. Archaeologists have re-kindled interest in Bourbourge's translation and with better facilities such as code busting computers, the document just may give up more secrets.

Another theorist who places Atlantis in the Atlantic is Maurice Chatelain, a brilliant French space engineer who worked with NASA on the Apollo space missions. He agrees with Plato in placing the island civilization at 9,000 B.C.E. Chatelain bases this belief on an ancient scripture from Tibet that supposedly records that in 9,564 B.C.E. a very large section of land sank into the ocean in what is now the Caribbean and the Gulf of Mexico. He also cites amazing evidence that a common language once existed on both sides of the Atlantic. Chatelain tells of a missionary from the Basque country in the Pyrenees of North-Central Spain, who traveled to Yucatan, the home of the Aztecs (and before them the Maya) only to discover that he could make himself understood among the Indians, by speaking his own native language. Basque (native name: Euskara) is distinct from all other European languages and its origin is still uncertain but the fact that it was understood by the natives of Yucatan really opens a can of worms.

Underwater Anomaly

There are many underwater sites still to be investigated today that would not qualify as Atlantis but nevertheless simply defy belief at the magnitude and the lack of any known history. An amazing find was discovered off the southwestern coast of Okinawa, Japan in October 1995. Now called the Yonquni Underwater Ruins, the first discovered artefact resembles a step pyramid or ziggurat and is measured at over 600 feet wide and 90 feet high, with precisely cut steps. Its artificial origins are beyond question but many detractors and scientists are still claiming the ruins are natural. There is nothing natural about them as the photographs show. As more divers joined in the search other structures were discovered nearby, along with what appeared to be long streets, buildings, boulevards, staircases, archways and enormous blocks of perfectly cut and fitted stone.

Professor Kimura, a marine geologist at the University of Okinawa, stated: *"This could only have been done by a people with a high degree of technology. There would have been some sort of machinery involved to create such a huge structure."* The Yonguni underwater ruins appear to be the remains of a massive city and are said to cover an area that stretches across many miles, yet because it sounds so highly implausible, the discovery has been greeted with skepticism by Western academia and its archaeological authorities. Regarding this reluctance, researcher Rixon Stewart states in his article, *'World's Before Our Own 2'*: *"But then these bodies rely on support and financial funding which invariably comes from the likes of the Carnegie Foundation and others of a similar ilk, in effect bodies created and financed by Big Money that investigate and pronounce on our past...or at least the official version."* (23)

The Yonguni underwater ruins Okinawa, Japan. They don't look like natural formations.

A report from America in 1976 documents the discovery by Captain Don Henry of a giant underwater pyramid forty miles off the southern coast of Florida. The immense structure showed up on sonar soundings and appeared to be a precise pyramid-shape. Subsequently, underwater closed-circuit TV equipment was employed, which confirmed that a 420 feet high pyramid (almost the size of the great pyramid of Egypt) was located 300 feet below the surface. It is interesting that this is right in the location said to be the resting place of Atlantis. We can only wait and see!

Baghdad Battery

Evidence has been unearthed which points to scientific and technical knowledge existing long before it was previously assumed possible. In 1938, Dr Wilhelm Kong, an Austrian archeologist, was rummaging around the basement of a Baghdad museum when he came across a six inch high pot of clay. The pot contained a cylinder of sheet copper which was soldered with a 60-40 lead-tin alloy, (similar to modern day solder) whilst the bottom of the cylinder was a crimped-in copper disk sealed with bitumen. Another insulating layer of bitumen sealed the top and held in place an iron rod suspended in the centre of the copper cylinder. With a background in mechanics, Dr Kong immediately recognized that what he was looking at was, in effect, a battery. What was truly amazing was that records showed that it had been unearthed from an archeological site dated from times B.C.E. and that other similar artefacts had been recovered from Sumerian ruins in southern Iraq that dated as far back as 5,000 years.

Michael Faraday only researched electromagnetic induction and the laws of electrolysis in the early 1800s and we see the modern battery as being a result of his discoveries. Are we to now believe that these artefacts are the forerunner of Faraday's discovery, or the vestiges of an ancient technically advanced civilization? [(24)] An exact model of the Baghdad battery when filled with grape juice (vinegar) was found to produce enough voltage to electroplate gold onto metal objects. When better acidic electrolytes were utilized its results matched batteries available today.

Before the Pharaohs

Another amazing find was also in the storage area of a museum whose curators had no idea what they held. To start this story at the beginning, Dr. Robert M. Schoch, a Boston University Professor of Geology, published a paper in

1992 suggesting that the Sphinx was carved at a time between 5000 and 7000 B.C.E. This conclusion was reached following a study of the erosion of the body of the Sphinx and adjacent exposures. Schoch stated that the '... *rolling and undulating vertical profile to the weathered rocks...*' was attributable to '... *precipitation-induced weathering.*' The Sphinx of Giza is conventionally attributed to the 4th Dynasty pharaoh, Khafre (ca. 2520 - 2494 B.C.E.) When faced with claims that the Sphinx is older than is generally accepted, Egyptologists frequently cite the 4th Dynasty of Giza, claiming that there is no evidence for any form of activity at the site before this time. It can now be proved that this assertion is not strictly true.

Following digs at the end of the 1800s, four complete ceramic jars were finally discovered in 1907 at the site of the Great Pyramid of Giza, (the precise location was not recorded). Following convention, these were tentatively attributed to the 4th Dynasty (as usual) and stored in the basement of the Cairo museum. In the mid 1980s an archaeologist, Bodil Mortensen, located these jars and was amazed to find that they were not from the 4th Dynasty at all but actually belonged to the era of the *Maadi people*, who existed 1000 years or more before the Great Pyramid was said to have been built. The pre-dynastic Maadi period was not known in 1907 when the jars were discovered and was only uncovered at Maadi, near Giza, in 1930. To add to this new knowledge, in the mid 1970s, an Austrian Egyptologist, Karl Kromer, investigated debris about a kilometre south of the Great Pyramid. From this site, Kromer reported finds from the late pre-dynastic, the First, Second and Fourth Dynasties. The work of both Mortensen and Kromer has demonstrated that there is certainly evidence for pre Fourth Dynasty activity at

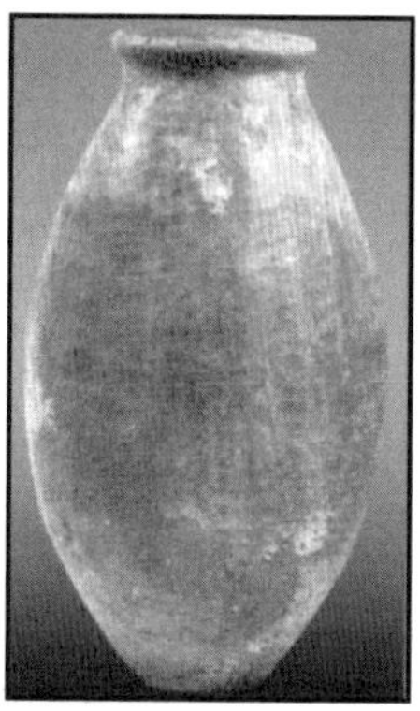

Four priceless vases from the Maadi era were found near the Great Pyramid.

The Cairo suburb of Maadi occupies the 1930's archaeological Maadi site.

Giza and it is consistent with earlier timescales on the basis of other, quite independent, considerations (such as the use of stone masonry in Ancient Egypt). The archaeological site of Maadi is now a suburb of Cairo that still bears that name. It is located on a desert ridge between two wadis at the southern city limits of Cairo. Unfortunately, the value of this pre-dynastic site was not realised in the 1930s and accordingly, insufficient controls were placed on the site. The high density living of Cairo City has meant that residential dwellings have intruded on the Maadi site, making further excavation most difficult. Nevertheless, we have considerable information from that location, highlighting pre-dynastic Egyptian communities.

The proven existence of the pre-dynastic Maadi people before any known Pharaohs certainly indicates that Egyptian settlement could be considerably older than previously thought. This evidence of activity at the site of the pyramid and sphinx prior to the 4th Dynasty of Giza could move towards quelling the conventional argument in dating these structures. (25)

Glazed Forts

Scotland's unique vitrified glazed forts are scattered from the Firth of Solway right up to the Central Western Highlands and then across to Aberdeen shire, with more along the north-western coast and some on the western islands. These are 'Iron Age' constructions, roughly circular in shape with a depression for catching rainwater and usually an accompanying well. The walls of the forts are made of piled up stones and are from 12 to 20 feet high. At some stage the stones have been subjected to intense heat that added a glasslike glaze. Whether this was deliberate as a form of strengthening or waterproofing or as the results of the inhabitants being blasted out with some form of ancient flame thrower, is simply not known. Scientists have calculated that the forts have been exposed to somewhere in the vicinity of 2,000 degree heat for some time to achieve the vitrification observed. It does not seem likely that this heat was applied deliberately since some walls have cracked and crumbled from too much heat. We can only wonder then at what kind of flamethrower or heat ray, available back in the Iron Age, could even approach the temperature required.

If this vitrification was caused by some advanced civilization, then what

It required immense heat to turn these rocks to glass.

exactly happened to that civilization? Could it be that it was engulfed in some kind of nuclear explosion? Evidence indicative of nuclear explosions has been discovered across the planet in the form of "fused green glass" found deep in the strata. Initially thought to only exist at nuclear testing sites, the glass has now been unearthed at various archeological digs as far apart as Gabon in west Africa, the Gobi Desert and Scotland.

Charles H. Hapgood postulated a theory that shifting displacements of the Earth's crust could introduce forces that were far more substantial than those manifested in earthquakes. He believed the forces involved could even introduce a nuclear explosion. This idea was subsequently backed by no less than Albert Einstein. Richard Noone took this idea further in his book, *'Hammer and the Pendulum'* where he postulated that the result would be like the cataclysmic triggering of a geological Armageddon. [26] Across the planet there would result a wave of earthquakes, floods and volcano's as the planet's rigid crust suddenly shifted and tore itself asunder. Noone considered that for those few who were not killed in the initial shocks there would be a desperate struggle to survive in the ruins of a shattered civilization. A few generations later there would be little else but stories of a golden age and myths of a great flood that had destroyed everything in its path. In addition, just maybe, there would be a few archeological anomalies that would one day baffle scientists of the future. [27]

Metallic Spheres

Over the past several decades, South African miners and rock hounds have collected hundreds of strange metallic objects, located in 2.8 billion year old pyrophyllite deposits mined by Wonderstone Ltd., near Ottosdal, South Africa. Known as the *Klerksdorp Spheres,* they are small, typically from 0.5cm to 10 cm in diameter, often spherical to disc-shaped, and sometimes have three parallel latitudinal grooves running around the equator. The spheres are of two types - *"... one of solid bluish metal with white flecks, and another which is a hollow ball filled with a white spongy center"* (28)

Roelf Marx, curator of the museum of Klerksdorp, South Africa, where some of the spheres are housed, said: *"The spheres are a complete mystery. They look man-made, yet at the time in Earth's history when they came to rest in this rock, no intelligent life existed. They're nothing like I have ever seen before."* (29) In 1979 several were closely examined by J.R. McIver, Professor of Geology at the University of Witwatersrand in Johannesburg, and Andries Bischoff, Geology Professor at Potschefstroom University. What they found only deepened the mystery. They were discovered to be a nickel-steel alloy which does not occur naturally, and is of such a composition that excludes the likelihood of meteoric origin. They don't appear natural and quite simply, they do not fit into any conventional prehistoric time-scale.

While playing with one of the stones on a very flat surface at a restaurant, Mr. John Hund of Pietersburg, realized it was extremely well balanced. An unsubstantiated report claims he took one to the California Space Institute at the University of California to have tests done to determine just how well balanced it was. Hund apparently explained: *"It turned out that the balance is so fine, it exceeded the limits of their measuring technology and these are the guys who make gyrocompasses for NASA. The stone is balanced to within one-hundred thousandths of an inch from absolute perfection."* There is no suggestion why this precision or balance would be required but this certainly denigrates the argument that they are formed naturally. Nobody knows what these objects are or can cast any light on their origins or proposed use.

Detractors argue that no matter how amazing they seem, these spheres must occur naturally. They believe they originated as concretions, which formed in volcanic sediments, after they accumulated some 3.0 billion years ago. Apparently, very similar concretions have been found within strata as old as 2.7 to 2.8 billion years, comprising part of the Hamersley Group of Western

Australia. [30] This would not explain the apparently man made grooves around the perimeter or the 'perfect' balance. If geologists were to prove this explanation correct, the Australian concretions and the Klerksdorp 'spheres' would be among the oldest known examples of concretions created by geochemical conditions known today. If not, we have no idea who made them or why.

Impossible Finds

Thousands of metal, corkscrew like objects, sized as small as 10 thousandths of an inch up to much larger examples have been found in the Ural mountains in Russia. The finds began at the beginning of 1991 and more are still being located by gold miners, today. They are found at depths from 3 to 40 feet and are thought to be more than 20 thousand years old.

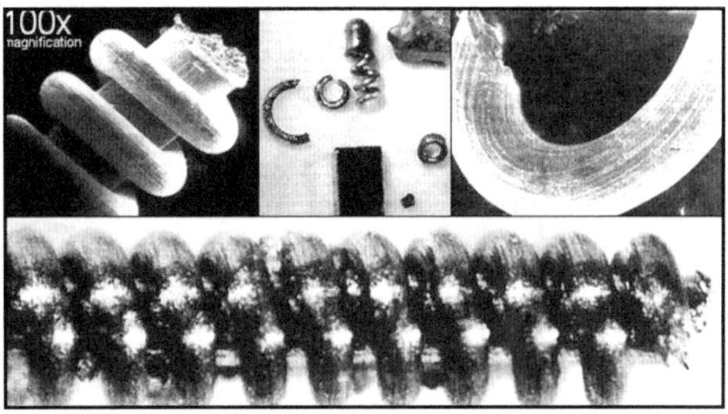

There are literally hundreds of these 'impossible' finds.

Often microscopically small they are made principally of tungsten, molybdenum, and copper. They were discovered as a result of official explorations aimed at exploiting the precious metals in that region of the Ural Mountains. Consequently geological and mineralogical analysis was done by the *Central Scientific Research Institute for Geology and Prospecting for Precious and Non Ferrous Metals* (ZNIGRI) in Moscow. Subsequently, ZNIGRI put out a report in which the author, Dr. Matveyeva, stated: *"The layer which contains the spiral shaped objects is characterized as gravel and detritus deposits ... From their orientation these layers can be dated to 100,000 years ago and correspond to lower regions of the Mikulinsk horizon of the upper Pleistocene."* [31] We have no clue what these items are but more are being discovered daily.

The Pleistocene era is the previous geological epoch, which began about 2 million years ago and ended around 10,000 years ago. This fact coupled to the depths at which they are located would make them very ancient indeed. Although I actually have no idea of the origins or use of these objects, I would have trouble believing they are extraterrestrial in origin, as some commentators believe. Rather they seem very terrestrial, so the only explanation is that they are the vestiges of a former hi-tech civilization in that region. [(32)] No other explanation seems tenable.

Last of the Pterodactyl

The pterodactyl supposedly died out over 140 million years ago, however, a group of French workmen tell a different story. When excavating a partially completed railway tunnel in north-eastern France between the St. Dizier and Nancy lines, in the winter of 1856, they had this amazing experience. In the dimness of the tunnel as the dust cleared following blasting, they heard something monstrous stumbling towards them from a great section of Jurassic limestone that had been split open. A monster appeared, tried to flap its giant wings, croaked horribly and died at the feet of the startled railway workers. This reptilian creature was covered in oily leather-like skin and had a wingspan of 10 feet 7 inches. It had four legs joined by membrane with long talons and a beak arrayed with long sharp teeth. A student of paleontology from the nearby town of Gray, identified the creature as a pterodactyl and claimed that the rock strata was of a commensurate age with the period these reptiles had lived. [(33)] The story is plainly impossible but it happened.

The myths of the Plains Indians of North America tell of the Thunderbird with massive wings that could carry away humans. Other Indian myths describe a huge, dark animal with wings and a long beak believed to live beneath bluffs along the Mississippi River. There is considerable documentation of these monsters:

- A story from the summer of 1873 claims that on a northeast Texas farm, five miles from Bonham, several men stared in awe at an enormous reptilian animal as it flew slowly overhead.
- In 1895, a massive bird in Webster County, West Virginia, carried off in succession a 10 year old girl, a hunting dog, a fawn and a sheep. It was supposed to have a wingspan of 15 to 18 feet. Similar

sightings continued into the 20th century.

- In Raymondville, Southern Texas in the evening of 14th January 1976, a man was attacked by a large, featherless flying creature that swooped down on him in the backyard of a relative's home. The creature was as big as a man and had huge red eyes, large talons, and a wingspan of 10 to 12 feet. Although the man's clothing was torn, he escaped, scratched but relatively unharmed, and the creature flew away.
- Another collaborated sighting occurred on 24th February 1976 near San Antonio, Texas. Three school teachers while driving to work, saw an enormous, low-flying, bird-like creature with a wingspan of nearly 20 feet. They decided later that it looked identical to a long extinct Pteranodon.
- An encounter recorded from the evening of 25th July 1977, from Lawndale, Illinois tells how six people saw an immense flying reptile descend from the southwest, seize a ten-year-old boy, Marlon Lowe, with its claws and attempt to fly off. His mother Ruth Lowe, sprinted to quickly grab hold of the boy. After carrying him forward some 35 feet, with his mother holding on, the giant bird dropped him, startled but relatively unharmed. The giant reptile was seen to continue flying to the northeast with its mate. They were observed to have beaks more than six inches long and wingspans of ten feet or more. [(34)] Crypto-zoologists have linked the Indians descriptions of Thunderbirds with surviving giant pterosaurs. They cite as support the fact that fossils of these creatures with wingspans up to an amazing 50 feet have been discovered on the North American continent.

CHAPTER THREE

WHO DISCOVERED AUSTRALIA?

'An error does not become truth by reason of multiplied propagation, nor does truth become error because nobody sees it.'

Mohandas Gandhi

Ancient Records

As far back as 481 B.C.E., the Chinese sage *Confucius* recorded the eclipses of the sun that had occurred on 7th April 592 B.C.E. and 11th August 553 B.C.E. The amazing thing, however, is that these were recorded back then, as seen from a latitude and longitude somewhere off Tasmania in Australia. Impossible as it seems, this is categorically confirmed and supported by computer models today and would show fairly definitely that the Chinese visited Australia in times B.C.E. In addition, the ancient Chinese book, *'The Classics of Shan Hai'*, written around 338 B.C.E., mentions a *'Great Southern continent inhabited by fierce black people who use a strange weapon'*. This weapon we now know from their description, to have been the boomerang.

A recently discovered map purportedly from 1418 (more than 350 years before Cook) states of the Australian natives, *'The skin of the aborigine is also black. All of them are naked and wearing bone articles around their waists. Those people also have anthropophagous (cannibalistic) habits.'* In a Taiwan museum there is a map believed to be over 2,000 years old that shows the southern coastline of New Guinea and the entire East Coast of Australia as far as the Northern Coast of Tasmania. Ancient records such as these, serve to indicate fairly strongly that China knew of the existence of the great South Land at a

An early Chinese map.

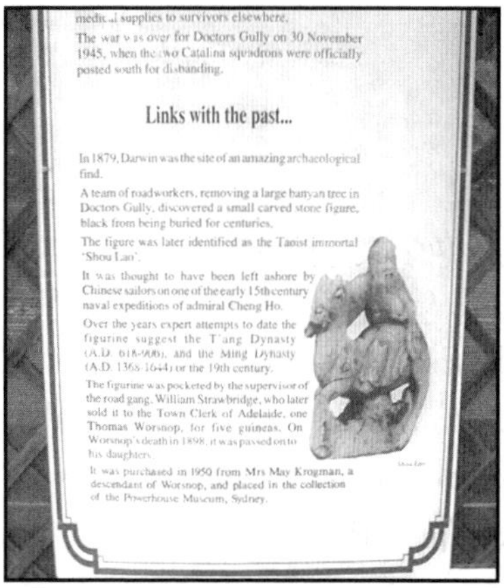

The plaque in Darwin showing the ancient figurine.

very early date and likely in times B.C.E.

In 1879 there was an amazing archaeological find in Darwin in Australia's Northern Territory. Council road workers removing a tree, uncovered a carved stone figure, black with age from centuries of burial in the ground. The carving when cleaned was found to be a statue of the Taoist immortal; 'Shou Lao' mounted on a donkey. Its position beneath the tree made it impossible to believe it could have been an ancient artefact that had been recently lost. Attempts to date the object would suggest the T'ang Dynasty, which would mean 618 A.D. to 906 A.D. but the likelihood of the figurine arriving in that timeframe would seem fairly remote. It has been suggested that this object could even have been left by sailors who voyaged here in the 1400s with Chinese Admiral Cheng Ho (Zheng He) who supposedly circumnavigated the entire world in seven voyages between 1405 and 1433. Many scholars are convinced that this brilliant navigator explored Australia as part of his sixth voyage in 1421, however, Cheng Ho apparently recorded the many countries he visited but left no mention of discovering new countries, new continents, new worlds or any land that would indicate Australia.

The supervisor of the road gang, Mr. William Strawbridge, pocketed the ancient figurine and later sold it to Thomas Worsnop, the Town Clerk of Adelaide, for 5 guineas. On Worsnop's death in 1898, his daughter inherited the artefact and in 1950 it was purchased from a family member and placed in the Sydney Powerhouse Museum where it resides today.

Marco Polo (c.1280 A.D.) described Java Major as the largest island in the world. Java, is a relative small island and the largest island in the world is of course Australia, so this suggests that the Great South Land must have been circumnavigated before the 14th century, (to know that it was an island). The confusion of Australia being linked with Java would indicate that Java may have claimed sovereignty over Australia at that time or that New Guinea, Java and Australia were considered to be joined as one giant land mass. Marco Polo's confusion of Java with Australia continued to lead people astray for more than 300 years. [(35)] One of Admiral Cheng Ho's Admirals, Hong Bao, documented *'Little Java'* indicating the area around Sumatra and *'Large Unknown Java'* by which he almost certainly meant the Great South Land.

Arabian maps made in 820 A.D. and 934 A.D. unequivocally show Western Australia, the Northern Territory, and northern Queensland, particularly detailing the Gulf of Carpentaria and Cape York Peninsula. Cornelious De Joad's World Atlas *'Specalein Orbus Terrae'* printed in Flanders in 1578 shows on the cover: a lion representing Africa, a Camel representing Asia, a Horse representing Europe and a Kangaroo with 2 joeys obviously representing the Great South Land of Australia. [(36)] The original Toscanelli map of 1474 A.D. in the Florence public library, unmistakably shows the Murray, Darling and McIntyre Rivers; the Channel Country south of Goondiwindi; the Diamantina; the Gilbert River flowing into the Gulf of Carpentaria; Cape York and many features of our East Coast. This confirms discovery pre-Cook but also suggests early inland exploration as well. There are some suggestions that these explorers were searching for the 'inland sea' that was probably located around Lake Eyre in prehistoric times. This would suggest that somewhere was a map or legend indicating the existence of this inland sea.

The British navigator, Matthew Flinders, anchored his ship off the entrance to Spencer Gulf on 20th February 1802 believing it was the lead in to either a river or to the Inland Sea. He even thought a passage could lead right through to the Gulf of Carpentaria at the extreme north eastern part of this new land. Flinders fully investigated the inlet of Spencer Gulf, and spent 9 days at the site of Port Lincoln exploring the region. Soon after, in April 1802 at Encounter Bay, Flinders met his French counterpart, Nicolas Baudin, who was charting the same areas. Despite the reports of these two mariners, the myth of an inland sea was entertained by future explorers for many years to come. Soon after Flinders, the explorer Charles Sturt recorded in his journal that the inland sea must have only recently dried up since the top section of vegetable matter still stank. It is of course possible that there had been a recent wet season but one would expect if that were so, Sturt would have recognized this fact. He discovered a bank of sea shells in central Australia that was 300 feet thick and left drawings in his journal. This would certainly be left over from the inland sea.

Early Explorers

Today, Australian children are taught in school that in 1770, the Englishman, Captain James Cook, was the discoverer of the east coast of 'New Holland'; the land that we today call Australia. Soon after Cook's voyage, Alexander Dalrymple, distinguished hydrographer and map expert, announced that Cook's discovery of the east coast of New Holland *'could not be described as a discovery at all'*. If Cook was the discoverer, how was it possible, he asked, that Cook took with him detailed charts showing Australia, New Zealand and New Guinea, featuring correct lines of latitude and longitude, accurately drawn by previous seafarers? In fact, an advance copy of Dalrymple's own 134-page octavo volume, *'An Account of the Discoveries made in the South Pacific Ocean Previous to 1764'*, was specifically taken along on the 'Endeavor' voyage by the naturalist, Joseph Banks. Cook, himself, recorded in his logbook as he explored the middle island of New Zealand, *'Geographers have indeed laid down part of Quiros' discoveries in this Longitude, and have told us that he had these signs of a continent, a part of which they have actually laid down in the maps; but by what authority I know not'*. Cook goes on to actually mention Dalrymple's charts. Research also shows:

- ***A Portuguese map showing Port Phillip Bay on the southern Victorian coast, had been made by Cristavio de Mendonca in 1522.***
- ***Australia's West Coast was explored by another Portuguese, Gomez de Sequeiro in 1525.***
- ***These two maps were joined together and later the Dieppe cartographers of France published their large hand-produced map in 1536 and even gave a copy to King Henry VIII of England.***
- ***This was known as the Dauphin Map and a copy was given to Joseph***

Banks by the British Admiralty prior to his voyage with Captain Cook. When the Endeavor struck the Barrier Reef, Cook knew exactly where suitable repairs could be affected. Cooktown Harbor and the Endeavor River are plainly shown on the de Mendonca map, and these details were transcribed to the compiled Dauphin Map, although the harbour is actually depicted as somewhat larger than it really is. This could be why Cook noted in his log that the entrance was narrower than he expected. He was, of course, comparing it to the map.

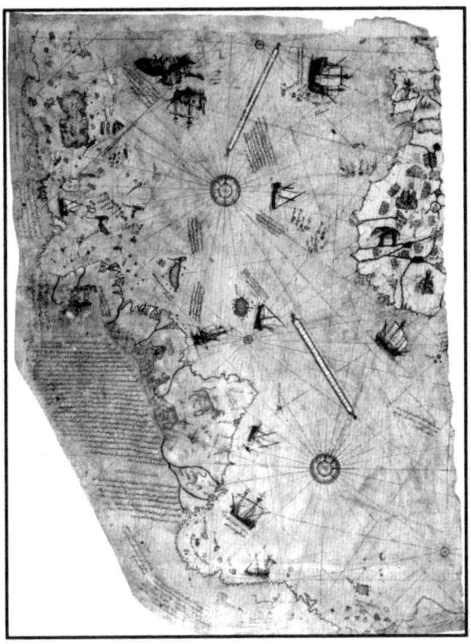

Captain Cook carried excellent maps with him on his Endeavor voyage.

From a time one hundred and forty years before Cook, the Dutch navigator Willem Janszoon (c. 1570 - 1630) is often said to be the first European to land on the coast of Australia. His ship the Duyfken was actually in Torres Strait in March 1606, just a few weeks before Torres sailed through. Because he didn't explore the straight, Janszoon returned to the Netherlands still believing that the south coast of New Guinea was joined to Australia. Dutch maps perpetuated this error for many years to come. Two Dutch mutineers; Wouter Loos and Jan Pellegrimsz de Beye were put ashore in Western Australia for their part in the murders of the passengers of the wrecked *Batavia* in 1629, possibly making them the first European settlers in Australia.

Although there have been many suggestions that earlier navigators from Egypt, Phoenicia, China, France, Spain or Portugal may have discovered parts of Australia, the *Duyfken* is the first European vessel historically known to have done so. On a later expedition in July 1618, Janszoon again landed in Australia at North West Cape on the Western Australian coast. Almost two years earlier, on 25th October 1616, Dirk Hartog came unexpectedly upon an island off the coast of Shark Bay, Western Australia, which is now called

Dirk Hartog Island. This made Hartog's expedition, the second recorded European landing on the Australian continent. Peter Pieterzoon sailed around the northern coastline in 1636. He was followed by Abel Tasman in 1644 and after Cook's epic voyage of 1770, Matthew Flinders in 1803.

Portuguese and Spanish Sailors

In the 15th century, Portuguese sailors were venturing further southwards along the west coast of Africa, looking for a passage that would allow a more direct trade route to India. Once around the Cape of Good Hope the south-westerly winds, *the Roaring Forties*, would take ships all the way to Batavia (Jakarta) or on to India. They were aware that to the east of this journey was the great *'Terra Australis'*. The Frenchman, de Gonneville is claimed to have landed on the western coast of Australia in 1503 and in the same year, French navigator, Binot Paulmyer, was blown off course in the Indian Ocean and is thought by some scholars to have also landed in Australia. [37]

The Intrepid Spanish seafarer, Alvaro de Mendana de Neyra.

Spain had established its empire in Central and South America, and in the 16th and early 17th centuries, began a series of expeditions from Peru into the South Pacific. Álvaro de Mendaña de Neyra discovered the Solomon Islands (north-east of Australia) in 1567 and further expeditions in 1595 and 1605 searched for gold and fortune for Spain and new lands for the Church. After these voyages failed to find either precious minerals or significant new lands, Spain was to abandon its interest and no further expeditions were mounted.

Although not really visible in the records, there is some evidence that Spanish adventurers explored the east coast of Australia in 1558 and it would be probable that at some stage they landed to make repairs, find water and to catch game. Many inhabitants of Gladstone, Queensland, are adamant that the Portuguese born Spanish explorer Pedro Fernández de Quirós was the one who actually discovered Australia, landing at Auckland Point on the Gladstone coast, in March or April 1606. Prior to excavating rock to construct the harbor breakwater earlier this century, carved inscriptions existed on a cliff there.

Local lore has it that the inscriptions were Spanish names including 'de Quirós' within a circle and beneath it, the date 1606. The inscriptions also suggested that de Quirós performed a ceremony atop Auckland Point in which he claimed this land for 'Spain and the Holy Church'. (38)

Pedro Fernández de Quirós, was appointed chief pilot of the expedition of four ships in 1595, under Álvaro de Mendaña setting out from Peru to colonize the Solomon Islands. On the death of Mendaña, de Quirós took command and decided for a multitude of reasons, that the place should be abandoned. He sailed westwards for two days seeking a more suitable location, but found no land and headed for Manila arriving 11 February 1596. After some time in the Philippines, he sailed for Mexico in December 1597 and on to Spain the next year. The expedition had given him the desire of discovering a great southern continent for Spain and for the Holy Church; however, so far it had eluded him.

De Quirós petitioned the Spanish king to allow another expedition into the Pacific, and in 1600 journeyed to Rome to seek Papal blessing for this enterprise. Finally, in March 1603, de Quirós was authorized to undertake another voyage to convert the heathen and extend the Spanish dominions. He was shipwrecked in the West Indies but reached Callao on 6 March 1605. In December he set out into the Pacific, intending to reach Santa Cruz, whence he would sail further west to eventually locate the Great South Land that he was sure existed 1000 leagues from Peru. After a long voyage, on 3 May 1606, de Quiros reached the islands of the New Hebrides or what he called Austrialis del Espiritu Santo.

After a few weeks of exploration to the south-east, because of contrary winds, his ship was blown out to sea and after several unsuccessful attempts at returning to the New Hebrides, de Quiros then supposedly sailed for Mexico. A visit to the Great South Land is missing from the historical record; however, it seems he located Australia on the way. One must remember this was his primary objective at the time. The second ship, the *'San Pedro'*, known affectionately as the *'Almiranta'*, with the brilliant pilot Luis Vaez de Torres, was left behind to fend for itself. Torres went on to locate the Great South Land and prove that it was a separate land mass from New Guinea by a straight that still bears his name. It is considered unlikely but possible that Torres made the landing at Auckland Point and left the inscription of *'de Quirós, 1606'* attributing the discovery to his Captain who for all he knew at the time, could have been lost at sea.

Finds in Australia

In 1912, Lawrence Hargraves (the Australian aviation pioneer) discovered carvings near the mouth of the George's River on the foreshores of Botany Bay, in the form of lettering and 2 outlines of a Carrick, a vessel steered by a sweep, (like an ancient Greek trireme), with the names Santa Barbara and Santa Isobel. The letterings beside the ship motifs were BALN on one line and beneath it ZAIH. The letter W was beside the symbol of a cross with an elongated circle. This is a known symbol of intended conquest for Spain and the Church. The identical symbol was emblazoned on the sails of the Spanish Armada and the ships of the Conquistadors. (39) Hargraves translated the Spanish-Latin shorthand to read, *"We in the Santa Barbara and Santa Isobel conquered W from point to point by the sign of the cross"*. Additional letters could have been the rock signatures of witnesses to the declaration. In the same area, Hargraves also examined two stout eye bolts that in ancient times had been painstakingly leaded into solid rock, far enough apart to hold ropes attached to the mast of a small ship. Nearby was an ancient indentation that could have been an excavation for collecting water. (40)

Historians speculate whether the Santa Barbara and Santa Isobel recorded here could have been the same 2 ships of those names which were lost from Álvaro de Mendaña's second pacific expedition to Australia in 1595, to establish a colony. His ships of these names were separated in bad weather and were never seen again. (41) Although history does not record it this way, it is of course likely that they were the same. How many ships of identical names were floating together around Australia, in that precise timeframe?

In 1970 the Australian adventurer and amateur archaeologist Rex Gilroy discovered Latin type doodling on a rock near Wollongong, NSW. These doodles were a similar form of Latin shorthand used during the 15th, 16th and 17th centuries. In September 1985, Gilroy was exploring dense scrub west of Gosford, at the mouth of the Hawkesbury River, when he discovered more faded images, which turned out to be of early European origin. The

Hawkesbury rock inscriptions were outlines of three vessels and letterings encircling a central human figure and three more letters plus a cross. Gilroy stated that the topmost ship outline resembles that of a Carrick, the ship to the left resembles that of a Caravel, and the ship to the right a Galleon. The central human figure is depicted with a helmet reminiscent of the morion worn by the conquistadores. Above this figure are the letters 'c.S.g.' Above the 'S' is a cross, and above this and slightly to the left, the date '1558' in archaic numerals. (42)

The translation is said to read: "We in the Almiranta, the Capitana and Concepcion, with colonists and soldiers claim this land for Holy Spain by the sign of the Cross, 1558." (43) Perhaps unrelated but certainly of interest is that shipping records confirm that the Spanish galleon 'Jesus Maria de la Limpia Concepcion', better known as the 'Capitana', was lost in 1654 after striking a reef system off Chanduy, Ecuador. The huge galleon served as the command ship, (the Captain's ship or 'Capitana') of the 1654 South Sea Armada, and due to her size and stature, carried the bulk of the fleet's treasure. Estimates place the quantity at nearly 10 million pesos of silver, well above the annual production of the combined mints of the Spanish Viceroyalty of Peru. After the 'Capitana' sank, it was partially salvaged, and its treasure transferred to the 'Almiranta' of the 1655 Fleet ('Nuestra Senora de las Maravillas'). The 'Capitana' sank again off Little Bahama Banks just two years later, in 1656. If this is the same ship associated with Gilroy's find, the century earlier date of 1558 becomes suspect. If Gilroy's finds are proved authentic, it indicates a visit that pre-dates the other Botany Bay carvings by 37 years. This in turn would pre-date James Cook by 175 years. Rex Gilroy also tells us that not far from the inscriptions are Aboriginal engravings of men in helmets, shirts and trousers with belts; and female figures in dresses from the 16th century age of the European letterings. This would certainly indicate very early planned colonization of Australia. (44)

Evidence of Spanish Colonization

In 2000, Greg Foster discovered more faded glyphs carved on a sandstone cliff right in the Sydney suburb of Baulkham Hills. He alerted Rex Gilroy who has devoted a lifetime to discovering anomalies within this country and researching its discoverers. Together, Foster and Gilroy cleared the rock surface and searched the location for more finds. The dilapidated condition of the carvings made chalking their outlines necessary for photographic purposes but it became apparent that these glyphs were more of the old Spanish-Latin 'doodles'. There was the familiar cross within a circle and two Spanish-type vessels outlines with the year '1595' in archaic letters among other glyphs. The rather lengthy inscription was eventually translated to read: *"We of the galleon Santa Barbara, of 51 crew in search of gold for Holy Spain, together with the San Filippe, with 51 crewmen, San Jeronimo, with 57 crew, Santa Catalina and Santa Isabel with 57 crew each, sailed in search of the West Land of Gold on 9th April 1595. Álvaro Mendaña de Neyra of the San Jeronimo is our leader; separated we sailed on. We claim this land for Holy Spain".* [(45)] Quite apparently there was a cold war situation among the various seafaring nations at the time. Secrecy was paramount and as a result many voyages of discovery were not recorded in history. We should also note other evidence of early colonization in Australia:

- Further upriver in the Colo area, an ancient Spanish morion soldier's helmet was found by a bushman 40 years ago. [(46)]
- About 1968 another old Spanish helmet was dug up near the river at East Hills. [(47)]
- In 1968 workmen digging a deep trench for a pipeline at Macquarie Fields, just south of Liverpool, at a depth of 3 metres, unearthed a dozen Spanish doubloons of the Cristavio de Mendonca - de Quiros period. [(48)]
- During the 1920s, bushwalkers in far north Queensland, found a stone Peruvian Idol, decorated in old Castilian jewelry. [(49)]
- On Prince of Wales Island close to Thursday Island and 60km west of Cape York, Queensland, a man investigating a cave found a huge rusty broadsword bearing finely engraved ancient Castilian designs beside a crumbling human skeleton. Nearby was a golden goblet. [(50)]
- In the 1930s an ancient human skeleton was found in a sandstone crevice in a deep rock shelter hidden in the mountains behind Mackay, Queensland. It was clothed in a morion helmet and breastplate. [(51)]
- Also in the 1930s two other skeletons clothed in Spanish armor were found preserved in a cave behind Cooktown, Queensland. From time to time, old Spanish coins continue to be washed up on the Cooktown shore. Maybe they are from a Spanish vessel wrecked in the same location that almost

claimed Captain Cook's *'Endeavor'.* [52]

- An aboriginal tradition of the Tweed River on the New South Wales side tells of strange men in stone garments attempting to mine the Mount Warning area, many generations before the British arrived. [53]
- A farmer dug up and old morion helmet at Kunghur, 15 km north of Nimbin in northern NSW. [54]
- Skin divers claimed years ago to have retrieved a number of 16th-century Spanish coins and other relics from the remains of an old wooden shipwreck off Tweed Heads (N.S.W.). [55]
- Aboriginal tales of apparent Spanish visitors still exist in the Grafton-Clarence River district (N.S.W.). For generations they told of a huge canoe with sails that ventured up the river from the coast bearing many white skinned men in garments of stone (taken to mean armor). [56]
- In 1953, a resident recovered a 16th century Spanish sword with a silver embossed hilt, from an old aboriginal shell midden. [57]
- South of Eden, (N.S.W.), sheltered amid dense scrub in a small inlet are the remains of what appears to be a stone fort. A badly weathered date 1524 is engraved into a stone forming part of the wall. Many years ago, the remains of an old Spanish breastplate are said to have been dug up nearby. [58]
- Off Gabo Island (Victoria), an angler's net brought up a 16th century Spanish wine jar. Scuba divers claim a Spanish galleon lies there. [59]
- Certain islands in the Great Barrier Reef are believed to have been the secret hide-outs of Spanish pirates during the 17th century. Credence was given to these tales, when Aboriginal children unearthed Spanish gold coins on one of these islands during the 1960s. [60]
- During his voyage up the Great Barrier Reef in 1770 Captain Cook is said to have seen the remains of a Spanish ship wrecked on Facing Island, off Gladstone. [61] He is believed to have soft-peddled this fact on his return to England as it would have proved a pre-British expedition to Australia. I have searched Captain Cook's log and discovered that the copy he submitted to the Admiralty has several departures from the original yet neither copy records this story. I guess we can never really validate this.
- A Canon embossed with the Portuguese rose and crown emblem of fifteenth or sixteenth century design was found on an island in Broome Harbor in 1916. [62]
- When I was a young man based in Darwin with the R.A.A.F. I was a member of the Darwin Sub-Aqua Club. A member called Tim Brooking located a huge square shafted anchor off Darwin, and as a club project we raised it using a raft of 44 gallon petrol drums. On one dive, I followed the chain,

> which was very long and some distance away, located a second anchor, almost completely covered with coral growth. It would seem a ship had scuttled these two anchors and chain a very long time ago. The one we recovered was eventually stabilized, restored then erected at our clubhouse as a monument. All our efforts could not date the square shaft but we believed it was ancient. The anchor is now outside the Darwin Museum.

The evidence would indicate certain interest in the South Land and possible colonization by the mariners of various countries well before the time of Cook. For Gilroy's date of 1558 on the Hawkesbury River site to be correct, we would have to accept that a colonization attempt probably followed the expedition of Spanish explorer Inigo Ortiz de Retes, who in 1545 extensively mapped the northern coast of New Guinea. He chose the name New Guinea because he believed the native islanders resembled the people he had seen in Guinea, Africa. On his chart de Retes wrote that he believed New Guinea was probably part of the 'great southern continent'. As we saw earlier, it took Luis Vaez de Torres to disprove this belief.

So was it Cook's own decision, back in England, to promote himself as the 'discoverer' of Australia and the first to explore the east coast? Was it a Government plot to downplay the contribution of the Chinese, Spanish, French, Portuguese and Dutch navigators who were viewed as the enemies of England? Did Cook milk his findings for all they were worth back in England and unwittingly create errors in our history books that tenaciously hold to this day? I guess that question will not be readily answered.

CHAPTER FOUR

WHO DISCOVERED AMERICA?

'The great enemy of truth is very often not the lie-deliberate, contrived and dishonest - but the myth; persistent, persuasive and unrealistic.'

J.G. Kennedy, delivered on 11th June 1962 at a commencement address at Yale University.

Another Discoverer

Young Americans are erroneously taught that the Italian, Christopher Columbus, discovered America in 1492 - despite the fact that the Chinese, Vikings and the Templar fleet, and no doubt many other Europeans had been there long before Columbus. We are still taught global untruths in history and the deception is so apparent that it would seem, certain that ruling forces have an agenda of falsifying history to keep us in the dark.

It all seems rather silly but a bigger question we may also ask ourselves is what right did Christopher Columbus have in 'discovering' America when it was already inhabited by the first nation, Red Indians, and had been populated for thousands of years? For that matter, under just what right did James Cook or any other explorer 'discover' Australia when the Aboriginal people had been living here for perhaps 40,000 years. For this reason, Adam Nordwall, the chief of the Indian Chippewa tribe, stepped off an Alitalia jumbo jet on 24th Sept 1992 and standing on the tarmac of Leonardo da Vinci International Airport in Rome, in the full dress of an Indian Chief, proceeded to take possession of Italy by right of discovery, claiming it for the Red Indian people. It really happened!

The fact that Italy has long been inhabited by people who consider themselves to be in full possession of their lands was precisely the point that Chief Nordwall was trying to make. In a bit of a reversal, the Indian Chief told the amazed inhabitants of Rome, *"What right had Columbus to 'discover' America when it was already inhabited by my people for thousands of years? The exact same right that I have now, to come to Italy and claim to have discovered your country"*.

Of course he made a relevant point but will the history books now show Adam Nordwall as the discoverer of Italy? Somehow, I don't think so!

The Naming of America

Four centuries before Columbus was born, the Vikings certainly had a settlement in the New England area of the New World and named it Vinland on their maps. In addition, Bishop Erik Upsi of Greenland is known to have visited this New World called Vinland in 1121, as recorded in the *Icelandic Annals*. Other ancient maps initially named it *Winland*, then later *Vinland*. Before the name 'America' was suggested, the New World was to be named 'Columbia' as a tribute to Christopher Columbus even though the Italian navigator landed at Puerto Rico and never even set eyes upon mainland America.

Christopher Columbus was born in Italy and lived in Portugal before receiving support for his voyage from the King and Queen of Spain.

Our history books claim that the name 'America' can be attributed to the Christian (baptismal) name of another Italian navigator, Amerigo Vespucci who was born in Florence 9th March 1451 and died at Seville 22nd February 1512. It seems that Vespucci also had very little to do with the discovery of North America and there is considerable evidence that the history of the New World, and even the source of its name, are shrouded in secrecy and conspiracy so we will look at an alternative scenario.

It was allegedly the Catholic priest, Martin Waldseemüller, who proposed the name 'America' and cited that it came from Vespucci's Christian name. In 1507 he published the celebrated work '*Cosmographiae Introductio*', at Saint-Dié, in Lorraine, calling the New World, by the new name '*America*'. He wrote: '*Now, these parts of the earth (Europe,*

Africa, Asia) have been more extensively explored and a fourth part has been discovered by Amerigo Vespucci. Insomuch as both Europe and Asia received their names from women, I see no reason why anyone should justly object to calling this part Amerige (from the Greek 'ge' meaning 'land of'), i.e., the land of Amerigo, or America, after the name of its discoverer, Amerigo, a man of great ability.' I believe that this was in fact a smoke screen and the Vatican masters of Waldseemüller may have held a hidden agenda.

A Star called Merica

From the influential book, *'The Hiram Key'*, authors Knight and Lomas state: *'Josephus, the historian of the first century, observed that the Essenes believed that good souls have their inhabitation beyond the ocean, in a region that is neither oppressed with storms of rain or snow nor with intense heat, but refreshed by the gentle breathing of the west wind which perpetually blows from the ocean. This idyllic land across the sea to the west (or sometimes the north), is a belief common to many cultures, from the Jews to the Greeks to the Celts. The Mandeans, however, believe that the inhabitants of this far land are so pure that mortal eyes will not see them and that this place is marked by a star, the name of which is 'Merica'.'*[(63)]

The Mandeans are one of the oldest pre-Christian ethnic minorities, living in southern Iraq as well as in the Iranian providence of Huzisian. They are also located along the river Karun in the province of Khuzestan with a sizable group now living in Australia. The name *'Mandeans'* is the Aramaic word which means *'knowledge'* (a translation from the Greek *'gnosis'*) which marks the Mandeans as a surviving Gnostic cult. They are followers of John the Baptist who they believe was the true Messiah. In their writings, Muhammad is called the 'demon Bizbat' and they view Jesus Christ as a false prophet who is depicted as somewhat evil. [(64)] The Mandeans are known to have adopted the 'mystery' doctrines of the Babylonian goddess, Ishtar (Astarte). Accordingly the 'star' that guides them to their Heaven on Earth (to the west) is in fact the 'Star of Ishtar' which is a 5 pointed star, not the stylized 8 pointed star adopted more recently. This is precisely the star symbol used by the U.S. government, as an emblem on the *Seal of Government*. The identical five-pointed star can be seen depicted on U.S. currency and as insignia on U.S. military aircraft and vehicles.

The followers of the virgin goddess Ishtar/Astarte, located the mysterious land called Merica somewhere to the west across the ocean. It was an idyllic place where they believed the spirits of the deceased go to reside after death. It may come as a surprise that such a concept also exists in the Christian Bible. The prophecy of Zechariah chapter 5 and Isaiah 18 : 1-2 mention a new Babylon which lies west of the old Babylon, and west of Egypt and the Nile river, beyond the seas. [(65)] The Knights Templar also included the star of Merica in their doctrine. Author Andrew Sinclair, (himself a descendent of the Templar, St Clair family) commented on the decoration within the chapel at the Scottish, Rosslyn Castle; *"Many Templar signs and seals are carved into Rosslyn Chapel. There are clusters of 5 pointed stars, reflecting the major graces of the Virgin Mary."* [(66)] In fact the 5 pointed stars reflect no such thing. Relating this icon to the 'Virgin' Mary is whimsical at best. They are representative of the Goddess Ishtar (the Queen of Heaven) and this was the star that guided the Templars of Rosslyn to the mystical land of Merica.

The Goddess Ishtar

In very early traditions, the God YHWH (Jehovah) had a wife and family. Ishtar (as Astarte or Ashtoreth) was said by some ancient documentation to be the consort of Jehovah and by other works to be the consort of Ba`al. Also the ancient moon Goddess Sin, was transformed to become Ashima, also documented as the wife of Jehovah. Clergy cannot overlook these Goddesses or simply dismiss them as mythical pagan deities because they are recorded - as members of the early 'Trinity'. They are mentioned no less than 40 times in the Christian Bible; once in Exodus, three times in Deuteronomy, five times in Judges, twice in Isaiah, once in Jeremiah, once in Micah and twenty-seven times in the books of Kings and Chronicles. [(67)] In addition the Christian celebration of the passion of Christ at Easter takes its name from this Goddess Ishtar/Astarte.

Ishtar of the Babylonians was called Astartu in Akkadian, Astarte by the Greeks, Ashtoreth among the Hebrew and Attart in the city of Ugarit. She is the equivalent of Inanna of the Sumerians and was worshipped as Atirat by the Assyrians and was also known as Elath, Ashratu, Atirat, and Sud. Anath was an early Hebrew Goddess initially said to be the daughter of Jehovah and

Astarte (Ashtoreth). We find in the Old Testament: Judges 3 : 31 *And after him was Shamgar the son of Anath, which slew of the Philistines six hundred men with an ox goad: and he also delivered Israel.* This same Shamgar was supposedly a son of El Elyon (YHWH) and Anath and is shown here as a 'flesh and blood' God putting in a valiant performance fighting against the accursed Philistines and killing 600 of them.

Anath became the equivalent of Astarte (whether her daughter or not) as a fertility goddess. This is quite apparent with the word Astarte actually meaning 'womb'. The Bible calls her Ashtoreth the Goddess of the Zidonians; however, she was mostly known as Asherah and certainly also worshipped by the Hebrew. Over time and through many aliases, these female entities tended to merge into one. Asherah (or Ashtoreth) is often referred to as the 'Queen of Heaven'. Under whatever names she may have been worshipped earlier, she was a Jewish cult figure since ancient times. Later Mary (Miriam) the mother of Jesus was adapted to replace her, becoming for a time the new 'Queen of Heaven'. For those who have never read these things in their Bibles or are having trouble believing this, here is one more item for you to research. The original Temple of Jerusalem was simultaneously dedicated to both Yahweh and to the Queen of Heaven. This is not made up, this is well documented fact. Groves of symbolic trees were planted in front of this Temple and called the sacred 'asherah'. This obviously relates to the Goddess Asherah and these groves, throughout Semitic lands, were associated with the female aspect of the deity within the trinity. [68] To appreciate this on a deeper level, we must understand that the Hebrew language was derived from ancient Egyptian and *Aser-t* actually means 'tree' in ancient Egyptian. As a word pun, *Asher-t* was an Egyptian word for a burnt offering explaining the symbolism in the 'asherah' groves in the foreground of the Temple.

Today, a modern representative of Ishtar (as Persephone, the Queen of the underworld) overlooks both New York harbour in the form of the *Statue of Liberty*, and Washington D.C.'s Capitol Hill as the *Statue of Freedom*. The depiction of the Statue of Liberty is purely Masonic and it was French Master Masons who proposed the gift to America where high-level Masons were entrenched in politics. An American sculptor, Thomas Crawford, then living in Rome, was commissioned to design a statue of Lady Freedom (freedom is very similar to liberty) to go on top of the newly constructed U.S. Capitol building. This occurred at the height of the Civil War in 1863. Initially, Crawford proposed a statue of a female wielding a sword and holding a shield with stars around a liberty cap; however, a liberty cap was a symbol of freed slaves, and the former *Secretary of War*, Jefferson Davis, strongly objected to this. The liberty cap was replaced by a helmet with an eagle headdress. It may concern some to know that the statues standing atop the American Capitol building and surveying New York's harbour are devices to denote ownership. Figure it out!

Knights Templar

The Mandeans are said to be descendents of the Nazoraeans, and subsequently the Essenes of Qumran whose recently unearthed scrolls indicate that more scrolls/treasures had been buried in the Temple of Solomon, precisely where the Knights Templar are known to have excavated. It seems the Knights Templar also believed in this land to the west called Merica (La 'Merica) or the Star of the West and this strongly links them with the pre-Columbus discovery of the New World.

By a completely different route, some scholars believe the *Merika* star comes from a Phoenician seafarers' name for Venus, the brightest star in the sky. This is likely true as well, and possibly could be the origins of the star Merica (Venus) that indicated the great land to the west. Knight and Lomas state that the medieval Knights Templar discovered a royal archive, dating from the supposed time of King Solomon, hidden deep under the Dome of the Rock in Jerusalem. Documents from this archive supposedly stated that in times B.C.E. Phoenician mariners from Tyre made trade trips from Eilat on the Red Sea to a westerly continent they named Merika after the star that guided them.

Just prior to the demise of Jacques de Moloy and the Templars in France at the hands of King Philip the Fair and the Vatican, part of the Templar fleet headed to a safe haven in Argyll and the Firth of Forth in Scotland, where they knew Robert the Bruce was engaged in a rebellion against England. Because they were skilled in warfare, the Templars knew that they could be very valuable to Robert and would be welcomed there. On 6th November 1314 the Scots were hugely successful at the Battle of Bannockburn. Initially, the battle went badly for Bruce's army until the intervention of a reserve force which quickly turned the tide of the whole battle and ensured victory for the Scots. Stories quickly spread that these mysterious warriors who had appeared from nowhere carried the Beausant (the battle flag of the Templars). The force was in fact led by the Grand Master of the Scottish Templars, Sir William St Clair of Rosslyn. The fact that Robert the Bruce was under Papal excommunication combined with the long St Clair family links with Rosslyn was the greatest attraction of Scotland as a sanctuary. It was also one of the few places in Europe where the Pope could not persecute them.

The Templar Fleet

Although most voyages of the Templar fleet appear to have been conducted in secrecy, there is evidence that links famous explorers with the Templars. The intrepid Portuguese seaman Vasco da Gama ventured out with the Templar cross insignia on his sails, as did Christopher Columbus and many others. Columbus' navigators were members of the extant Portuguese Templar Order, and the Templar cross was featured prominently on the sails of his ships in 1492. Evidence suggests that the Templars discovered America almost a century before Columbus and his voyage was simply a later formality. We do know that another Scottish Masonic Lodge leader and Templar descendant, Henry Sinclair (the Earl of Orkney) is known to have undertaken a mysterious voyage to the New World, well before Columbus. Henry was the son of William Sinclair, Laird of Rosslyn, and Isobel of Strathearn, a daughter of Malise of Strathearn, Earl of Orkney. On his father's death in 1358, Henry succeeded as Laird of Rosslyn and Earl of Orkney.

In *'The Hiram Key'*, Knight and Lomas note that the ornate embellishments within the Temple at Rosslyn Castle depict Aloe Vera plants and cobs of Maize. These plants were both specific to the New World and since Rosslyn Castle was built in the 1330's and decorated well before the time of Columbus, this strongly supports the Sinclair voyage to the New World where he viewed these exotic plants and likely brought back drawings and samples. This belief is also based on letters written in the late 1300s by the Zeno brothers of Venice. The *Zeno Narrative* tells of a mysterious ocean voyage to the west, by a Prince Zichmni who set up a colony in the New World. Indian legends and a number of clues suggest that the landfall was Nova Scotia. In *'The Fisherman's Tale'* from the Zeno Narrative, a nameless ancient mariner tells the Earl of Orkney (Henry St Clair) about the New World to the west and what he might find there and this inspires the 'Prince' to undertake the voyage for himself. (69)

The *Zeno Narrative* describes this voyage throughout the North Atlantic, said to be in 1398, under the command of Prince Zichmni utilizing his fleet of ships equipped for war. The Earl of Orkney was in fact the only ruler in this area with a war fleet at the time, a fact that caused Johann Reinhold Forster to reasonably speculate in 1784 that it was in fact Henry St Clair (as Prince Zichmni) who explored Greenland and may have founded a settlement among the Micmac Indians of present-day Nova Scotia. St Clair is also thought to have settled present-day Massachusetts and Rhode Island in line with annotations on the Zeno map. A descendant, Nicolo Zeno admitted that he had destroyed his ancestors' original book, and in his writings he worked from an ancient sailing chart that was rotten with age. This has been cited by detractors as a stratagem to excuse errors and discrepancies in his narrative and his map but that is a thin argument at best. Regardless of any supposed error, the narrative and map were utilized by many future generations of seafarers.

To indicate the credibility of this document, the Correr Museum of Venice displays a large globe made in 1693 showing the geography of the known world including the Arctic Circle. This globe had been based on the Zeno map dating from some three centuries before. Modern day writer, Andrew Sinclair, fully investigated this scenario and strongly supports this theory. He wrote: *"The chief interest of the Zeno Map was its placement of two cities in North America, appearing to confirm a colonizing expedition there after 1390, the previous date given for the Zeno voyage by Marco Barbaro. Yet there has also been significant other cartographical evidence for North American colonization by knights, who knew how to build fortifications and wore a Templar or Engrailed cross."* (70) The ancient archaeological sites in America, of the Newport tower and the Westford knight carved in the rock face, support this pre-Columbian settlement. Being a descendent of the Rosslyn St Clair's, Andrew Sinclair was able to gain access to records that were likely closed to other researchers. His work would certainly indicate that the Knights Templar not only possessed the charts of pre-Columbian voyages to America; they actually took part in the exploration and settlement. As a result we can see that the tale we were taught that Columbus was the discoverer of the New World is just so much rubbish. The question is: Why are things of our natural history so often shrouded in deception?

Drake's - New Albion

It is well known in American history that Sir Francis Drake visited California in 1579. He and his crew were warmly welcomed by the local natives who saw them as Gods and offered him their lands. According to reports of the voyage, Drake accepted their offer and left a plaque acknowledging this fact, nailed to a post, proclaiming this land of *'New Albion'* to Queen Elizabeth of Great Britain.

Bee it knowne unto all men ...: This plaque gives England the legal title deed to the State of California.

In 1936 Mr. Beryle Shinn, a San Francisco shop assistant, was picnicking near the Golden Gate Bridge when he moved a rock and discovered underneath a brass plaque that he thought may be useful for car repairs. Eight months later he noticed the plaque still in his garage and com menced cleaning it with soap and water. He noticed the word, 'Drake' and wondered if it was valuable. Shinn had the plaque sent to Dr Herbert Bolton at the University of California where it was further cleaned and deciphered to read:

BEE IT KNOWNE VNTO ALL MEN BY THESE PRESENTS
17TH IVNE 1579

BY THE GRACE OF GOD AND IN THE NAME OF HERR MAIESTY
QVEEN ELIZABETH OF ENGLAND AND HERR SVCCESSORS
FOREVER, I TAKE POSSESSION OF THIS KINGDOME WHOSE KING

AND PEOPLE FREELY RESIGNE THEIR RIGHT AND TITLE IN THE WHOLE LAND VNTO HERR MAIESTIES KEEPING NOW NAMED BY ME AND TO BEE KNOWNE VNTO ALL MEN AS NOVA ALBION.
FRANCIS DRAKE

There were the usual cries of 'fake'; however, everything about the plaque checked out except one thing. Drake recorded that he had landed near white banks and cliffs and this certainly did not match with the spot near the Golden Gate Bridge. Amidst the publicity and controversy, out of the blue came a chauffeur called William Caldeira. He told how he had been waiting for his employer at 'Drakes Bay' Laguna Beach four years before and had picked up the plaque which he though contained Chinese writing except for the word, 'DRAKE' that he recognized in English. Caldeira had taken the plaque home but had subsequently thrown it away right near the spot where Mr. Shinn found it. After being missing for 357 years, this plaque is now residing in the University of California and in fact, gives England the legal title deed to the State of California.

Mystery Plaque of Kansas

The history of Kansas, U.S.A. tells us that the Spanish conquistador Francisco Vazquez de Coronado, was the first European to explore Kansas in 1541. New research by a resident of Leoti, Kansas, amateur historian Dean Jeffries has suggested a different theory - one that puts Europeans in Kansas well before Coronado's landmark journey and at least half a century before Columbus. Jeffries contends that ancient European sun-worshippers who crossed the state in about A.D. 500 inscribed an old stone tablet which was reportedly dug up in the Westfall area around 1913 by a local farmer. The stone features a carefully inscribed area containing various characters. It was donated in 1920 to the State Historical Society in Topeka where it was briefly studied and then stored until 1993 when it was returned to Lincoln County. It is currently on display in the Kyne House Museum in Lincoln, Kansas. [71]

After 7 years study, Jeffries released a translation of the 16-symbol inscription on the tablet, which he says is engraved in an ancient language once common in the Iberian Peninsula and known as Gaelic-Punic. Jeffries contends the tablet marks the grave of a fallen comrade and is a death chant: *"Thy song. - Strength which powers the journey above. The one who strengthens all. Oh! Thy Song!"*

State archaeologist Tom Witty, said the stone, which he first examined in 1960, was chiseled in very sharp lettering and lacked any considerable weathering or oxidation characteristics, which he expected would be evident on any similar stone exposed to the elements for 1,500 years. (72) On viewing the stone, however, it becomes apparent that it was carved by an artful stone worker who was meticulous about his work and who spent considerable time precisely working a very hard and durable stone. This degree of diligence is not likely to be undertaken by a hoaxer. It is not disclosed how Jeffries arrived at the date of A.D. 500 since what appears to be a date of 1322 is recorded on the artefact. Either way this is a tough one for those who categorically see Columbus as the discoverer of America in 1492. The more we research, the more we see that much in our modern world is based on falsehood and fabrication. There is plenty of evidence to suggest that many others from many nations had visited America long before Columbus and this apparently included mariners from ancient Egypt, Phoenicia, China, Scandinavia and medieval Europe as well as the Templar fleet from Scotland. Despite this, modern authorities continue to push the untenable line that *"Columbus discovered America"* when in reality Columbus never even set eyes upon mainland America.

When Christopher Columbus arrived at Puerto Rico during his second voyage on 19th November 1493, the island was inhabited by a group of Arawak Indians known as Taínos. They called the island *'Borikén'* whereas Columbus named it *'San Juan Bautista'*, Spanish for Saint John the Baptist. Later the island took the name of Puerto Rico (Port of Riches) while the capital was named San Juan in line with the name given by Columbus. We must ask ourselves why the authorities still promote Christopher Columbus as the discoverer of America when there is a plethora of evidence readily available to counter that stance. Further, why would they promote the mariner Amerigo Vespucci as giving his name to the New World when he had nothing to do with it and that too is plainly false?

CHAPTER FIVE

PRIMITIVE LIGHTING

'As we acquire knowledge, things do not become more comprehensible, but more mysterious.'

Will Durant

Lamps That Burn Forever

Both the ancient Egyptian *Book of the Dead* and the *Pyramid Texts* make striking references to *'The Light-Makers'*, a body of people responsible for lighting the subterranean areas of their complexes. These reports, however, seem to lose something in the translation as these 'Light-Makers' appear to be revered well above a simple torchbearer or lamp lighter. It seems that these folk tendered or maintained the ancient lamps that burned forever.

Iamblichus Chalcidensis, (c.245 - c.325) was a Syrian neoplatonist philosopher who recorded a fascinating account that was found on a very ancient Egyptian papyrus held in a mosque in Cairo. It was part of a story by an unknown author from around 100 B.C.E. about a group of people who gained entry to underground chambers around Giza for exploratory purposes and encountered these amazing lamps. He described their harrowing experience: *'We came to a chamber and when we entered, it became automatically illuminated by light from a tube being the height of one man's hand and thin, standing vertically in the corner. As we approached the tube, it shone brighter ... the slaves were scared and ran away in the direction from which we had come! When I touched it, it went out. We made every effort to get the tube to glow again, but it would no longer provide light. In some chambers the light tubes worked and in*

The Egyptian Book of the Dead mentions the Light makers.

others they did not. We broke open one of the tubes and it bled beads of silver-colored liquid (now thought to be mercury) *that ran quickly around the floor until they disappeared between the cracks. As time went on, the light tubes gradually began to fail and the priests removed them and stored them in an underground vault they specially built southeast of the plateau. It was their belief that the light tubes were created by their beloved Imhotep, who would someday return to make them work once again'.* (73) We can only wonder!

Free Energy Lights

Completely different illumination is also disclosed in other writings. In its entirety, this following ancient text purports to describe and then give two recipes for the construction of ever-burning lights. It is ascribed to an expert in cryptography and the occult arts called Johannes Trithemius (1462-1516), a German Benedictine Abbot of Sponheim, leading scholar and counselor to Emperor Maximilian I. In its original form it reads:

'Two eternall unquenchable burning temporall lights of Mr. Trittemio Abbot at Sponheim, described by the hande of Bartholomeus Korndorffer:

"Two unquenchable eternall lights are founde and to be seen hearin, which I Bartholomeus Korndorffer have written of a disciple of Mr. Trittemius Abbot of Sponheim, which did affirme with an oath that they were never published nor opened before, only that his Mr. the Abbot had bestowed one of them unto a great potentat. This famous Maus Trittemius, which lived in time of the great Emperour Maximilian the first, and none like unto him was to be founde in his age, hath done much good with his artes, not mingled with divilish worcke, as some malicious men doe accuse his, butt he did knowe all what was done in the world of what he desireth by the starres of ministerie, he hath also tolde of things to come manie times. Once as was travaling, came to S. Moritz, and found an acquaintance to whome I spoke,

he was glad to see mee, he invited mee to dinner, and another named Servatius Hohel, which had been with the Abbot at Sponheim and served him 12 years. He was very civill, yet sometime he spoke a word of this arte. Now as wee came together, and dinner being past Mr. Hohell desireth mee to goe with him to his chamber, which I did discoursing of diverse matter of artes and seying he was an antient man, I desired to leave him allone to his studie butt he would not let mee, and bespoke a meale by his hostess, which wee two did take in his chamber. Mr. Hohel did bestowe uppon mee that time, the handwriting of Mr Trittemius whearin thease two incombustible lights were wrytten, and some magick pieces, which I did trye to prouve affterwards & founde them to be very true & right. Mr. Hohel tolde mee also that his Mr. Trithemius had bestowed one of those lights unto this great potentat the Emperour Maximilian, and placed it in a glass in his chamber, which the sayd potentat had kept very well, and many had seen the lightning thereof. After that a sickness aryseth that the Emperour did departe from that place, & came not to this place again in 20 years: but as he came theither at the least, Mr. Trittemius beying dead long before, he remembered this light & went presently to see it, which was found theare with all tokens unquenchable as Mr. Trittemius had lefft it, & the people of that castle tolde the Emperor that they had seene continually a lightning in that place, like a lampe in a church. Wherefore this Emperour lefft the light years still burning wheare it shall burne still at this daye, which is a great secret in this worlde. The Emperour Maximilian hath given 6,000 crownes for those temporall ever-lasting lights." (74)

Recipes

For those of you who are concerned with your electricity bill and would like to try this at home, the document states: *"Hearuppon followeth the process & practica"*;

"Take 4 unces of sulphur, & so much of calcyned alume, bruise them together, put it into an earthen sublimatorie, place it into a coale fier, well lited, let the sulphur ascend through the Alume, and in 8 houres is it prepared. Thearof take at the lesse 2 1/2 unces, and one unce of good christallick venetian porras, bruse them two small togeather, put it into a flat glasse that it may lye flatly, poure uppon it a stronge sharpe 4 times distilled spirit of wine uppon it, & extracte it in ashes sofftly to the oyle, poure it uppon again, extracte it to the oyle, poure it uppon again & drawe it of agayne; take a litle of the sulphure, laye it uppon a red hott copper

plate, and when it floweth like wax without smoking then is it prepared, if not then must thou extract theareof more of the spirit of wine, till it sustineth the proove & it is prepared.

Nowe take alumephume, make therof a top not as long as a little finger, and halfe as thicke, foulde it about with whyte silke, put it thus whole into a venetian little glasse, & joyne thearunto of the prepared sulphure, place it a day & night in hott sande, that the top be continually in the sulphur. Nowe take the top thearout, and put it into such a glasse, that the top looke out a little, adde thearunto of the prepared incombustible chyburals, place the glasse into hott sand till the sulphure melteth, and cleaveth beneath and upward about the top, that it be seene but a little above, kindle the top with a common light, & it beginneth to burne presently, and the sulphure remaineth flowing, take the light and place it wheare you wilt, and it burneth continually for ever." [(75)] Of course, this also saves on running wiring and would be handy on a camping trip. It may be just the thing to light that dark cupboard or the backyard tool shed but wait, there's more:

- Theosophist, Helena Blavatsky, mentions the ever-burning lamps of the ancients. In her work, *'Isis Unveiled'* (v.I, pp. 224-232 & 522) she reveals a wealth of ancient accounts of *"Inextinguishable lamps"*. [(76)]
- Numa Pompilus, the second king of Rome, had a perpetual light shining in the dome of his temple.
- Plutarch wrote of a lamp which burned at the entrance of a temple to Jupiter-Ammon, and its priests claimed it had burned since antiquity.
- A beautiful golden lamp in the temple of Minerva which could burn for a year was described by Pausanius (second century A.D.)
- St. Augustine (A.D. 354-430) left a description in his work, *("De Civitate Dei", lib. xxi., cap. 6)* of a wonder lamp. It was located in Egypt in a temple dedicated to Isis, and Saint Augustine says that neither wind nor water could extinguish it.
- Fortunius Licetus describes a similar lamp in his work *'De Reconditis Lucernis Antiquorum', cap. vi.* On page 44 , he mentions a preparation of quicksilver (mercury) filtrated seven times through white sand by fire, of which, he says, lamps were made that would burn per-

petually.

- Both Maturanthus and Citesuis firmly believed that perpetually burning lamps could be achieved by a purely chemical process. (77)
- An ever-burning lamp was found at Antioch during the rein of Justinian of Byzantium (sixth century A.D.). An inscription indicated that it had been burning for more than five hundred years.
- During the middle ages a third-century perpetual lamp was found in England and it had burned for several centuries.
- When the sepulcher of Pallas, son of Evander, immortalized by Virgil in his *Aeneid*, was opened near Rome in 1401, the tomb was found to be illuminated by a perpetual lantern which had been alight for more than 2,000 years.
- A sarcophagus containing the body of a young woman of patrician stock was found on the Via Appia near Rome in April, 1485. When the dark ointment preserving the body from decomposition had been removed, the girl looked lifelike with red lips, dark hair, and shapely figure. It was exhibited in Rome and seen by 20,000 people. When the sealed mausoleum was opened, a lighted lamp amazed the men who broke in. It must have been burning for 1,500 years!
- In his *'Oedipus Aegyptiacus'*, (Rome 1652) the Jesiut, Kircher, refers to lighted lamps found in the subterranean vaults of Memphis in Egypt.
- Ever-burning lamps were found in the temples of India supporting the age-old tradition of the magic lamps of the Nagas - the serpent Gods and Goddesses who live in underground abodes in the Himalayas.
- The *Agastya Samhita* text states that speculation of ever-burning lamps is not extravagant. History shows that the priests of India, Sumer, Babylon, and Egypt, as well as their confreres on the other side of the Atlantic, were custodians of amazing lighting science.
- Tibet is also said to have had miraculous lamps that burned for long periods. Father Evariste-Regis Huc (1813-1860), who traveled extensively in Asia in the nineteenth century, left a description of one of the ever-burning lamps which he had seen himself in that country.

- One of these lamps is also mentioned by the Rev. S. Mateer of the London Mission. In the temple of Trevandrum, in the kingdom of Travancore, South India, *'there is a deep well inside the temple, into which immense riches are thrown year by year, and in another place, in a hollow covered by a stone, a great golden lamp which was lit over 120 years ago, still continues burning'.* (78)

Primitive Lighting

At a conference on street lighting and traffic control held in Pretoria, South Africa, in 1963, it was purported that C. S. Downey discussed, *'a system of artificial illumination, equal, if not superior to, the 20th century technology'.* He referred to the natural lighting of *'a village in the jungle near Mount Wilhelmina, in the Western half of New Guinea' (West Irian).* (79) This is but one of the references to ancient lighting to be found in a book by Andrew Tomas, called; *'We Are Not The First'.* Tomas also tells us: *"Traders who penetrated this small hamlet lost amid high mountains said they were terrified to see many moons suspended in the air and shining with great brightness all night long. These artificial moons appeared to be huge stone balls mounted on pillars. After sunset they began to glow with a strange neon like light, illuminating all the streets."* (80) This is quite unbelievable but several other references to *'glowing stones'* are found in literature from around the world:

- Barco Centenera, a memoirist of the conquistadors, wrote about their discovery of the city of Gran Moxo near the source of the Paraguay River in the Matto Grosso region of Brazil. In a work dated 1601 he paints a word picture of this island city and says: *"On the summit of a 7.75 meter pillar was a great moon which illuminated all the lake, dispelling darkness."*
- Colonel P. H. Fawcett set out in 1925 on an expedition into this unexplored Matto Grosso interior of Brazil from which he failed to return. In an article written not long before his departure, he documented that he hoped to find a large ruined city of the remote past and described the original discovery of that city. Colonel Fawcett was an English surveyor and explorer. He was originally hired to define the boundaries between Brazil, Bolivia and Peru. It was the

time of the rubber boom, and at that time there were no plantations, and gatherers had to go into the jungle to find rubber trees to tap. Because the boundaries were not certain and the three countries in volved could not really trust each other they asked the English Royal Geographical Society to find an independent surveyor. It was Fawcett who noted a green cola drink enjoyed by the natives in Brazil which was the forerunner to Coca Cola.

Fawcett with his eldest son was searching for the fabled lost city of *'Ciudad de los Cisares'* somewhere in the Chilean jungle. They both disappeared on that expedition. It was considered at the time that he had not died but may have been captured by an Indian tribe and was supposedly sighted on more than one occasion. While twenty years later, in 1953, Colonel Fawcett was still missing, his letters, manuscripts, and other records were collected and published by his youngest son, Brian Fawcett, in a volume replete with stories of adventure covering the beliefs and customs of the native tribes of South America. (81) It is stated that some fifty years ago Colonel Fawcett was told by the native inhabitants of the Matto Grosso that mysterious cold lights had been seen by them in the lost cities of the jungles. Writing to the British author, Lewis Spence, at that time he said: *"These people have a source of illumination which is strange to us - in fact, they are a remnant of a civilization which has gone and which has retained old knowledge"*. Col. Fawcett was in search of the ruins of that vanished civilization, and he laid claim to having seen a lost city in the jungle which he was to explore. We can likely believe in Colonel Fawcett's sincerity because he apparently sacrificed his life in that expedition. (82)

- Lucian of Samosata (c. A.D. 120-180) was a well traveled, celebrated author of witty essays and dialogues. Born in Samosata, in Syra, Lucian's first language was probably Aramaic but he became famous for his works such as *'True History'*, in Greek. In Heirapolis, Phrygia, he reported seeing a shining jewel in the forehead of the goddess Hera which brilliantly illuminated the whole temple at night. In the same locale the temple of Hadad or Jupiter in Baalbek was provided with another type of lighting – that of glowing stones. (83)

- The Cabbalists assert that the secret of perpetual illumination was known to Moses, who had learned it in Egypt; and that the lamp ordered by the Lord to burn in the tabernacle, was actually an inextinguishable lamp. *Exodus 27 : 20 'And thou shalt command the children of Israel, that they bring thee pure olive-oil beaten for the light, to cause the lamp to burn always'.*
- Even Erich Von Daniken mentions ancient glowing stones in his works.

Quite enlightening! The truth is out there somewhere!

CHAPTER SIX

THE PLAIN OF JARS

'The important thing is to never stop questioning;
Curiosity has its own reason for existing.'

Albert Einstein

Laos

In southeast Asia the country of Laos is a land-locked communist state officially known as the Lao People's Democratic Republic. This region traces its history to the Kingdom of Lan Xang *(The Land of a Million Elephants)* which existed from the fourteenth to the eighteenth century. By the late 1880s the French had resolved to annex the Lao territories, believing that they held deposits of precious metals and that the Mekong River offered a 'back door' into China. After almost 70 years as a French protectorate, Laos gained independence in 1949. This country was extensively bombed in secret by the Americans as part of the Viet Nam war in the early 1970s and the communist Pathet Lao movement finally came to power in 1975 after a long and bloody civil war.

Archaeological Anomalies

Laos has many mysteries for the archaeologist to contemplate and uncover. In Houaphanh Province groups of hilltop standing stones, or menhirs, likely dating from around 1000 B.C.E., mark the entrances to stone crypts containing human remains, ceramics, beads and bronze artefacts. Southern Laos boasts one of the world's largest deposits of dinosaur bones. During the 1930s French geologist Josué Heilman Hoffet discovered deposits of fossilized herbivores, freshwater mollusks, crocodiles and tortoises in the region of Ban Tangvai, about 120 kilometres east of Savannakhet. The most enigmatic attraction in Laos, however, must be the remote Plain of Jars, which contains literally thousands of massive ancient stone jars, scattered throughout the Xieng Khouang area. While most ancient Asian sites, such as the Angkor temples in Cambodia, have now revealed many of their secrets, modern archaeologists, anthropologists and historians are still completely baffled as to where these jars came from, how old they are, their original use and what they represent. They are actually very ancient, quite mysterious and just a bit unsettling. There is an almost total lack of local myths, legends or even a good tenable folklore story that begins to explain their origins or use.

The mysterious stone jars of Laos.

Indiscriminate American Bombing

Unfortunately, this region is now simply littered with un-exploded American bombs and landmines, the result of massive US bombardment during the Secret War. Regarding this situation John Perkins lucidly described America as: '*... an Empire that does not flinch at inflicting brutal and often totalitarian measures on any who have resources we covet.*'[84]

Some of the hardware the Americans left behind.

Unfortunately the resources in this case were opium poppies and became part of the CIA's illicit drug trade. The entire area is now quite unsafe and reports of explosions causing serious injury to locals, are a regular occurrence. Because of this, the Plain of Jars remains one of the most dangerous tourist or archaeological sites in the world today, and although visits are discouraged, further injuries to local children and tourists are reported almost every week. Phonsovan is the nearest town to the Plain Of Jars, and devastation caused by the American bombing is still well in evidence almost everywhere. Despite being the destination of virtually all visitors who come to see the Jars, Phonsovan still feels like tourism has barely touched it.

Uses in Folklore

One obscure story tells us that a race of giants once inhabited the area and created the giant sized jars to hold their wine. An ancient giant king called Khun Jeuam, supposedly fought a long, battle against his enemies who may or may not have been giants (In Asia, 'Khun' is a respectful title somewhere between Mr. and Sir). This king apparently celebrated his eventual victory with rice wine brewed in the jars. To give that particular legend any credence, we must accept that after that one massive boozy celebration the whole tribe went teetotal and for some reason the jars weren't ever re-cycled or used again. From my own experience in S.E. Asia, this is not really hard to believe, because one night out on the local rice wine would cause even a seasoned drinker to swear off the booze forever. They also brew a rough whisky called 'Mekong' which I firmly believe is scraped off the bottom of the Mekong Delta. It really is a shocker! Nevertheless this explanation is considered unlikely to be true.

The jars are made of sedimentary rock, usually sandstone but also granite, conglomerate or calcified coral are found to have been used for some. A few are so large that entire families use them for housing, actually living in the stone jar. They range from 3 to 13 feet (1-4 meters) in height and can weigh up to 17 tonnes. Some have disks nearby that appear to have been lids but certainly not the sort that would seal wine. There are also earthenware urns on the plain and some of the urns were decorated with motifs such as cats, stars, or the strange figure that the modern Lao people call the 'frog man'.

Original Discovery

This timeless communist country of Laos has only been open to tourists for a relatively short time and still holds many of its ancient secrets. The French archaeologist, Henri Parmentier visited the site in 1923 and was instrumental in locating within the huge jars, glass beads, drilled carnelian beads, earrings of stone or glass, bronze bells, black cooking pots, one or two hand axes, a bizarre object which he thought was a lamp and the debris of human bones. Parmentier documented that the stone jars were originally brought to the attention of the Western world in 1909 by a French customs official named Vinet, however, none of this man's notes or correspondence appear to have survived. The first westerner to seriously catalogue the Plain of Jars was another French archaeologist, Madeline Colani of the *École Française d'Extrême Orient*. In two large volumes of her 1930s work, *'The Megaliths of Upper Laos'*, Colani documented that the jars may have been funerary urns carved by a vanished Bronze Age people who cremated their dead. Evidence to support this conclusion was established when she excavated a nearby cave and found human remains, burned bones and ash. Nevertheless, Madeleine Colani also speculated that the Plain of Jars connected a caravan route from northern India, for which there is some evidence. Since the jars appear to be gathered in clusters along a major road network that was probably a trade route at some ancient time, she suggested that it is possible that they may have held water for camel caravans and thirsty travelers. The size and shape does not appear to lend itself to efficient water storage and the sheer number of jars in clusters would not really support this purpose. This also begs the question of how monsoon rainwater would be collected and channeled into the jars and why literally thousands were required in clusters. There are indications that the ancient Plain of Jars civilization engaged in international trade with neighboring societies evidenced by foreign beads and grave tributes found there.

The Plain of Jars is rich in salt, and this highly valued commodity would have secured its place on the spice trade routes of China and India. Excavated material from the plain has been dated between 500 B.CE. - 800 A.D., but it is believed the area was habited well before this timeframe. There is evidence that suggests the jars were used 1,500 to 2,000 years ago, by an ancient Mon-Khmer race whose culture is still fully unknown. More recently, Australian universities, among others, are conducting studies of the jars and surrounding area in the hope of finding some clue to help throw some light on this enigma. Till the riddle is solved, the jars remain a mystery of a lost stone age culture and their purpose remains entirely unknown.

CHAPTER SEVEN

FISHERS GHOST

'Truth is strange - but true - for truth is always strange:
stranger than fiction; if it could be told ...'

Lord Byron in his epic poem *Don Juan*

Frederick Fisher

The story of *'Fisher's Ghost'* is one of the best known and enduring ghost stories in Australia and is actually known the world over. Frederick George James Fisher was a 35 year old *ticket-of-leave* former convict who originally came to Australia from England on a convict ship named the '*Atlas*', arriving in the colony in 1816. Forged banknotes had been found in his shop in England and whether he had acquired these accidentally or not, he was sent to the colony for 14 years. Because of food shortages, a *ticket-of-leave* was something convicts who were particularly well behaved could gain for themselves to be allowed to buy land and work it, rather than remain imprisoned. Frederick Fisher acquired 30 acres of land at Campbelltown not far from Sydney; however, in 1825 Fisher had an argument with a local carpenter and received a light prison sentence. Worried about his farm, he gave his neighbour, George Worrall (also a former convict) power of attorney during his sentence. After his release on 17 June 1826, Fisher mysteriously disappeared, and George Worrall gave out that Fisher had returned to England - leaving him with power of attorney to use his hut and land. He was even seen in Campbelltown wearing Fishers pants.

Suspicions were raised when Worrall tried to sell Fisher's horse and obtain the deeds to his property. One evening another neighbour called John Farley was returning from market and saw Fisher sitting on the fence rail of his paddock. Never suspecting this was an apparition, he walked towards it but saw it leave the fence and retreat into the field beside a watercourse, where it was lost from sight. Still unsuspecting, Farley let people know that Fisher was back and a lot of pressure was put on Worrall. When Fisher could not be found, Farley was sure something was amiss but was equally certain that he had viewed Fisher sitting on the fence rail. The ghost of Fisher is said to have then been viewed several times on the fence by various other people and is said to have pointed to the location of his grave in a nearby paddock.

In time, Farley made a deposition before magistrates. It is also alleged that others who had seen the ghost supported him. A native tracker was taken to the fence where the ghost of Fisher had been seen and discovered 'white man's blood' on it, marking it as the murder scene. Finally, the body of Fisher was located buried in the paddock next to a string of waterholes. Fisher's brother had his remains re-buried locally in St Peter's Graveyard at Campbelltown, however, no headstone was erected. Worrall tried hard to blame others and claimed Fisher had been murdered by a man called Lawrence along with his neighbour, Nathaniel Cole. This was the story he gave in court but under intense questioning, Worrall finally confessed that he had murdered Fisher and tried to steal all his property and goods. In time, the condemned former convict was hanged, his fate secured by the ghost of the man he had murdered. [(85)]

Historical Records

'The Truth about Fisher's Ghost', first appeared in the famous monthly *Blackwood's Magazine*, issued by the Edinburgh publishing firm William Blackwood & Sons, who published the periodical from 1817 to 1980. This version was reprinted, with little change, in the book, *'The Valet's Tragedy and Other Studies'* by Andrew Lang, published in 1903 by Longmans (London). Lang was able to confirm that both Frederick Fisher and George Worrall were recorded as former convicts living in the Campbelltown area and the characters and events are a true record. Fredrick Fisher was murdered on 17th June 1826 after his release from prison. The trial of George Worrall is reported in

the *'Sydney Gazette'* of 5th February 1827. Not surprisingly, there is not one word printed about Fisher's ghost leading to the capture. The tale is told in *'Tegg's Monthly Magazine'* (Sydney, March 1836); in *'Household Words'* for 1853; in Mr. Montgomery Martin's *'History of the British Colonies'*, vol. iv. (1835) and also in another of John Lang's books called 'Botany Bay' (about 1840), where the yarn is considerably dressed up.

Worrall's Trial

At the trial, James Coddington deposed that on 8th July 1826, when Fisher had been missing for three weeks, Worrall tried to sell him a colt which Coddington believed to be Fisher's. Worrall again averred that Fisher had left the country. A few days later Worrall showed Coddington, a receipt issued by Fisher for the sale of his horse to Worrall. The receipt was sworn to by Lewis Solomon as a forgery and the court record shows: *'A witness, from having seen Fisher write, had considerable doubt as to the genuineness of the receipt'.* James Hamilton swore that in August 1826 he bluntly told Worrall that foul play was suspected; he *'turned pale, and endeavored to force a smile'.* He merely said that Fisher *'was on salt water'*, but would not name his ship. Later he claimed it to be the *Lord St Vincent* (also reported as the Lady St Vincent in some accounts) but no ship of this name had visited Sydney, which aroused further suspicion. Samuel Hopkins, who lived under Fisher's roof, last saw Fisher on 17th June 1826, in the evening. Some other people, including the man named Lawrence, were in the house but left shortly after Fisher went out that evening. They later remarked how strange it was that he had not returned. Nathaniel Cole gave evidence to the same effect. In short, Fisher strolled out on 17th June 1826, and was never seen again (except as a ghost). [86]

Fisher's body was not easily found. A twenty pound reward for its discovery was offered by the Government on 27th September 1826, when Fisher had been dead for three months, and this may have stimulated all that was immortal of Fisher to perch on his own fence-rail, to draw attention to the position of his body. It appears that though the reward was offered, the local magistrates (to whom the ghost-seer, John Farley supposedly went) did not bid their constable make searches till 20th October. Chief Constable Robert Burke, of Campbelltown, deposed to having apprehended Worrall after the body was found by George Luland. Nobody saw the murder committed and Chief-Justice Forbes said in summing up (on 2nd February 1827) that although it was impossible for the evidence to be stronger, it was wholly circumstantial. The jury returned a verdict of guilty and the death sentence was passed. George Worrall was hanged and buried at what is now one of Australia's most valuable pieces of real estate, overlooking Sydney Harbour at The Rocks.

In the *'Sydney Gazette'* of 6th February 1827 it reported: *'George Worrall, convicted on Friday last of murder of F. Fisher, yesterday suffered the last penalty of the law. Till about 5 o'clock on the morning of his execution, he persisted in asserting his innocence, when he was induced to confess to a gentleman who had sat up with him during the night, that he alone had perpetrated the murder, but positively affirmed it was not his intention at the time to do so. We need not follow Worrall's attempts to explain away the crime as an accident. He admitted that he had deliberately intended to have both Lawrence and Cole hanged for the crime'.*

It is ironical that had they not found the body and ultimately obtained the confession, Worrall would have walked free. We are therefore left wholly in the dark as to why the police began their investigations at the fence rail and can only attribute it to the ghost reported by Farley and perhaps others. To this day, that string of waterholes at Campbelltown is still called 'Fisher's Ghost Creek'. [(87)]

Postscript

A correspondent adds another similar example from Australia's past. Long after Fisher's case, this gentleman was himself present at a trial in Maitland, New South Wales. A servant-girl had dreamed that a missing man told her who had killed him and where his body was concealed. She, being terrified, wanted to leave the house but her mistress made her impart the story to the chief constable, a man known to my informant, who also knew and named the judge who tried the case. The constable excavated at the spot pointed out in the dream, unearthed the body, and arrested the criminal - who subsequently confessed, was found guilty, and was hanged. Not a word was allowed to be said in court about the dream. All the chief constable was permitted to say was that *'acting on information received'* he went to Hayes's farm, and so forth.

There are now several cases on record of a murder victim communicating from the grave to bring about the conviction of the murderer. An early account was reported from County Durham, England, in 1681 where a miller called James Graeme was accosted by the hideous ghost of a young woman with five open head wounds and drenched with blood. She told Graeme that her name was Ann Walker and she had been murdered with a pickaxe by a man called Mark Sharp acting for a relation of hers, also called Walker, by whom she had become pregnant. She told him her body was buried in a pit and made it clear that she would continue to haunt Graeme until he went to the Magistrate with her story. Refusing to believe what he had seen, Graeme did nothing but when the apparition continued to appear, pleading and threatening, he went to the authorities with her grizzly tale. On checking the pit Ann Walker's apparition had indicated, her body was indeed found. Sharp and Walker were arrested and finally confessed. They were both hanged and Ann's spirit was finally able to find peace and never appeared again.

CHAPTER EIGHT

ANGELS

'The things that you're liable to read in the Bible; ain't necessarily so!'

(From the musical, *Porgy and Bess.*)

Are They all Angels?

Angels have enjoyed a renaissance in recent years and some enlightened souls even pray to Angels rather than to God. Strictly speaking, this is not scriptural, but many reasonable and intelligent people today claim to have seen Angels while others believe they have Angelic spirit guides to assist them and watch over them. These people are quite sincere in their belief and it leads one to question just what substance there is to support this phenomenon. There appears to be an ingrained need within mankind for the comfort of these intercessory supernatural beings.

Many of the clergy identify every Bible reference from *'Heavenly Host'* to *'Sons of God'*, as Angel beings. Every one of the Biblical designations including: Rapha, Rephaim, Zuzim, Anakim, Elohim, Nephilim, Emim, or Zamzummin, has been taught at some stage as Angels or fallen Angels and we must now look beyond the superficial anthropomorphic imagery to see what is going on here. This is important because, in reality, these Biblical names have nothing whatever to do with the modern concept of Angels! Some basic research into the meanings of these names shows that:

- Rapha in Hebrew, means 'giants' and accordingly Rephaim really meant 'spirits of Giants';
- Zuzim meant 'evil roaming things';

- Anakim were a race of giants descended from the Giant Anak (the son of Arba) of the Nephilim.
- Emim and Zamzummin were local names for Anakim. Zamzummin were also lumped together with Rephaim.
- Now the difficult one to grasp is that Elohim and Nephilim were the original *plural words* used for the *(obviously plural)* Sky-Gods and the Sons of the Gods that have been altered to the (singular) God in today's Bible.

This is a straight out mistranslation and enduring Biblical error. To be fair though, this is bigger than individual clergymen and has become an international, theological scotoma (blind spot). [88]

Plural Gods

For Christians who choose to believe that there is and was only ever one God called Jehovah, well go right ahead; however, that is not what the Bible states. For example; Deuteronomy 32 : 16-17 *They made Him jealous with their foreign Gods and angered him with their detestable idols. They sacrificed to demons, which are not God - Gods they had not known, Gods that recently appeared, Gods your fathers did not fear.* Note that it does not anywhere say 'false' Gods or 'make believe' Gods; just foreign Gods, other Gods and Gods that recently appeared. According to the Bible there seems to have been no shortage of these Gods. In addition we find Gods called, El, El Elyon, El Shaddi, Adoni and others within the Jewish and Christian religions. These were not a pre-existence of YHWH Jehovah, they were other Gods. The Hebrew psyche was that they had selected a good macho, warlike God, YHWH-Sabaoth, one of many from the global pantheon. It seems in the Bible that this God YHWH supports the existence of other foreign Gods, some who had only recently appeared. A thinking person will acknowledge that there had to be other Gods for Jehovah to stand in the midst and judge them. *Psalm 82 : 1 God standeth in the congregation of the mighty; He judgeth among the Gods.* Today the clergy attempt to portray the early Jewish history as having always been monotheistic when in fact nothing could be further from the truth. We can find another clue in the following Bible passage where these other Gods are told: *Psalm 82 : 7 But ye shall (now) die like (mortal) men, and fall like one of the princes.* Take the time to read the entire chapter in your Bible. It is very enlightening!

Author L. Michael Barré PhD. had this to say about this Bible passage: *"Psalm 82 relates to the plural Elohim and shows Jehovah-El in a position where He; 'judgeth among the other Gods'. Psalm 82 is remarkable in that it has El 'firing' all his own sons and condemning them to mortality. Although this Psalm shares the same view of El and his sons, this tradition descends from northern tradition and in this respect differs from the Jerusalem tradition found in Deuteronomy 32 : 8-9. In Psalm 82, Yahweh is not explicitly mentioned even though this passage would place him among the "sons of Elyon" (v. 6)."* Barré continues; *"Apparently, among his reforms, intended to distance Israel from Judah and to promote national identity, Jeroboam I and his court thought it best to announce El's decision that the Gods of the other nations had been condemned to death and that El was now forced to rule alone."* (89)

Through incorrect teaching, the laity now believes in one God when the early Bibles clearly depicted multiple Gods and even today's modified Bibles still give hints of multiple Gods. Today's parishioners also desire glorious angels with majestic wings in their Christian walk but this doesn't alter the fact that the modern concept of angels is an anti-scriptural created Christian fantasy. We can read an original Biblical passage:

- ***Genesis 6 : 1-4 'And it came to pass, when men began to multiply on the face of the earth, and daughters were born unto them, that the Nephilim saw the daughters of men that they were fair; and they took them wives of all which they chose. And the Elohim said, our spirit shall not always strive with man, for that he also is flesh: yet his days shall be an hundred and twenty years. There were giants in the earth in those days; and also after that, when the Nephilim came in unto the daughters of men, and they bare children to them, the same became mighty men which were of old, men of the shem.***

The translation of 'men of the shem' as 'men of renown' is also quite incorrect. We can argue until we turn blue in the face but a *'shem'* was shown in ancient depictions as a transport vehicle of the Elohim Sky-Gods or in other words a fiery rocket. (90)

Teach Your Children Well

Most depictions of Angels are as some form of white-robed servants of God, flying with magnificent wings from the heavenly host; to watch over the pious, to intercede, to assist the needy, or to deliver messages on behalf of God. When not gainfully employed, these immortal beings float around on clouds playing harps or worshipping God. They also have a fabulous choir for singing praise to Him. Children are told, 'Mummy died and went to be with God; she is now an angel.' If you are a Christian and believe the Bible's scripture, why would you believe stuff like that? The Bible tells us the deceased are in a deep sleep; *Ecclesiastes 9 : 5 "They are conscious of nothing at all."* Ask yourselves this: Why would the dead in Christ need to rise first, when Jesus returns, if they are already with him, as Angels? Surely, Angel beings were not included in the Bible to be an embarrassment.

Ma`at

Included in the ancient Egyptian pantheon was a Neteru Goddess named Ma`at, the daughter of the Creator God. She was depicted as a human woman with symbolic, birdlike wings and her symbol was an ostrich feather in her hair. She held a Sceptre in one hand and an Ankh in the other and this particular Neteru was the prototype of today's Biblical angels. The Bible tells us that there were also evil angels; not controlled by Satan as you would expect, but actually controlled by Almighty God:

- ***Psalm 78 : 49-50 'He (God) cast upon them the fierceness of His anger, wrath and indignation and trouble, by sending evil angels among them.'***

It is interesting to note that there was some derision of this angel subject even back in the time of St. Paul, with the Sadducees vehemently denying their existence:

- ***Acts 23 : 8 'For the Sadducees say that there is no resurrection, neither angels, nor spirit; but the Pharisees confess both.'***

Messengers

This is a book about mysterious and peculiar things and I certainly don't mean to ridicule Angels or those who believe in them. To me truth is paramount and as a result, I feel it is my duty to certainly point out the mistranslations in the Bible. In reality, the word *'angel'* simply meant *'messenger'*. It still does mean that. Where confusion came in was with the Christian reporting. Persons undertaking a journey or a religious work were said to be led by God and it would be documented; *'And God caused an angel to be sent unto Gideon'*. This was immediately seen as a winged creature flying down from Heaven. All it really meant was that a messenger (in God's service) was dispatched from somewhere nearby, with a message for Gideon. In the same way, men of God call themselves His servants and when they set out on a journey in the Lord's work, the writers recorded; *'And God sent His servant.'* Really, all that occurred was a messenger was sent to deliver a message. Possibly, on many occasions, these messengers would have been Essenes and since the Essenes wore white robes, scriptures exist correctly describing 'angels' in shining white robes.

- The word used for messengers in the original Hebrew Scriptures was *'Mal'akhim'* (Hebrew for messenger).
- This was translated into Greek as *'Aggelos'* (Greek for messenger).
- The Latin, *'Angelus'* (meaning messenger) was the first to give this connotation of heavenly flying men.
- Then, English translators, instead of translating the Latin *'Angelus'* to the appropriate English word *'messenger'*, created the new word *'Angel'* and carried on the fallacy.

In *Genesis 19 : 1* we read where Abraham's nephew Lot, met with men who told him to get out of Sodom and he talked and ate with them for some considerable time before he realized that they were Angels. They were simply men (or messengers) with a message. If more evidence is required, read this instruction from the Bible:

- ***Hebrews 13 : 2 'Be not forgetful to entertain strangers: for thereby some have entertained Angels unawares.'***

I maintain that it would be quite difficult to unawares, entertain men who were disguising a set of hang-glider sized wings beneath their robes. When Daniel met with the archangel, Gabriel, did he meet a man who was a special messenger or did he meet with a strange winged creature? Read for yourself:

- ***Daniel 9 : 21 'Yea, while I was speaking in prayer, even the man Gabriel, whom I had seen in the vision at the beginning, touched me about the time of the evening oblation.'***

Now, we were taught that winged angels were present when Jesus was 'taken up'; however, this is simply not what is recorded in the Bible. It seems that the Church is ever ready to promote esoteric angles into a very Earthly scenario. Let's read it:

- ***Acts 1 : 9-11 'Now when He had spoken these things, while they watched, He was taken up and a cloud received Him out of their sight. And while they looked steadfastly toward heaven as He went up, behold, two men stood by them in white apparel, who also said, 'Men of Galilee, why do you stand gazing up into heaven? This same Jesus, who was taken up from you, will so come in like manner as you saw Him go into heaven.'***

Two men who stood by in white apparel were almost certainly Essenes and there is nothing at all here, to promote winged angels.

- ***Galatians 1 : 8-9, An angel who preaches a gospel contrary to that of Paul will be accursed.***

This passage doesn't seem to accord the usual measure of respect, to an angel of God. Does it sound more like a white winged creature, or a church messenger who is actually a junior preacher and subservient to Paul? [91]

Flying Sky-God

It seems from the Bible that God cannot fly by himself; I always understood that he was omnipresent and really didn't need to. In the following passage, he has to hitch a ride with a passing cherub. This really interferes with my 'mind picture' of God; however, this is what the Bible states:

- ***2 Samuel 22 : 11 'And he (the Lord) rode upon a cherub and did fly: and he was seen upon the wings of the wind.'***

I can't begin to explain this one; it is apparently a later addition to the Bible. Let's just say the scribes were at the altar wine and move on! In the Bible, there are some other bizarre creatures to look at. The Bible mentions six winged creatures called seraphims; who use two wings to cover their face, two to cover their feet and two with which to fly (so they have 10 limbs). I must confess that I have no idea what they are, but if I saw one I would be concerned about the coming hangover.

- ***Isaiah 6 : 2 'Above it stood the seraphims: each one had six wings; with twain he covered his face and with twain he covered his feet and with twain he did fly.'***
- ***Isaiah 6 : 6 'Then flew one of the seraphims unto me, having a live coal***

in his hand, which he had taken with the tongs from off the altar: and he laid it upon my mouth and said lo, this hath touched thy lips; and thine iniquity is taken away and thy sin purged.'

An easy explanation is that Angels are often seen in visions, and in that event, the unearthly forms are surely not required to be anatomically or biologically viable. This must be balanced against the true meaning of Angel which is 'messenger'. It would seem that practicing Christians have a need for anthropomorphic Angelic beings in their lives and are not averse to accepting conjured up images that are way outside those in the Bible. These same people would likely never deviate from other Biblical scripture, so this would perhaps indicate that the original Bible dogma falls down in this role. The Holy Ghost is meant to be the comforter in the Christian religion, but the image of a ghost is not one that would usually afford comfort. For this reason, a beautiful puissant entity such as an Angel would be an easier image from which to accept empathy and comfort, and would seem to fit the role of a 'comforter' far more altruistically than would a Ghost. Accordingly, perhaps the whole motif may be explained simply by supply and demand. There must be a desire for the current anti-scriptural depiction of winged Angels, so since the market existed, the clergy simply supplied it.

CHAPTER NINE

MIN MIN LIGHTS

'How sweet my life would be, if I were wise!
Wisdom is well known when it is no longer seen or thought of.
Only then is understanding bearable.'

Monk, Thomas Merton

Ghost Lights

Ghost lights are an unusual visual phenomenon that appears in specific areas around the world and this term describes the strange appearance of lights where one presumes there should be none. The lack of any reasonable sources or explanations for this phenomenon, has at times, led them to be associated with the paranormal. Australian Aboriginals used a name Min Min Lights for the unexplained lights seen particularly in Queensland, Australia. I had heard of these things but only ever associated them with the western parts of the state. I was in for a shock.

Adventure Holiday

Just after Christmas in 1976, I threw my diving equipment and a few things in the 4WD and headed north up to Queensland's *Great Barrier Reef* for a well earned break. Out from Shute Harbour I arranged to be dropped at Cid Harbour, along with two people I had met, to experience a 'deserted' Island for a few days. For some reason the boat could not get us ashore at the popular camp site at Cid Harbour so instead the skipper dropped us along with another two of his passengers on Henning Island a few kilometres from Hamilton Island Resort.

For shelter, I located a fallen tree just back from the beach and trimmed away some branches. With a canvass cover over the top and the sand scooped out and leveled, this made a perfect shelter for the 'balmy' nights in the tropics. I speared a few Coral Trout and cooked this magnificent fish in the coals, laid it on a bed of rice with garlic and ginger and made a sauce from fresh North Queensland pineapples. We had a feast on the beach, in the wild, and were all happy and at peace. The weather was magnificent and next morning we relaxed, explored, swam and fished and in the evenings sat up talking until sleep overtook us.

About 2.00am on our last night on the Island, I was awakened by one of the girls who pointed out a light in the distance. *"It's just a shipping beacon... its solar powered"*, I said still half asleep. About 3.45am, I woke again to find the others in a fairly scared state. Eight small, fairly dull lights had surrounded our camp. I was the only 'bushman' so I had to show some bravado to prevent outright panic. With my powerful diver's underwater torch, I crawled out of the shelter and walked inland towards the nearest light. As I did it slowly moved away. When I put the torch on it, there was nothing there and the torch shone right through it. Although this would have been scary if I had been alone, I found it interesting and amusing and played with the lights running towards them and then away from them and set a jovial mood in the others. There was unquestionably some intelligent control of this light phenomenon and they apparently presented no danger to us. We then sat up and talked until daybreak, watching the lights, telling ghost stories and the like. As the morning sky lightened, the lights slowly moved away and disappeared.

Local Knowledge

Next day back on the mainland, I met a local sugar cane farmer called 'Frosty' who was a keen angler and invited three of us out fishing in his boat. When we relayed our story to him, he laughed and said, *"They were Min Min lights!"* On his charts, he showed us two islands known locally as the 'cow and calf' and explained how local fishermen would not go anywhere near these islands at night, because of the fear of the mysterious lights.

Since then I have heard many tales and Aboriginal folklore about Min Min lights in the bush and have even contributed to other people's research with the encounter presented here. Near Boulia in Western Queensland is the abandoned Min Min Hotel which at one time was known as Hamilton Hotel. I was told by locals that on a property near there, several times each month around 7pm, what appears to be car lights are observed coming up the long driveway to one homestead, causing the station owners to 'put the billy on' anticipating company. As they near the homestead, however, the lights simply disappear. This would further suggest intelligent control and it was even reported to me that the lights appeared to 'bounce' in unison as if going over bumps along the roadway. I have spoken to bushmen who fired their rifle at Min Min lights and noted the bullet 'sparking' as is went through the light. There are many Aboriginal legends of children following them and becoming lost in the bush, but for all that, we still have no idea what they are.

Fata Morgana

As a child, living in a farming community on the Jimbour plain, on the Darling Downs of Queensland, I was familiar with an early morning mirage-like anomaly that in mid-winter often allowed us to see 20 kilometres distant grain silos very clearly but upside down in the air. Once we watched a man on a horse (riding upside-down) who was in fact some 8 kilometres away. This early morning phenomenon results from a temperature inversion and is termed 'Fata Morgana' and across the world allows objects on the horizon, such as islands, cliffs, ships or icebergs, to appear elongated and elevated, like fairy tale castles. Fata Morgana is a Latin name for Morgan le Fay, the mythical fairy half-sister of King Arthur (both 'fata' and 'fay' mean fairy). The phrase is also used to depict an illusion, and many scholars now attempt to explain the strange nocturnal properties of the Min Min lights by the unusual optical conditions of the Fata Morgana. They stress the human factors that supposedly operate under these highly-reduced stimulus conditions involving a single isolated light source without reference landmarks. These scholars have quite obviously never experienced a Min Min light and I am here to say that having experienced both phenomena, they hold no similarities whatsoever. Aboriginals say Min Min lights are lost spirits and in the absence of any better explanation, we should consider that, just maybe, they are right.

CHAPTER TEN

UFO'S IN ANCIENT RECORDS

'When you get reports from professors at MIT, engineers on balloon projects,
military and commercial pilots and air traffic controllers,
you might one day sit down and say to yourself,
"Just how long am I going to keep calling all these people crazy?"'

Dr. J. Allan Hynek. OMNI 1984;
Professor Emeritus and Chairman of the Department of Astronomy - Northwestern University.

An Ancient Report

Among the papers of the late Professor Alberto Tulli, former Director of the Egyptian section of the Vatican Museum, fragmentary documentation was discovered from the Royal Annals of Pharaoh Tuthmosis III, covering the sighting of UFO's in ancient Egypt, which translates as follows:

> ***'In the year 22 [c.1482 B.C.E.] in the third month of winter, in the sixth hour of the day, the scribes of the House of Life noticed a circle of fire that was coming from the sky [...]. From the mouth, it emitted a foul breath. It had no head. Its body was one rod long and one rod wide. It had no voice and from that the hearts of the scribes became confused and they threw themselves down on their bellies [...] then they reported the thing to the Pharaoh [Tuthmosis III.] His Majesty ordered [that all the writings...] should be examined [...] and he was meditating on what had happened, that it was recorded in the scrolls of the House of the Life. Now after some days had passed, these things became more and more numerous in the skies. Their splendor exceeded that of the sun and extended to the limits of the four angles of the sky [...] High and wide in the sky was the position from which these fire circles came and went. The army of the Pharaoh looked on with him in their midst. It was after supper. Then these fire circles ascended***

higher into the sky and they headed toward the south. Fish and birds then fell from the sky. A marvel never before known since the foundation of our land [...] And Pharaoh caused incense to be brought to make peace with Earth [...] and what had happened was ordered to be written in the Annals of the House of Life so that it be remembered for all time forward.' (92)

There is also a separate report about these same circular craft suggesting that they are relatively small, about 5 Metres in diameter. Egyptian documents also claim that: *'His majesty (Tuthmosis III) was taken aboard and flew up to the sky and there learned the secrets of Heaven.'* (93)

Biblical Flying Machines

There is no cause for Christians to smile about these strange reports since the Bible contains some quite unusual UFO records too. For example, could the Sky-God, who brought the children of Israel out of Egypt, have actually used a form of flying machine to achieve this rescue? *"No way"*, I hear you say. OK, then consider what the Bible records:

- ***Exodus 19 : 4 'Ye have seen what I did unto the Egyptians, and how I bare you on eagles' wings, and brought you unto myself.'***

This could be just another nonsensical Bible passage except for two things:

- The first Hebrew coin minted in the 'Promised Land' depicts the God YHWH seated in a winged chair or flying chariot.
- The Jewish Zohar contains a passage that draws on a third century mystical work by Rabbi Eleazar ben Pedath that states:

The first Hebrew coin depicts YHWH God on a flying chariot that certainly resembles the depiction of Triptolemus of Greek mythology.

'As Pharaoh came out of Egypt, to follow the Israelites, he raised his eyes to Heaven, and saw the Prince of the Egyptian Angels flying in the air.' (94) Now in addition we can read in the apocryphal *Book of Adam and Eve*, how the angels of the Lord, *"de-*

scended to the Gates of Paradise, where Eve was mourning the death of Adam." At this point the Sun, Moon and stars grew dark, the Heavens opened and the eagles appeared. [95] These are unusual passages recorded in the Bible and the Hebrew scriptures from which it was derived. The clergy have never satisfactorily explained these things and we are left to wonder.

My Own Experience

As a child, along with my parents, I watched a cigar shaped unidentified flying object for close to three hours in the skies above our farm near Dalby in Queensland, Australia. Now there is no question that we saw something solid, real and unexplained, hovering with no detectable sound. We were joined by a number of neighbors and altogether, about nine of us watched the object with the naked eye and through binoculars, for this extended period. Today, I would say we saw a UFO 'mother ship', but the occurrence was around 1960 and I had never heard of UFO's back then.

I now advocate caution, since UFO reports over the last century have gone through stages of Zeppelin sightings in the late 1800s, followed by mystery rockets around the time of World War II, then disc shaped 'flying saucers' from the 50s and today, more commonly, encounters with alien entities and the invasive testing of abductees. This causes some apprehension because the supposed alien technology we have observed through the years has remained just a little ahead of our own. The sheer number of UFO sightings by rational people, makes it obvious that this is, indeed, a real phenomenon; however, the question must be asked: Is there something additional occurring in the brains of those having the experience? Is someone teasing us with technology just out of our reach, or are our brains hardwired to receive and interpret an evolving, changing message?

Aliens

There is a tendency in religious circles to associate flying vehicles with the transport vehicles of the Gods and for this reason religious works hold many UFO descriptions. If for a moment, we look at a Gnostic work attributed to Seth the son of Adam; *The Three Steles of Seth*' (vii, 5), in verses 119 & 120, talking to the Almighty it states: *"Thou hast appeared in order that thou mightest reveal the Eternal Ones. Therefore thou hast revealed those who really are and thou art from another race for thou art not similar but their place is over other races for their place is in (eternal) life".*

Firstly, the Anunnaki Sky-Gods are called the 'Eternal Ones' at times in the Sumerian clay tablets and the entities recorded here are rulers. As eternal beings and clearly from another race we would have to pose the question: Just who was this ancient writer talking about?

Accepting the ancient Sumerian, Chinese, Egyptian and Biblical data as factual goes a long way towards acknowledging the existence of extraterrestrials. The Sumerians called them 'Anunnaki', the Chinese called them 'Sons of Light', the Egyptians called them 'Neteru' and in the Bible they were 'Elohim' and 'Nephilim'. America's late President Ronald Regan must have considered the existence of Extra-terrestrials possible - or perhaps he had classified information on alien contact. Many times he broached the subject in major speeches. For example, in his address to the United Nations on 21st Sep 1987 he had this to say: *"In our antagonisms of the moment we often forget how much unites all the members of humanity. Perhaps we need some outside, universal threat to recognize this common bond ... I occasionally think how quickly our differences would vanish if we were facing an alien threat from outside this world."*

From the 1950's, this appears to be a genuine picture of an alien from a crashed UFO.

There was an interesting report on the net involving Emmy award winning TV producer, and famous conspiracy and UFO author, Linda Moulton Howe, that claims she has "inside information" about this very subject, gained via the considerable influence she has in high places. *"Perhaps the most noteworthy example is the now well-known incident in April of 1983 when Air Force intelligence officer Richard Doty invited her to Kirkland Air Force Base in Albuquerque to a secured room and read, under observation, a classified government document entitled "Briefing Paper for the President of the United States of America."* Linda Moulton Howe holds a lot of integrity, and later reported that the paper revealed the Government had reliable information that extra terrestrials had been visiting earth for thousands of years, and had helped to create the human race, as we now know it, by genetically manipulating the DNA of the native primate population. [96]

Bingo! It seems the EBE's (Extra-terrestrial Biological Entities) are now confirming to American Military Intelligence what the Sumerians tried to tell us from thousands of years ago and it is reassuring that the American President was briefed on this. There remains to this day a belief that President Eisenhower met with extraterrestrials on 21st-22nd Feb 1954 at Muroc Field (now Edwards Air Force Base). This belief is kept alive by a very convincing letter dated 16th April 1954 from Gerald Light to Meade Layne, the then director of Borderland Sciences Research Associates; that alleges a meeting with extraterrestrials took place. Gerald Light claimed he was part of a delegation of community leaders to be invited to this meeting. If he was lying it would be inane to send such a letter and in any case his document carries an aura of authenticity in its very verbalization. In a subsequent article, Meade Layne described Light as a 'gifted and highly educated writer and lecturer'. Light was also a well known metaphysical community leader in the Southern California area. The alleged purpose of his selection and that of others on the delegation was said to be to test public reaction to the presence of extraterrestrials. Light described the circumstances of the meeting as follows:

"My dear friends: I have just returned from Muroc [Edwards Air Force Base]. *The report is true - devastatingly true! I made the journey in company with Franklin Allen of the Hearst papers and Edwin Nourse of Brookings Institute (Truman's erstwhile financial advisor) and Bishop MacIntyre of L.A. When we were allowed to enter the restricted section (after about six hours in which we were checked on every possible item, event, incident and aspect of our personal and public lives), I had the distinct feeling that the world had come to an end with fantastic realism. For I have never seen so many human beings in a state of complete collapse and confusion, as they realized that their own world had indeed ended with such finality as to beggar description.*

The reality of the 'other plane' aero forms (UFO vehicles) is now and forever removed from the realms of speculation and made a rather painful part of the consciousness of every responsible scientific and political group. During my two days visit I saw five separate and distinct types of (alien) aircraft being studied and handled by our Air Force officials - with the assistance and permission of the Etherians! I have no words to express my reactions. It has finally happened. It is now a matter of history. President Eisenhower, as you may already know, was spirited over to Muroc one night during his visit to Palm Springs recently and it is my conviction that he will ignore the terrific conflict between the various 'authorities' and go directly to the people via radio and television - if the impasse continues much longer. From what I could gather, an official statement to the country is being prepared for delivery about the middle of May."

Of course, President Eisenhower made no such announcement, and now, over 50 years later, the UFO cover-up continues. [97] I cannot say for certain that the events detailed here actually occurred or not; however, they certainly read like a genuine 1954 report. Despite considerable research and checking by scholars, this story cannot be disproved and has proved to be extremely tenacious. In addition the author of it has needlessly added the names of colleagues who also attended, necessitating that if his report is not a true one, then they would be in a position to immediately debunk his story. I do not believe he would needlessly put himself in that position, which in turn suggests that he is telling the truth. Dr. Boyland also reports on experts who testified under oath to the Congressional and White House official hearing. One such person was Stephen Lovekin, a lawyer from North Carolina who worked with a Top Secret security clearance in the Pentagon during President Eisenhower's White House term in the 1950s, as a cryptologist. He was the military aide who regularly briefed President Eisenhower on UFO evidence and developments. Another was rocket scientist and consultant to NASA, David Adair, who stated that he could back up Lovekin's report because in

Germany was reportedly flying circular aircraft at the end of WWII and further secret development of these craft appears likely.

These amazing photos are genuine and depict a German circular aircraft from the closing stages of WWII and two U.S. saucers from the 1950s. They are said to be the result of back-engineering advanced Alien craft and could certainly account for a percentage of today's UFO sightings.

1960 he was taken 20 stories underground at Area 51, to help figure out how an extraterrestrial engine worked (back-engineering); an engine taken from a UFO, he claimed. According to Adair the engine cowling displayed 'hieroglyphic' symbols which he later saw Lovekin display at the Congressional briefing. Adair said that they eventually identified the UFO device as an electromagnetic fusion-containment engine. [(98)]

Today we have important information that brings to light the possible alien reality and our interactions with these beings. This is Dr. Steven Geer's initiative, "The Disclosure Project". Since August of 2000, the USA based Disclosure Project has recorded the testimony of over 100 military, government and related witnesses to UFO events and projects from around the world. It involves hundreds of military and corporate personnel in high places, all willing to testify before Congress to their personal UFO experiences within Government projects, from back-engineering of alien devices and actually working with aliens.

On 9 May 2001, a historic event took place at the National Press Club, Washington, D.C. Over 20 selected witnesses to UFO activity and related Government projects came forward as a group to disclose the 'truth' to the world. Although "The Disclosure Project" has been active since 1993, this was the kick-off of The Campaign for Disclosure, a campaign to get open hearings in the Congress, ban weapons from space, and work in harmony with EBEs with a view to benefiting from back engineering their propulsion technology. In addition, this group is striving to remove the secrecy surrounding UFOs and to enact legislation to explore space peacefully. We have certainly heard of less noble motives.

Interesting Conversations

Astronauts are in the perfect job to evaluate the existence of UFOs. Many astronauts along with airline pilots have made numerous reports of their encounters. On the Oprah Winfrey Show of 19th Jul 1991, Dr. Edgar Mitchell stated, *"...there is a lot more known about extraterrestrial investigation than is available to the public right now (and) has been for a long time. It's a long, long story and goes back to World War II when all that happened and it's highly classified stuff."* Most conversations between Astronauts and the Command Centre are heavily edited for reasons of National Security but some pretty wild stuff gets through. Here are a few of many examples:

Apollo 11 – 20th July 1969; Michael Collins remained in orbit while Neil Armstrong and Bud Aldrin landed in the Sea of Tranquility. According to Otto Binder, who was a member of the NASA space team, something strange happened when the two moon-walkers, Armstrong and Aldrin were making their rounds some distance from the Lunar Module. Armstrong clutched Aldrin's arm excitedly and this was recorded:

- Armstrong: ... ***What was it? What the hell was it? That's all I want to know! These babies were huge, sir! ... Enormous! ... Oh, God! You wouldn't believe it! ... I'm telling you there are other space-craft out there ... lined up on the far side of the crater edge! ... They're on the Moon watching us! ...***

Otto Binder, tells us: *"There has, understandably, been no confirmation of this incredible report by NASA or any authorities, one can surmise that mission control went into a dither and then into a huddle, after which they sternly ordered the moonwalkers to forget what they saw and carry on casually and calmly as if nothing had happened. After all, an estimated 600 million people around the world were hanging on every word spoken by the first two men to leave footprints on the Moon".* (99)

Although there was a two minute interruption in the live broadcast, blamed on an overheating TV camera, here are a few bits of conversation that hackers and ham radio operators who had their own VHF receiving facilities that bypassed NASA's broadcasting outlets, were able to glean. Christopher Craft at Houston is talking with Neil Armstrong and Bud Aldrin on the Moon. Unfortunately it is impossible to delineate the excited voices of Armstrong and Aldrin so they have been lumped together:

- Craft: ***......there are other spaceships?***
- Armstrong & Aldrin: ***...Those are giant things. No, no, no, this is not an optical illusion. No one is going to believe this!***
- Craft: ***...What...what, what? What the hell is happening? What's wrong with you?***
- Armstrong & Aldrin: ***... They're here ...under the surface!***
- Craft: ***... What's there ...***(muffled noise) ... (interference) ***Control calling Apollo11 ...***
  [Space]
- Armstrong & Aldrin: ***... We saw some visitors. They were here for a while observing the instruments.***
- Craft: ***... Repeat your last information!***
- Armstrong & Aldrin: ***... I say that there were other spaceships. They're lined up in the other side of the crater!***
- Craft: ***... Repeat, repeat!***
  [Space]
- Armstrong & Aldrin: ***... Let us sound this orbiter... in 625 to 5 ... Automatic relay connected ... My hands are shaking so badly I can't do anything. Film it? God, if these damned cameras have picked up anything – what then?***
- Craft: ***... Have you picked up anything?***
- Armstrong & Aldrin: ***... I didn't have any film at hand. Three shots of the saucers or whatever they were that were ruining the film.***
  [Space]
- Houston: (Not Craft) ***... Control, control here. Are you on your way? What is the uproar with the UFO's over?***
- Armstrong & Aldrin: ***... They've landed here! There they are and they're watching us.***
- Houston: ***... The mirrors, the mirrors – have you set them up?***
  Armstrong & Aldrin: ***...Yes they're in the right place but whoever made those spaceships surely can come tomorrow and remove them. Over and out!*** (100)

For those who believe the astronauts did not go to the Moon and the TV images were shot in a studio, you just may be partly correct. I am convinced that they really did land on the Moon but by the conversation here, it is possible that the entities already on the Moon, *'were ruining the film'*. If this assessment is true, and 600 million people on Earth were watching and waiting for the TV coverage, with the advertising all ready booked and paid for, it just may have necessitated a cut to plan 'B'. They would have had a studio mock-up waiting just in case. Perhaps they had to use it!

Apollo 15 - 30th Jul 1971; David Scott and Alfred Worden land on the Apennine Mountains.

- Capcom: ***... You talked about something mysterious?***
- Orion: ***... OK Gordy, when we were coming about 30 or 40 feet out, there were a lot of objects – white things – flying by.***
- Capcom: ***... We copy that.***

Apollo 16 – 21st Apr 1972; Thomas Mattingly stays in orbit. Charles Duke, and John Young land on the Descartes Highlands.

- Duke: ***... You got ... YOWEE! Man! - John, I tell you this is some sight here. Tony, the blocks in Buster are covered - the bottom is covered with blocks, five meters across. Besides the blocks seem to be in a preferred orientation, northeast to southwest. They go all the way up the wall on those two sides and on the other side you can only barely see the outcropping at about 5 percent. Ninety percent of the bottom is covered with blocks that are 50 centimeters and larger.***
- Capcom: ***... Good show. Sounds like a secondary ...***
- Duke: ***... Right out here ... the blue one that I described from the lunar module window is colored because it is glass coated, but underneath the glass it is crystalline ... the same texture as the Genesis Rock ... Dead on my mark.***
- Young: ***... Mark. It's open.***
- Duke: ***... I can't believe it!***
- Duke: ***... you'd have to be here to see this to believe it – those domes are incredible!***
- Mission Control: ***... OK could you take a look at that smoky area there and tell me what you can see on the face?***
- Duke: ***... Beyond the domes, the structure goes almost into the ravine, you can't see the delineation. To the north-east there are tunnels; to the north they are dipping east to about 30 degrees.***
  [Space]
- Casper: **...** (Mattingly in lunar orbit overhead): ***Another strange sight over here. It looks - a flashing light - I think it's Annbell. Another crater here***

looks as though it's flooded except that this same material seems to run up on the outside. You can see a definite patch of this stuff that's run down inside. And that material lays or has been structured on top of it, but it lays on top of things that are outside and higher. It's a very strange operation.

Apollo 17 – 11th Dec 1972; Ronald Evans stayed in lunar orbit, while Eugene Cernan and Harrison Schmitt land in the Taurus-Littrow Valley. They find something startling, and are ordered to immediately switch to code:

- Command Module Pilot: ***... Mode is going to HM. Recorder is off. Lose a little communication there, huh? Okay, there's bravo. Bravo, select OMNI. Hey, you know you'll never believe it. I'm right over the edge of Orientale. I just looked down and saw the light flash again.***
  [Space]
- Jack: ***... Was there any indication on the seismometers on the impact about the time I saw a bright flash on the surface?***
- Capcom: ***... Stand by. We'll check on that, Jack.***
- Jack: ***... A UFO perhaps, don't worry about it. I thought somebody was looking at it. It could have been one of the other flashes of light.***
- Capcom: ***...Roger. We copied the time and ...***
- Jack: ***... I have the place marked.***
- Capcom: ***... Pass it on to the back room.***
- Jack: ***... O.K. I've marked it on the map, too.***
- Capcom: ***... Jack, just some words from the back room for you. There may have been an impact at the time you called, but the Moon is still ringing from the impact of the S-IVB impact. So it would mask any other impact. So they may be able to strip it out at another time, but right now they don't see anything at the time you called.***
- Jack: ***... Just my luck. Just looking at the southern edge of Grimaldi, Bob, and - that Graben is pre-Mare. Pre-Mare!***
- Capcom: ***...OK, I copy on that Jack. And as long as we're talking about Grimaldi we'd like to have you brief Ron [Evans] exactly on the location of that flashing light you saw ... We'll probably ask him to take a picture of it. Maybe during one of his solo periods.***

Notice that Capcom reiterates that it was a 'flashing' light. It was therefore not a meteor impact that they were witnessing and that the Moon was 'ringing'. Notice also that the Lunar Command Pilot specifically mentions a 'UFO'.

[Space]

- Mission Control: ***... Go ahead Ron.***

- Evans: ***... OK Robert, I guess the big thing I want to report from the back side is that I took another look at the ... the ... cloverleaf in Aitken with the binocs and that southern dome*** [garbled] ***to the east.***
- Mission Control: ***... We copy that Ron. Is there any difference in the colour of the dome and the Mare Aitken there?***
- Evans: ***... Yes there is ... That Condor...Condorsey, or Condorcet or whatever you want to call it there ... Condorecet Hotel is the one that has got the diamond shaped fill down in the [uh] floor.***
- Mission Control: ***... Robert. Understand. Condorcet Hotel.***
- Evans: ***... The area is oval or elliptical in shape. Of course the, ellipse is towards the top.*** (101)

Obviously there is more going on than we have been told. A certain Professor, who wishes to remain anonymous, was engaged in a discussion with Neil Armstrong during a much later NASA symposium:

- Professor: ***What really happened out there with Apollo 11?***
- Armstrong: ***It was incredible, of course we had always known there was a possibility ... the fact is, we were warned off! There was never any question then of a space station or a Moon city.***
- Professor: ***How do you mean 'warned off'?***
- Armstrong: ***I can't go into details, except to say that their ships were far superior to ours both in size and technology - Boy, were they big! ... and menacing! No, there is no question of a space station (on the Moon).***
- Professor: ***But NASA had other missions after Apollo 11?***
- Armstrong: ***Naturally - NASA was committed at that time, and couldn't risk panic on Earth. But it really was a quick scoop and back again.***

According to a Dr. Aleksandr Kasantsev, Buzz Aldrin took color movie film of the UFOs from inside the module, and continued filming them after he and Armstrong went outside. Armstrong confirmed that the story was true but refused to go into further detail, beyond admitting that the CIA had instigated the cover-up. (102) It seems strange that America put in such a huge effort to get to the moon by 1969, then after the Apollo missions, with our much improved technology, appear to have lost interest. Perhaps they were '*warned off*' as stated.

Where Are They Now

- Neil Armstrong – was in the United States Navy and saw action in the Korean War. He served as a test pilot at the National Advisory Committee for Aeronautics (NACA) High-Speed Flight Station, now known as the Dryden Flight Research Center, where he flew over 900 flights in a variety of aircraft. After his trip to the Moon, he was appointed Deputy Associate Administrator for aeronautics for the Office of Advanced Research and Technology (DARPA). He served in this position for only 13 months, and resigned from it and NASA as a whole in August 1971. He accepted a teaching position in the Department of Aerospace Engineering at the University of Cincinnati. Later Armstrong worked for Chrysler and served on the board of several companies before settling down on a farm in Ohio, zealously guarding his privacy and granting no interviews.
- Buzz Aldrin - wrote a book, *'Return to Earth'* in 1972, about his post-moonwalk nervous breakdown. He became head of Starcraft Enterprise, a California firm that promoted his ideas for reinvigorating the space program. Some of these were so left field that they earned him the sobriquet 'the Nutty Professor' back at NASA.
- Alan Bean retired from NASA in 1981 and now devotes himself full time to his passion of painting, mostly moonscapes. His artistic credo: *'I am the only artist in all of history who has been to another world and can paint it.'*
- Charles Conrad - began working for McDonnell Douglas in California, involved in developing a single-stage rocket intended to dramatically reduce the cost of sending payloads into orbit.
- Alan B. Shepard - was already a millionaire from banking ventures even before his moonwalk. He expanded his business activities after leaving NASA in 1974. He was president of the scholarship-bestowing Mercury Seven Foundation. Shepard, was the first American to fly in space and one of only 12 humans who walked on the Moon. He died in 1998 at the age of 74.
- Edgar Mitchell - believed his experiences in space provoked a *"blissful alteration of consciousness"* that led him to found the Institute of

Noetic Sciences in Sausalito, California, which pursues such topics as ESP and the mind. Despite this consciousness raising (or perhaps because of it), he was targeted in 1984 for a paternity suit by a former Playboy bunny.

- David Scott - was caught in a NASA scandal for carrying more than 400 stamped and canceled envelopes into space for later resale; the affair cost him his place in the astronaut corps. He moved on to head up a space-transportation consulting firm in California.
- James Irwin - his co-moonwalker was involved in the same envelope scandal but whilst on the Moon, *"felt the power of God as I'd never felt it before"* and subsequently founded an evangelical Christian organization whose activities included expeditions to Turkey to look for traces of Noah's Ark. He died of a heart attack in 1991.
- Charles Duke - became an evangelical Christian six years after his 1972 moonwalk. He became a speaker to religious groups around the world.
- Harrison Schmitt served a single term as a Republican Senator from New Mexico before suffering a narrow defeat in 1982; his opponent's campaign slogan was, *'What on Earth has he ever done?'* Schmitt became an independent consultant in science, technology and public policy in Albuquerque, New Mexico.
- John Young was the only moonwalker who remained working for NASA, as a technical overseer for a range of upcoming space projects. Young stated, *"I think it is absolutely amazing that 25 years later, we do not have a base up there with human beings exploring that weird place"*.

We may wonder about the very same thing! If the American Government is really proud of its space achievements, why is there a need for super secure places such as Area 51 and all the secrecy. We really need to be open minded on this entire issue because it seems fairly apparent that there is much going on that we don't know about.

The Pleiades

The Pleiades have captured man's attention since very early times. This group of stars known colloquially as the Seven Sisters, were used by ancient agrarian societies in both hemispheres, as critical timing devices to track agricultural seasons and for primitive time keeping. Today, many theorists claim this is the home of the aliens who visit our planet and the origin of the UFO's seen in our skies. This particular group of stars holds considerable mention in the Bible and ancient literature and is thought to be the central point of our galaxy. The sacred Temple of Hathor in Egypt houses a 'star clock' that allowed the priests to plot the 25,920 year precessional cycle through the zodiac, utilizing the Pleiades as the pivot. Various global constructions from the magnificent Parthenon in Greece and the Torreon Temple of the Three Windows at Machu Picchu in Peru, to the great Pyramid of the Sun at Teotihuacán outside Mexico City, are oriented to the setting of the Pleiades. Ancient Magi referred to this star group with names such as the *'Centre of Heaven'*, the *'Seat of God'* and the *'Creator of the Universe'* and it seems, an inordinate amount of consideration was given to this constellation. Ancient man believed his Gods lived there in *"The Centre"* of our Galaxy.

To give some idea of the impact the Pleiades have had on our planet, author Moira Timms recorded this amazing revelation in her book, *'Beyond Prophesies & Predictions'*: *"If a star map is superimposed over the Earth with the pole star placed over the terrestrial North Pole, we have a celestial clock making one revolution daily. The noon point of that map (like Greenwich) is the Great Pyramid of Giza. Thousands of years ago, Egypt was known as the land of Khem. The Khema were the group of seven major stars (in the constellation of Taurus), known today as the Pleiades. If the map is positioned with the Khema over the Land of Khem (Egypt) - directly over the apex of the Great Pyramid - then Taurus falls over the Taurus Mountains of southern Turkey; Ursha Major, The Great Bear, rambles over Russia; the head of Draco the dragon coils up over China; Orion (the warrior) over Iraq/Iran; Aries the Ram over Rome, and Capricorn (identified with the god Pan) falls over Panama, Panuco, and the Mayapan (the old name of the Yucatan). Aquila the eagle spans the United States. The analogies are obvious, and quite impressive. This is one of the clearest examples of the law of, 'As Above, So Below'."*

Were the ancients sufficiently versed in geography and astronomy to organize this global fit, or were they assisted by the Sky-Gods as they recorded? It would not be normal human nature for man to credit the Gods with his own meticulous achievements. Therefore we have to consider that the diverse ancient records of Sky-Gods who assisted man, may be true.

CHAPTER ELEVEN

THE GOLDEN MEAN

'Geometry has two great treasures: one is the theorem of Pythagoras;
the other, the division of a line into extreme and mean ratio.
The first we may compare to a measure of gold;
the second we may name a precious jewel.'

Johannes Kepler (1571-1630)

The Golden Section Ratio

Geometry has been sacred to man since time began. Any number of sacred paintings contain hidden geometry. The Church Father, Saint Bernard, defined Almighty God as, *'length, width, height and depth'* whilst Pythagoras stated that, *'number is all'*. The one point in Nature that 'proves' that there is a harmonious Good or Light Force controlling the Universe is possibly that manifested in the Golden Mean. This is encapsulated in the mathematical sequence of .6180339887.... The dots at the end indicate that this is a nonrecurring decimal number and that the numbers after the decimal point would actually go on forever. The ancients knew about the Golden Mean which was also called the Divine Proportion and they used it to achieve the harmonious proportions in great buildings and in works of art that would be most pleasing to the eye. [(103)]

For some reason in architecture, a point almost 62% of the way along a line or a ratio of 618 : 382 is the optimum dimensional way to appeal to the senses of man. When this proportion is utilized for Length is to Width, it somehow produces a 'classic' look. This is also called the Golden Section or

Golden Number and its calculation is really fairly simple;

A C B

The point C is located so that the ratio of AB : AC is equal to the ratio of AC : CB

This is the 'Golden Mean' and equates to 1.618033989 or Phi, (not to be confused with Pi which is used for calculating the area or circumference of a circle and equals 3.14159265.)

So Phi = 1.618033989 and 1/Phi = 0.618033989

Phi is a Greek letter, its name originally taken from the Greek sculptor Phidias Phobias (c.493 - c.430 B.C.E.), one of the greatest sculptors of all time. He closely studied the Divine Proportion and was selected to supervise the sculptural program for the Parthenon, which is also built to this ratio. Throughout history Phi has been observed to evoke pure emotion or aesthetic feelings in man and is considered the epitome of pleasing architecture. The ancient Egyptians used it in the construction of the great pyramids and even in the proportion of hieroglyphs. The ancients of Mexico embraced Phi while building the Sun and Moon Pyramids at Teotihuacán. [104]

Pythagoras

The Greek geometer, Pythagoras (560-480 B.C.E), was especially interested in the Divine Proportion, and demonstrated that it was the basis for the proportions of the human figure. He showed that the human body is built with each part in a definite proportion to all the other parts, all of which correspond to the proportion of .618. For example, whether he is short or tall, the height of a man divided by the height from the floor to his navel calculates at precisely the Golden Mean.

In fact it can now be noted that even the DNA molecule, the program for all life, is proportioned on the Golden Mean. This molecule measures approximately 34 angstroms long by 21 angstroms wide for each full cycle of its double helix spiral. When you divide the precise figure that is approximately 21, by the figure that is approximately 34, this gives exactly 0.618033989 or the Divine Proportion. Leonardo da Vinci (1451-1519 A.D.)

certainly displayed an ardent interest in the mathematics of art and nature, as did others such as Michelangelo and Raphael. The Golden Mean proportion can be found incorporated in most of their famous paintings, proving that they knew of its appealing aesthetic qualities to the viewer. Even subtle landscape features in the background of the Mona Lisa are proportioned to the Golden Mean, indicating just how passionate da Vinci was about maximizing the impact and appeal of his work.

It can also be shown that all music reverberates in line with the Golden Mean; however, classical music composed by Mozart, Beethoven, and Bach specifically reverberates precisely to mathematical formulae that embrace the ratio of Phi. Whether this was purely intuitive, the result of absolute genius, or simply occurred by accident as written to be entirely appealing to the ears, can only be guessed at. [105]

Fibonnaci

Formalization of the Divine Proportion was said to be derived from one of the most competent mathematicians of the Middle Ages; Leonardo of Pisa (c.1175 AD - 1250) who produced the Fibonacci sequence that follows the exact same proportion or possibly from which that proportion is derived. In this sequence, each term is equal to the sum of the two preceding terms, for example:

0 1 1 2 3 5 8 13 21 34 55 89 144 233 377 610

Leonardo was the son of Guglielmo Bonaccio and the name 'Fibonacci' derives from the Latin 'filius Bonacci', which means 'son of Bonaccio'. Surprisingly, Leonardo would take no credit for discovering this sequence and stated that he did not calculate the sequence that was credited to him. He claimed that it had been in use by Indian mystics and other learned men for millennia. The fact that ancient buildings and monuments such as the pyramids of South America and of Egypt correspond precisely to this ratio would certainly date this knowledge to distant antiquity.

The Golden Mean

It is almost impossible to comprehend that across every land mass of the ancient world, examples exist of the usage of the Golden Mean. How is it humanly possible that something that personifies such ultimate perfection could have developed independently in such diverse, remote and unconnected cultures? What is even harder to grasp is not only that the ancients were fully conversant with this system, but that the ratio appears to occur naturally in the Universe in many guises! Nature effectively shows that a common principle is at work here that appeals to the human senses. It can be found everywhere in Nature, in the harmony of music and the beauty in art and architecture. (106) For example:

- There are always more female than male bees in a hive and anywhere in the world the number of female bees divided into the number of male bees equals .618033989 .... (107)
- The ratio of the slant height of the Great Pyramid to the distance from ground center is precisely 1.6180339 ... and this is the basis for the proportions that provide the 'perfect' 51 degrees 58 minutes for the diagonal angles. (108)
- Regardless of the plant species, the spacing of leaves or buds on a living stem each sit 61.8033989% closer towards the tip, also conforming precisely to the Golden Mean and the Fibonacci sequence. (109)
- The spirals of the seeds within a sunflower conform precisely to the Golden Mean. (110)
- A living Nautilus seashell (cephalopod mollusk) injects gas in order to pump water from its spiraled tube and thus minutely adjusts its buoyancy. Amazingly, the spiral ratios of this crustacean are again precisely in line with the Golden Mean. (111)
- The spirals of Galaxies in the Universe are again in this exact proportion. (112)
- This proportion can be observed in the behavior of light and atoms. (113)
- The design of plants, flowers, fruit and vegetables, from the skin of pineapples to the pattern of pine cones and palm fronds, all work with the Fibonacci sequence and the Golden Mean. (114)
- The length and breadth proportion of the magnificent Greek Parthenon is precisely in line with the Golden Mean. (115)
- There are now computer programs available that allow one to play the stock market in line with this proportion. It seems the human

element behind the rises and falls correspond to increments within the proportion of the golden mean.

Nature

The technical term for the study of the arrangements of leaves and of seed heads in plants is phyllotaxis. Growth occurs from a single tiny group of cells right at the tips of any growing plant, called the meristem. There is a separate meristem at the end of each branch or twig where new cells are formed and grow in size. New cells are only formed at such growing points as cells earlier down the stem expand so that the growing point rises. These cells grow in a spiral fashion to become a new branch, or perhaps a bud or flower. The amazing thing is that the consistent angle of the spiral produces the optimal design no matter how big the plant grows. It works so each leaf will least obscure the leaves below and be least obscured by any future leaves above it to maximize the benefit of the sun's light and the rain upon the plant. This phenomenon was only proved mathematically in 1993 by Douady and Couder, two French mathematicians, who were amazed to find that the fixed proportion is precisely equal to Phi. [(116)]

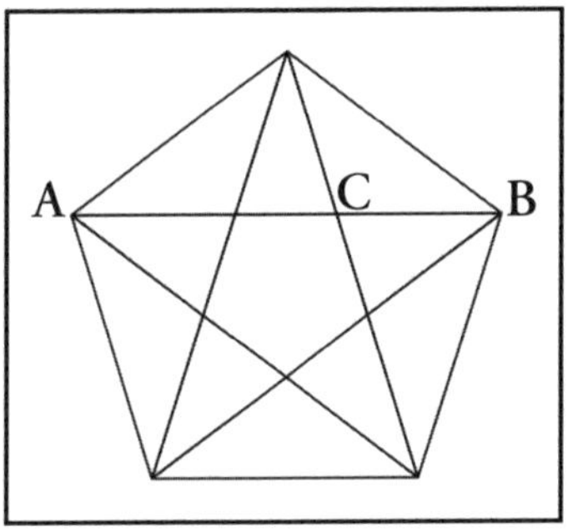

The figure of the Pentagram with its inherent Golden Mean proportion.

The figure of a pentagon is a classic example of the Golden Mean ratio and demonstrates graphically that this particular design is rather special. If we construct a pentagon and join the points forming a pentacle (five pointed star) then an inverted pentagon results inside the pentacle. The ratio of the points thus formed AB : AC is equal to the ratio of AC : CB again showing that the Golden Mean occurs naturally within this most ancient symbol. [(117)]

The Golden Mean is seen as a harmonious force within the Universe. It is a thing of naturally occurring beauty in nature and in music and if we analyzed the songs of birds and the sounds of Nature, I'm sure we would find it there too. It is pleasing to the eye in architecture and art as identified in the works of the past Masters. It closely follows the tranquil concept of Ma`at sought by the Egyptian Pharaohs and is the nemesis of chaos and yet the purity of the pentagon diagram contains within, an inverted pentagon, which is the symbol of Satanism.

In like manner the *I Ching* operates on the same harmonic principle of *'yin and yang'* which conveys this infinite truth to us, housed within this simple concept: *'Within the greatest Good is contained the seed of the greatest Evil and within the greatest Evil is contained the seed of the greatest Good.'* We must recognize that most religions work around a dualistic system of Good vs. Evil. We all hope and pray that Good overcomes Evil for the common good of Mankind. Accordingly, the Golden Mean and the Fibonacci sequence found occurring within Nature spotlights an 'intelligent design' within our universe. In its auditory and visual forms, it is a Godly concept that Nature has shared with man.

The yin and yang of the Asian philosophy, are always in harmony as opposed to the eternal conflict contained in other classic dualities.

CHAPTER TWELVE

BUSTING TENACIOUS MYTHS

'Man's biggest problem is that he just doesn't think.'

Albert Schweitzer

Pushing the Button

We've all done it and we have often seen others do it; impatient people giving the button a thorough work-out to speed up the green signal or elevator cab. The rationale is that each push represents a person present and will convince the system that myriads of people are waiting for that green signal or elevator cab. Thus by sheer weight of numbers it will be coerced into reconsidering its electronic priorities and actually arrive more quickly. The reality is however quite different.

Traffic light controllers in most Cities are time controlled during daylight hours and use traffic detectors (inductive loops under the road surface) to measure traffic density and regulate its timing accordingly. During business hours in most areas, the button is merely non-operational 'street theatre'. Only outside business hours or in lighter traffic areas will the button become active. At these times, you may also see bicycle riders or those on small motor scooters get off their 'steed' and walk over to push the button, since there is insufficient metal in their cycle to register on the inductive loop activator.

With both Traffic light controller buttons and those that signal elevator lifts, the first button push causes a 'latch' within the system and further pushing regardless of the passion and vigor expended, is entirely superfluous and totally ineffective. [(118)]

Shakespeare & the Bezoar

For a lot of reasons, I sincerely believe that William Shakespeare was the pen name of Sir Francis Bacon and I believe he left us a clue to this. Bacon was commissioned by King James I of England, (James VI of Scotland) to edit the 1611, King James Bible and apparently spent 18 months in this endeavor.

The mythical William Shakespeare of Stratford-upon-Avon, was said to be born in the year 1564, which would have made him 46 years old during 1610 when the finished KJV Bible was handed to the King. The name William Shakespeare is an anagram of, *"Here I was, like a psalm."* It may have been to acknowledge Shakespeare's 46th birthday or just a silly prank, however, if we go to Psalm 46 in the KJV Bible and count down 46 words from the top, we arrive at the word "shake". Omitting the added salutation *Selah'* count back 46 words from the end of the psalm and we arrive at the word "spear". This is an obvious Bible code and was almost certainly left by Bacon as a sign. The odds of the 46th word from the front and back of the 46th Psalm spelling out the name of Shakespeare right in his 46th year; are simply astronomical. Whether or not he was really Francis Bacon is a mystery that has not been solved in 400 years, so we won't dwell on it.

William Dugdale was acquainted with the Shakespeare family. His depiction of the bard from 1653 bears little resemblance to the promoted image of William Shakespeare we all know.

The only Shakespeare I remember from school days was an interesting quote from the play *'As You Like It'*, where the bard (whoever he was) wrote:

"Which, like the toad, ugly and venomous,
Wears yet a precious jewel in its head."

In Shakespeare's time, it was believed that an old male toad had a growth in its head called a 'borax' or 'stelon' which would repel poison and could be utilized as a cure for wounds and to combat infection. Right through the middle ages folks believed in the overall antidote generically called a 'bezoar'. The word bezoar comes from the Persian word *'padzhar'* which means, 'pro-

A bezoar was believed to guard against poisoning.

tects from poison'. A bezoar or enterolith is a sort of concretion, a foreign body found in the intestines of mostly ruminant (cud-chewing) animals, but also occurring among others including cats and even humans. [(119)]

Shakespeare's contemporaries wore rings, to which were attached certain highly valued bezoars cut from the heads of old toads or taken from the stomachs of animals. The upper class were never quite sure where the loyalties of their friends lay and at functions, made a habit of clandestinely dunking their bezoar in their wine to render any poison harmless. The common folk were assured of the effectiveness of a bezoar and that, *'touching any part envenomed by the bite of a rat, wasp, spider or other venomous beast, ceases the pain and swelling thereof."* Strangely, it would appear that this treatment did have some positive medicinal value.

Chinese healers still go to toads for a substance they call *materia medica*. The dried venom of certain of their toads, is prescribed to break up colds and utilized to treat everything from toothache to local inflammations. The apparent effectiveness of Chinese toad venom was recently evaluated scientifically and it was found that the toad secretes a fluid whose components are both animal and vegetable. One ingredient is *ergosterol*, which is also found in cod liver oil. Another is *adrenalin* exactly like that taken from the suprarenal glands of animals. Two other ingredients act like digitalis, which is produced by the purple foxglove plant. The scientists' claim that they do not know how the Chinese dry and prepare their toad venom. It seems that strange things may be added, befogging a true analysis. [(120)] Regardless, this medicine seems to be quite effective in Asian countries.

Judas Iscariot was the Baddie

To many of us, the Easter holidays are simply a time to enjoy a break from work and spend quality time with friends and loved ones. Christians of course see Easter as an occasion to celebrate the redemption found in the sacrifice of Christ their Saviour, who was supposedly betrayed by Judas Iscariot and crucified at this time.

Recent news items told of the ancient scriptural *'Gospel of Judas'* being found in the Egyptian desert and National Geographic published details of this find. This is actually not a new find at all. This 1,700 year old document was actually found in the 1970s and has been lying in a Safety Deposit box slowly deteriorating and has only just now been brought to light. This version is written in Coptic (the last stage of the ancient Egyptian language written in Greek lettering) and is a copy of an earlier version. Bishop Irenaeus of Lyon mentioned this ancient document about 180 A.D. and although it pre-dated the Catholic Church's newly manufactured 'orthodoxy', he somewhat ludicrously claimed that it was 'heretical' to the Church.

Of interest is that the ancient *'Gospel of Judas'* paints Judas as the most trusted and loved Disciple of Christ and not the 'bad guy' of our Sunday School days. In fact, Judas was the treasurer for Christ and the Disciples so this scenario is likely true. Thinking people will recognize a somewhat ludicrous Christian prejudice in the Bible, where Satan is blamed for the actions of Judas Iscariot prior to the crucifixion:

- ***Luke 22 : 3 "Then entered Satan into Judas surnamed Iscariot".***

We are told a Christian rejoices in the salvation achieved from the sacrifice of Jesus, their Saviour. Paramount is the belief that Jesus died for them as a personal Saviour! Thus, logic tells us Judas obviously played a crucial and pivotal role in achieving that sacrifice. (No Judas, no betrayal, no sacrifice, no resurrection, no redemption, no salvation.) If the whole thing was prophesied and planned for the salvation of mankind, then Judas was simply acting out a role orchestrated for him by Jesus, and the Bible makes this clear:

- ***Luke 22 : 37 For I say unto you, that this which is written, must yet be accomplished in me.***

We can see that this role was fully orchestrated. Recall that when the time drew near, Judas even received a cue from Jesus:

- ***John 13 : 27 What thou doeth, do quickly.***

To blame Satan in line with Luke's passage above, Christians would need to believe that the Devil actually worked to achieve their salvation, found in the crucifixion of Jesus. This entire Biblical story of Jesus being betrayed by a kiss from Judas is indeed fraught with problems; let's move on to that:

- ***Matthew 26 : 49-50*** Jesus is betrayed by Judas with a kiss, and then he is seized.

- ***Mark 14 : 44-46*** The same story from the same original Quelle source.
- ***Luke 22 : 47-48*** Jesus anticipates Judas' kiss but no actual kiss is recorded.
- ***John 18 : 2-9*** Jesus voluntarily steps forward to identify himself negating any need for Judas to identify him. Again no kiss is mentioned.

The 'cue' we just looked at is from this same Book of John involving Judas who is then not even required when Jesus steps forward.

We appear to be a people obsessed with 'justification' and the same can be particularly stated for the early, warlike, Hebrew people. The Jewish religion is a religion of 'justification' and by association, so is Christianity. As people become educated the quaint myths of the past will finally lose their tenure and Biblical characters like Judas may finally overcome their evil image.

Cinderella Wore Glass Slippers

The concept of the 'glass slippers' in the Cinderella story is so entrenched that it is now central to the story. To remove them would ruin the story for many. In the original French version of this fairy tale, Cinderella wore 'pantoufles en vair' meaning, *'slippers of fur or white ermine'*. By the 14th century the French word 'vair' was no longer in use, and the author Charles Perrault (1628-1703) selected instead, 'verre' meaning glass, when he re-wrote the story in 1697. Thus by a mere chance the story was changed and children now desire glass slippers as a pivotal part of their Cinderella story.

Cook an Egg With our Mobile Cell Phone

I have had the emails and no doubt, you have too. You must have stopped and thought, *'Hey, if you can really cook an egg with two mobiles, what is it doing to my brain'*. The email is enough to scare you silly at the thought of sizzling your brain with each and every call you make or receive. So! Would that Indian telemarketer you can't get off the line really cause your mobile phone's radiation to actually fry your brain? The answer is No!

The simplest way to prove this to yourself is to try a simple experiment. Place a fresh egg in an egg-cup. Using rubber bands sandwich the egg between two mobile phones. Now phone one mobile from the other and start a timer.

After an hour, two hours, three hours, the result will be the same. When you crack the egg, it will still be raw. If you have free calls to a particular number try it overnight; the egg will not be cooked.

Actually the phones do not talk to each other directly but rather back through the station or cell, so really only one phone is needed. A mobile phone transmits a maximum of 2 watts peak power but it is in pulses that average about 0.25 watts depending on how close you are to the base station or cell. Close to the base station it could be as little as 2 milliwatts (two thousandths of a watt). Now you can cook an egg in a microwave oven in about 2 minutes but the microwave is around 1,200 watts; so you can see the miniscule radiation from our mobile phone and the 1,200 watts from our microwave are simply poles apart. Thus if it took 1,200 watts to cook an egg in 2 minutes it would likely take 2,400 watts to cook it in 1 minute. If your mobile put out a quarter of a watt, it should take 2,400 X 4 = 9,600 minutes (160 hours); however, there is another consideration. The egg would actually cool faster than the tiny quarter watt appliance could heat it, so the 160 hours would blow out to infinity. In other words it is not possible to cook an egg using a mobile phone. [(121)]

So…how did the ridiculous story start? A 61 year old archiver by the name of Charlie Ivermee, who works for a legal firm in Southampton in the U.K., keeps a web page he calls the *Wymsey Village Web*. Under the pen name of *Suzzanna Decantworthy*, Charlie recounts the goings on of his fictional village of Wymsey. He 'fessed up that he started this ridiculous myth on his site. The whole concept of mobile phones frying your brain was really silly so he wrote the send up story of cooking an egg and posted it. He was truly amazed that people took it seriously and passed the story on. [(122)]

Stonehenge was Built by Druids

Lord Colin Renfrew, Professor of Archaeology at Cambridge University acknowledged in 1998 that much of prehistory was now in turmoil and certainly headed for a review of paradigm shift proportions. This is because many of the hypotheses formulated by various historians and archaeologists alike were based on assumptions that are no longer tenable. Lord Renfrew stated: *"Archaeologists all over the world have realized that much of prehistory, as written in the existing text books, is inadequate. Some of it is quite simply wrong."* [123]

These things die hard, however, and it is certainly taking an extended amount of time. For example, it was once proposed that Stonehenge was built by the Druids. Now today we know for a fact that Stonehenge predates the Druids by many millennia. Somehow the totally wrong supposition still remains in vogue today with the populous at large, and they will inform you with certainty that Stonehenge was built by the Druids, even though this is nonsense.

The Pyramids were Pharaohs' Tombs

In the late 1800s, British and French archaeologists encountered a practice in Egypt where the bodies of Pharaohs were often removed from their tombs to simulate that they had ascended to the Gods. [124] It was wrongly stated by Herodotus that the Great Pyramid of Khufu (Cheops in Greek) was built to be that pharaoh's tomb, even though his body was not contained there. This was put down to the belief that he had ascended or at least this had been simulated and it became widely believed that the pyramids were the Pharaoh's tombs. This totally incorrect assumption is still widely believed today and is even regurgitated by the Egyptian tour guides whose dialogue goes unquestioned. Pharaoh Khufu did do some renovation of the pyramid that bears his name; however, it was extremely ancient long before he was born. Generally, Pharaohs were buried in tombs such as those in the Valley of Kings, not in the Pyramids. Despite not one mummy or body ever being found in the "Great Pyramid of Khufu" and despite no evidence at all of grave robbers or any other device that might have removed the body, it is accepted as historical fact.

In 1954 a stele in the shape of a scarab was found with engravings showing where Khufu was really interred and it surely wasn't in the pyramid that incorrectly bears his name. Zechariah Sitchin showed that the Great Pyramid of Khufu is a total misnomer. The British Army archaeologist, Col. Richard Howard-Vyse, confirmed in 1837 that he had found a cartouche inside depicting Pharaoh Khufu, but Sitchin was able to show that Howard-Vyse, totally despondent that he was running out of time and money before returning to Great Britain, actually forged the cartouche himself (complete with errors and incorrect ancient Egyptian grammar) in an attempt to write his name in the history books. This all goes to prove that once a paradigm is set, the unlearning is a long and difficult process indeed.

The Theory of Evolution

The above point also applies to much of the information surrounding the Darwinist theories, which after years of rejection by the Church, are now taught and accepted as fact despite a general lack of supporting evidence. We can't just point the finger at Darwin however. We must appreciate that Charles Darwin was an intelligent, studious and hardworking pioneer of the origins of man, who traveled the world and expended enormous efforts in a relentless search for the answers. In 1859 Darwin published his work, *'On the Origins of Species by Means of Natural Selection'*, then followed it in 1871 with, *'The Descent of Man'*. Darwin did not suggest that man descended from apes as is commonly stated. He suggested that man and apes may have a common ancestor.

We should understand and appreciate that the man, Darwin, was not a fanatical supporter of his own theory. He was patently aware of several shortcomings. For example, all primates have 48 chromosomes, while humans have 46. Further, the primate gestation cycle is something between 5 and 8 months, varying from monkeys to chimpanzees and apes, while for humans it is 9 months. Their sharing a common ancestor was always particularly difficult to reconcile and now with DNA sampling, it is shown to be near impossible. Coincidently, 'estrus', the phenomena of coming into season, colloquially called 'on-heat', is common to all mammals except modern woman and orangutans. It seems that over the millennium, nature has caused this practice to become extinguished in just these two species. Another piece of trivia is that man and orangutans are the only species that are ticklish and utilize tools.

To gain further perspective on the shortcomings of the evolution theory, man, though a mammal, is unique among the land animals in that he has a descended larynx, a channel from nose to mouth and can breathe equally well through either. Only diving mammals (the sea lion and dugong) share this feature. Animals have the channel from nose to lungs (the wind pipe) and another channel from mouth to stomach (the gullet) and unlike man; this allows them to breathe and drink at the same time. The land animals, however, do not have the connection from nose to mouth. It is this unique configuration that allows the passage of air across the voice box to create human speech. For this reason, animals can only make snorts, grunts, growls etc.

It is likely that Darwin became disenchanted with this theory as he approached old age. He is said to have made a statement in his twilight years to the effect that, *"I created a hypothesis because I wanted man to think. Man took that theory and turned it upside down."* (125)

A Hand and a Name?

The prophet Isaiah relayed God's specific promise that he would send a yad and a shem, but you might never know it today, because of spurious translations in the Bible:

- ***Isaiah 56 : 5 "Even unto them will I give in mine house and within my walls a yad and a shem, better than of sons and of daughters: I will give them an everlasting shem, that shall not be cut off..."*** (126)

Now a *'yad'* is known by archaeologists to be a monument with a sharp pointed pyramidion shape, whilst one with a curved top like a fairly sharp, half oval, is known as a *'shem'*. Great reverence and even worship was given to these monuments in antiquity and there seems no doubt they were always associated with the 'Sky-Gods'. They were depicted with flames shooting out the bottom, like a child would draw a rocket. It may stretch belief a little but it seems that these shapes depict two 'space vehicles' of the Gods, one apparently for passengers only and the other to carry greater payloads. This may be difficult to accept but if you prefer the quite ridiculous translation in today's Bible; *'will I give in mine house and within my walls a hand and a name...'* well go right ahead, but be cautioned that the translation is not correct. In fact, it actually makes no sense at all. The association of the Sky-Gods with 'shem' vehicles can be taken a step further with the Jewish people actually calling their G-d of Avraham, Yitzchak, and Ya'akov (God of Abraham, Isaac and Jacob), *'Ha-Shem'*. Whether you like it or not this name means, *'God of the fiery rockets'*.

King Hiram's Journey

Ezekiel had this to say about the King of Tyre, who according to the Bible, apparently went for a journey with the Sky-Gods in one of their 'Shem' vehicles;

- ***Ezekiel 28 : 12-14 "Thus saith the Lord God; Thou sealest up the sum, full of wisdom, and perfect in beauty. Thou hast been in Eden the garden of God; every precious stone was thy covering, the sardius, topaz, and the diamond, the beryl, the onyx, and the jasper, the sapphire, the emerald, and the carbuncle, and gold: the workmanship of thy tabrets and of thy pipes was prepared in thee in the day that thou wast created. Thou art the anointed cherub that covereth; and I have set thee so: thou wast upon the holy mountain of God; thou hast walked up and down in the midst of the 'stones of fire'."***

The 'shem' were usually documented as 'shem stones' or called 'stones of fire' and if these in reality were the Gods' transport vehicles, this may indicate that they were made of a metal that to primitive man was solid like stone. They also sprouted flames and fire and there is no shortage of documentation and depictions of this. The above 'stones of fire' from Ezekiel are again translations of that 'shem' word:

- ***Genesis 6 : 3-4 "... when the sons of God came in to the daughters of men and they bore children to them. Those were the mighty men who were of old, men of the shem."***

Again we see a faulty translation of that 'shem' word with the current KJV Bible recording 'men of renown'. Remember Enoch was called to pass on God's punishment to the sons of the Sky-Gods (Watchers) who 'went native' with the daughters of men. It is highly improbable that their offspring would be considered 'men of renown' or 'men of the name'. This is simply an obvious translation error and despite any clerical protests, this original, 'men of the shem' certainly referred to 'men of the fiery rockets'. [127]

The Thomas Crapper Story

Thomas Crapper was born in Yorkshire and was baptized on the 28th September 1836. Crapper had a successful career in the plumbing industry in England from 1861 to 1904; however, the inventor of the flushing toilet was not Thomas Crapper as is commonly stated. It was actually John Harington

who invented the WC and the manufacturer Thomas Crapper who promoted it. Sandringham, Windsor Castle, Buckingham Palace and Westminster Abbey all benefited from the Crapper Company's quality goods and services. Today, the manhole covers in Westminster Abbey, emblazoned with the name 'Crapper' are popular for students to make brass rubbings for projects or to take home as souvenirs!

Thomas Crapper's name was synonymous with quality sanitary ware. He is shown (top) as a sanitary engineer.

Eskimo's Have Hundreds of Names for Snow

There are two major Eskimo languages:

- *Inuit* - spoken in Greenland, Arctic Canada and northern Alaska and
- *Yupik* - spoken in Siberia and southwestern Alaska.

Outside these languages, Eskimo and Inuit people speak many different languages and dialects. [128] From these languages, only four names for snow can be quoted:

- Snow on the ground - *aput*
- Falling snow - *qana*
- Drifting Snow - *piqsirpoq*
- A snow drift - *qimuqsuq*

Back in 1940 an article called *'Science and Linguistics'* by Benjamin Lee Whorf made the claim that, we have the same word for falling snow, snow on the ground, snow packed hard like ice, slushy ice and wind-driven flying snow, whereas an Eskimo would have different words to describe each. Actually this is not true. In English, we would use different words and phrases such as *rain, hail, snow, fluffy snow, melting snow, driving snow, blizzard, sleet, slush, ice* and *black ice* in a very similar way to the Eskimo. Then in English we have *snowfall, snow tyres, snow goose, snow job, snow plough, snow shovel* and so on.

A 1958 work by Roger Brown called, *'Words and Things'* took the Whorf generalizations and made them fact. By 1978, a play called 'The Fifth of July' by Lanford Wilson made the claim that there are 50 Eskimo words for 'snow'. In the New York Times, *'journal of record'* in 1984 it misquoted Whorf, claiming Eskimo's had 100 words for 'snow'. Soon after the Cleveland Ohio TV station WEWS, broadcast that Eskimos had 200 words for 'snow'. [(129)]

Eskimologist, Professor Anthony Woodbury from the University of Texas in Austin is one of the world's top authorities on the Eskimo and Inuit peoples. When this situation was put to him, he stated that there is no single Eskimo language and the number of words would depend on your precise definition of *'Eskimo'* and of *'snow'*. With so many languages and dialects among people generically called 'Eskimos', this could introduce additional words in other languages and dialects. The fact probably remains; however, that Eskimo's have no more words for snow than we have.

Rain from the Gods

Today, the concept that an invisible, immortal God continues to regulate all natural phenomena in the Universe, does not stand up to even mild scientific scrutiny. Of course, the fact that God is supposed to be invisible gives him a lot more latitude but really does not change a thing in this argument. In ancient times the belief that prayer could influence that regulation was widespread, even if apparently misguided. The Gods were called upon to provide that which was perceived as necessary for survival.

Most civilizations in their early history worshipped pagan Gods in an attempt to guarantee the supply of basic needs, such as protection from the elements and food for their sustenance. Early man praised Gods who they believed controlled the elements that could affect the tribe's harvest. Hence, the worship of Sun Gods and Rain Gods. Obviously, procreation was deemed important too; and as a result fertility Gods and phallic Gods were common. Sacrifice began with token offerings to the Gods, of a portion of a successful hunt or harvest. Next came tokens of appreciation for a successful birth. In time gifts of appeasement were offered and later, birds, lambs, goats, oxen and even humans were sacrificed to ensure clemency, good seasons and fertility. A God who could be relied on to provide basic needs was attractive, indeed. [(130)] We see all this as a little naive and quaint within the context of today's modern world and yet in the Christian Bible we can still find a record that appears to depict a pagan rain God who requires obedience and sacrifices to bestow good harvests;

- ***Leviticus 26 : 1-7 'I am the Lord. If ye walk in My statutes and keep My commandments and do them; then I will give you rain in due season and the land shall yield her increase and the trees of the field shall yield their fruit. And your threshing shall reach unto the vintage and the vintage shall reach unto the sowing time: and ye shall eat your bread to the full and dwell in your land safely. And I will give peace in the land and ye shall lie down and none shall make you afraid: and I will rid evil beasts out of the land, neither shall the sword go through your land. And ye shall chase your enemies and they shall fall before you by the sword.'***

The fact that this passage remains in our Bible is of considerable embarrassment to senior clergy. The whole concept is quite primitive. Robert Gillooly understood the point I am making. He states: *'Certainly, Christianity did nothing to dispel a belief in spirits when it taught that the Almighty hung out the stars each night with his giant hand, set the sun on its course each day and kept in touch with an Earthbound audience by means of various signs and wonders - comets, for example, were flung across the night sky to register his displeasure (although some theologians believed they were piloted across the sky by lesser spirits). And angels, the minions of the Almighty and themselves spirits, performed such duties as opening the 'windows of heaven' to let the rain fall from heaven's great cistern. So, from the earliest of ages, humanity hazarded a guess that unseen spirits orchestrated the universe. The more powerful of the spirits became Gods and those of evil intent became demons. But all were merely creatures of the imagination, born of a need to understand the natural world and cope with the problems of life.'* [131]

Early man attributed to the Gods that which was not easily attained for himself, but this lessened as he gained education. As science allowed man to perform the magic that had previously been solely the realm of the Gods, the Deity's requirement was naturally lessened. We are seeing exactly the same thing occurring in the Churches today, where education of the masses is rendering the Church dogma somewhat redundant. Man has recently obtained medical and scientific abilities that would have appeared Godlike to ancient peoples. Now that man can utilize computers, irrigate the desert, clone life, detonate weapons of mass destruction, fly to the moon and communicate across the globe in seconds, then the power and attraction of Almighty God for today holds considerably less relevance. (132) As science and education reduce the potency and requirement of mythical guiding spirits in the Churches, the better-informed congregations begin to stay away in droves. In the time of Jeremiah, God's wrath appeared to be focused plainly on those who lived in Egypt.

- ***Jeremiah 44 : 13 'I will punish those who live in Egypt with the sword, famine and plague, as I punished Jerusalem.'***

The Lord was really down on the Egyptians, even over the Feast of Tabernacles;

- ***Zechariah 14 : 18 'If the Egyptian people do not go up and take part, they will have no rain. The Lord will bring on them the plague He inflicts on the Nations that do not go up to celebrate the Feast of Tabernacles.'***

This is certainly a strange one. It seems that the public were avoiding this feast, hosted by Almighty God! The way it is written, this cannot have been a very appealing or entertaining celebration, if he had to wave the big stick and threaten and demand that the crowd be there. Free tickets and free refreshments wouldn't do it. You will attend or else! Again, we see a poor management style, with threats and ultimatums. Maybe a Dale Carnegie course could have subdued all that wrath and made for a much happier God. (133) Like many other nations, the Egyptians did not support the Hebrew tribal God YHWH, yet here for some unspecified reason he required their participation in the Hebrew festivities – that doesn't make a lot of sense.

The Bible also depicts YHWH as a storm God on whom all were to rely for their rain and good harvests; however, it is worth noting that the Biblical scribes must not have known that the Egyptians did not get rain anyway; they relied on the Nile River. An Egyptian legend claimed that the *'mighty drop'* they called *Leylet el-Nuktah* at the rivers source, caused the rise of the Nile. Their crops were then planted in the fertile mud and silt, deposited in times of the annual flood. They were watered manually by irrigation from the Nile. It is recorded that there was not even a precise Egyptian word for 'rain' because they had never experienced it. On journeys to foreign countries, such as Lebanon, the Egyptian scribes were literally 'lost for words' when first experiencing this phenomenon called 'rain', and actually documented that *'the*

Nile fell from the sky.'[134] For Almighty God to threaten that they would have no rain was a fairly hollow threat when they had lived for decades without it anyway.

Paganism involves Witchcraft and Devil Worship

The concept is that Christianity is the religion of a benevolent, kind and loving God unlike the 'Pagan' religions that are involved in evil of all sorts including human sacrifice. The term 'pagan' now carries derogatory undertones and is considered the spiritual equivalent of 'heathen', although it was never meant to be that. The term Pagan stems from the Latin *paganus*, meaning *'a rustic country dweller'*. Accordingly, paganism denotes a set of spiritual or cultic beliefs and practices in the format of folk religion and folklore (that includes any rustic, primitive or native religion and in turn any polytheistic religion). Regardless of this meaning, any religious traditions outside the Abrahamic, monotheistic group of Judaism and its offshoots Christianity and Islam, are now broadly classed as *pagan*. This also includes the most ancient Eastern Dharmic religions such as Hinduism, Buddhism, Jainism and also the Shinto religion.

Theosophical pioneer, Alvin Boyd Kuhn, (born 1880) believed he located a continuing theme of paganism within the Christian religion and included this in the many early books he wrote. Dr Kuhn blamed its introduction on the apostle Paul: *'To-day we have to face a problem that is one of the most difficult; it is my object to prove that Paul was the opponent and not the apostle of Historic Christianity. It is well known to all serious students of the subject that there was an original rent or rift of difference between the preacher Paul and the other founders of Christianity, whom he first met in Jerusalem - namely, Cephas (or Peter), James, and John... It is likewise more or less apprehended that two voices are heard contending in Paul's Epistles, to the confounding of the writer's sense and the confusion of the reader's. They utter different doctrines, so fundamentally opposed as to be for ever irreconcilable; and this duplicity of doctrine makes Paul, who is the one distinct and single-minded personality of the 'New Testament', look like the most double-faced of men; double-tongued as the serpent. The two doctrines are those of the Gnostic, or Spiritual Christ, and the historic Jesus. Both cannot be true to Paul; and my contention is that both voices did not proceed from him personally.'* (135)

In the Bible, there are two distinctly separate Jesus doctrines about a hundred years apart, each with its own adherents. Despite any concerns Christians may have with this evidence, it can be proven factual, since in a documented decree of the Fifth Council of Constantinople in 553 A. D. the Roman Church had to actually decide between the two prevailing Jesus myths. Tony Bushby confirmed that:

'... the Fifth Ecumenical Council of Constantinople made the most extraordinary decision that can be found recorded in Christian records. Under the direction of its Pontifex Maximus, the Roman Catholic Church decreed that Emperor Constantine's deified entity, Jesus Christ was 'truly the son of God' and Rabbi Jesus' faith was officially declared heretical.'

I personally find this mind boggling and am fairly certain it is not known by many Christians today. The Rabbi Jesus extolling peace and love from the shores of Galilee became heretical, while the Jesus manufactured in Rome as a more marketable figure, became orthodox. Of course the self imposed infallibility of the Church would have ensured that they culled the correct one, now wouldn't it? This means by definition the Christian religion is as Pagan as a religion can get. This is way outside what we were led to believe.

Gypsies & Tarot Cards

We were taught by the clergy to avoid those 'devilish' Tarot Cards, because they were handled by soothsayers and Gypsies - and thus, must be inherently evil. They were actually firmly outlawed by the Church in the Thirteenth Century, so we just assumed they were devilish and probably never even con-

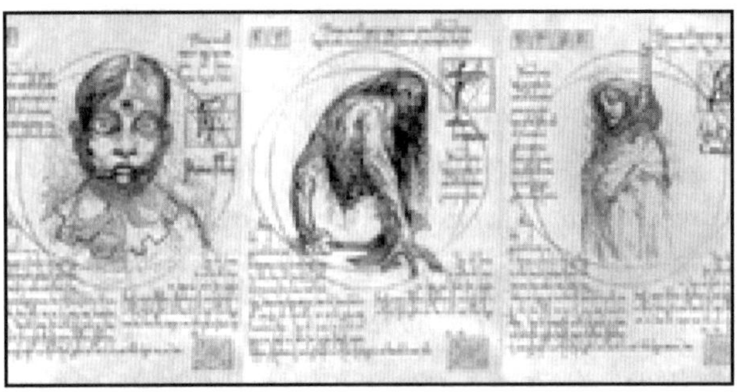

What mysteries are contained in the ancient Tarot Cards?

sidered whether they might carry any special information or be in any way useful in our search for truth.

The Tarot deck consists of 78 elaborately decorated cards, which are divided into two groups, called Arcana. The Minor, or Lesser Arcana, (the precursor of the modern playing card deck) is made up of 56 cards, divided into four suits. The wands suit corresponds with the modern clubs; cups with hearts; swords with spades; and pentacles (coins) with diamonds. These suits, in medieval times, were said to represent the various classes of society; cups for the clergy, pentacles (coins) for the merchant class, swords for the nobility and wands for the peasantry. Each suit has 14 cards, with numbered cards from ace to ten and four face cards: king, queen, knight and knave. The four knight cards have been eliminated in the modern deck of playing cards. The Major, or Greater Arcana, consists of 22 cards, each bearing a title and a picture, such as the Hanged Man, the Wheel of Fortune, Judgment, the Moon etc.; each one supposedly rich in occult and astrological symbolism. The number 22 corresponds to the letters of the Hebrew alphabet. Twenty-one of the cards are numbered. The twenty-second card, the Fool, numbered 0, is analogous to the modern joker. In modern fortune telling, usually the Major Arcana alone is used. Despite the message we accepted from our Sunday School teachers, we will now discover, with some degree of amazement, that a part of our Bible has a direct correlation to the Tarot pack. This is a crucial point and we will get to it soon.

In 1781, the French author and amateur scholar, Court de Gébelin (1725-84), somewhat surprisingly referred to the Tarot as 'a book preserving the pure wisdom of ancient Egypt'. [136] This is likely the first written suggestion that occult wisdom had been encoded in the Tarot cards, despite their having already been in use for at least 300 years. The French astrologer and cartomancier, *Etteilla*, produced Tarot cards in 1789 which he called *'The Book of Thoth'* (the Ibis-headed Egyptian Moon God). This seemed to support what Court de Gébelin had documented. Versions of the Etteilla cards are still produced today, under the name *'Grand Etteilla'*, or *'Egyptian Gypsies Tarot'*. What could this mean?

In the highly romanticized versions of popular lore, 'Gypsies' are shrouded in mystery and although perhaps associated with secrets and mysteries, are not usually thought to be the holders of ancient wisdom, particularly from Ancient Egypt. Many historians generally agree that they originated in the area of Northern India and Pakistan, and traveled a northern route towards the Balkans. There are others, however, who maintain that Gypsies reached Andalusia, Spain, after sailing along the coast of Africa from Egypt. The Spanish Gypsies had a total absence of Arabic words in their vocabulary and this fact alone seems to spoil that theory. The Spanish writer, Gérard-Anaclet-Vincent Encausse, under his adopted name, *Papus*, also alleged that the Tarot has strong links to the Christian Bible and holds secret information that originated in ancient Egypt. Papus stated: *'Yes; the game of cards, called Tarot, which the Gypsies possess, is the Bible of Bibles. It is the book of Thoth Hermes Trismegistus, the book of Adam, the book of the primitive Revelation of ancient civilizations.'* (137) This is pretty amazing stuff and indicates that the Gypsies certainly warrant further investigation. Some experts have shown that many Gypsies still claim that they originated in Egypt (the so-called Egyptian Gypsies) and actually left India with Alexander the Great and were the blacksmiths and camp followers of his army as it traveled back from India to Egypt. Many Gypsies themselves came to believe they were descended from the Egyptian Pharaohs and this thought is still held by many. In fact, it is referred to in the Gypsy songs and legends. They believe that they were originally called 'Egyptians', 'Gypsians' and then Gypsies. In Fifteenth century Spanish, 'Gitano', the name given to Gypsies in that country, was a direct translation of the word *'Egyptian'*. We need to look further at this!

Samuel Roberts wrote: *'Just when Gypsies originally arrived in England is very uncertain. They are first mentioned in our laws by several statutes … in which they are described as 'an outlandish people calling themselves Egyptians; who do not profess any craft or trade, but go about in great numbers with secret books.'* (138) Under Turkish domination, the 'Kosovar Egyptians' were called *Hashkalija*, which in Turkish again means nothing more than Gypsy. Since 1990, the Gypsies have been classified into three groups, *Roma, Hashkalija* and *Egyptian*. The idea that the Gypsies held ancient wisdom and arcane secrets in the tarot cards they used, is not entirely new; however, few people could agree on what the secret knowledge might be or how it was to be decoded. Try it for yourself. Get hold of a pack of tarot cards, spread them out on the table and try to ascertain precisely what secrets and mysteries of Ancient Egypt are captured there. For that matter, try to seek out the devilish content that might have caused them to become taboo to God-fearing folk. You will probably soon give it up as a fruitless and nonsensical exercise!

In the 1896 version of the Oxford Bible, we can read in Genesis 26 : 5, that the word 'Tarot' is simply a plural form of 'Torah'. The word 'Torah' actually refers to 'The Law', with a connotation of 'instruction.' This supports the idea that if the Torah is a singular body of instruction in the laws of the Gods, then the Tarot is a plural version, with the Greater Arcana, containing 22 individual picture cards of instruction and guidance in these laws. [(139)] We can also see that 'Tarot' derives from 'Tora(h)' spelled backwards, but what does that mean?

By skipping letters in the Hebrew Torah, a code known as the 'Torahcode' is revealed and one such pattern is the traditional 5-word hermetic sentence, composed utilizing only four letters. It reads: *Rota Tarot Orat Tora Ator*, that means, *'The wheel of Tarot tells the law of Hathor.'* Now, this would change the situation considerably if the 'Torahcode' actually reveals that Egyptian secrets of the God Hathor are contained within these mysterious cards.

In Egypt, the ancient *'Book of Thoth'* supposedly contains the wisdom and secrets that the Sky-Gods chose to reveal to mankind. Much of this information, however, *'went over the heads of the un-initiated'*, and in times B.C.E. it seems, the priests were concerned that its secrets were in danger of falling into oblivion. [(140)] To allay their fears, twenty-two miniature reproductions of the original symbolic illustrations from the *'Book of Thoth'* were made by the initiates and these twenty-two illustrations became what we now call 'Tarot Cards'. This vehicle for ensuring continuation of the significant parts of the God's wisdom and secrets from the *'Book of Thoth'* was known to the Egyptian Priests as *'The Book of Truth'* and today is known as the *'Book of Tarot'* and still clandestinely contains the secret Egyptian information. [(141)] *The Encyclopaedia of Occultism of 1889*, contained the following passages, which certainly echoes the thoughts of Papus, shown above; *'The Gypsies possess a Bible; yes, this volume is called the Tarot, which is the Bible of Bibles. It is a marvelous book and immense antiquity is claimed for it. Under the names of Taro, Tora, Roto, this collection has formed successively the basis of secret teachings of all the ancient peoples.'*[142] This is like a beacon to those familiar with the 'Torahcode'. *Rota Tarot Orat Tora Ator.* Who would have thought our research would show that ancient Egyptian mystery school information was actually spread far and wide by the Gypsies, yet this is what the evidence now shows. To prove we are on the right track, we find that remains of the original Tarot designs can still be seen today in the artwork of the ruins of temples at Thebes in Egypt. We also find that the 22 major cards are found paralleled in the *'Book of the Dead'* and are not unlike the cards the Biblical Ezra must have had in his possession, when he re-wrote the Torah after the captivity in Babylon. [143]

4 Ezra (2 Esdras 14 : 21-22) 'For your law has been burned and so no one knows the things which have been done or will be done by you. If then I have found favour with you, send the Holy Spirit into me and I will write everything that has happened in the world from the beginning, the things that were written in your law, so that people may be able to find the path and that those who want to live in the last days may do so.'

It is highly implausible that every available copy of the ancient scriptures was totally burned and I suspect Ezra had a hidden agenda to introduce his mystery school dogma. It certainly seems that, in addition to the secrets in the Tarot, Ezra set out to preserve the stories he had learned in Babylon and the experiences of his initiation in the Panther Mystery Schools of Egypt. It seems apparent that Ezra re-wrote the Bible to preserve these things; some parts for the initiated and some parts for the laity. Did Ezra care about getting historical facts correct? No, he did not! This may really surprise you, but we can be certain Ezra used the Tarot and that he included Tarot information when he re-wrote the Old Testament. Let's look at that now:

Psalm 119, in the Hebrew Bible, has 22 separate verses of 8 lines each; each line of these 8 line stanzas commences with a particular Hebrew letter; the next 8 lines with another Hebrew letter and the stanzas proceed through all 22 letters of the Hebrew alphabet. The King James Version has the separate stanzas, written under a heading of each Hebrew letter. This immediately alerts us that something is coded in this part of the Bible. I have never heard these passages read in any Church and am not sure if the clergy are aware of this secret. Here is what it is: Each 8 'same letter stanza' gives a precise description of one of the sacred images from the Book of Thoth and by default, of the 22 Major Arcana cards of the Tarot pack. [144] This is not esoteric meanderings or fanciful guesswork; it is quite obvious and apparent to any serious student and there can be no mistake. Whether we are comfortable with this or not, this Tarot information is unequivocally preserved in the Christian Bible. How would your clergyman handle this fact? What about the Vatican dictators who in ignorance outlawed Tarot cards, never suspecting they were part of the Bible?

It becomes quite apparent that Ezra was privy to the Gypsy secrets and was likely initiated in the mystery schools of Egypt. He certainly utilised both the Book of Thoth and the Tarot. Remember, the Bible collection did not exist *(per see)* at that time and Ezra probably taught from a composite scripture collection in his worship services for the Hebrew people he led out of Babylon. We have been wrongly told that the tarot cards are devilish and evil. The Church outlawed them in the 13th century and yet they are part of the Biblical Book of Psalms and accordingly, it follows, part of the ineffable Word of God.

What Are The Pharaoh's Holding?

The Egyptian psyche was one of order and perfection. Pharaohs had a responsibility to dispense *Ma`at* within their rule. Ma`at was a peaceful Egyptian concept that meant roughly the opposite of 'chaos'. The closest English translation would be something like 'tranquility' but suggesting a tranquil state achieved through meditation and purity of thoughts. We can read Pharaoh's throne names today that translate as, *'He who lives with Ma`at'*, or *'He who rules through Ma`at'* and so on. Freemasons still use the ancient Egyptian word Ma`at in their ceremonies today.

Achieving this state was taken very seriously and Pharaoh's would expend great discipline in their meditation and purity of thoughts. They would also ingest a white powder form of gold, which was claimed to vastly heighten awareness and allow users to enter a new dimension, virtually as Gods. The success was virtually instantaneous and the associated feeling of wellbeing, promoted its continued use. The white powder gold was also utilised within the most secret, 'God-making' initiation ceremonies at the coronation of Pharaohs. There is considerable evidence to support this, with traces of this gold

Pharoahs were often depicted holding their personal 'Wands of Horus'.

being found by Egyptologists, as well as a huge supply found by the archaeologist, Flinders Petrie, stored in a lined cave at Mt. Sinai. These esoteric masters ingested the gold powder by drinking it dissolved in water, by putting about a third of a teaspoon under their tongue and allowing it to be absorbed into their bodies or alternatively, by eating it in special conical cakes they called *'Shem-an-na'*. We can still see these shem-an-na cakes in several Egyptian frescoes, particularly in those depicting the induction of new Pharaohs, and the actual powder is recorded in dozens of inscriptions as *'mfkzt'*. I know this sounds a bit like we are reading an eye-chart, but that was the name the ancient Egyptians gave it.

Many statues of Pharaohs and Priests can also be seen with arms by their sides, holding objects like small cylinders or dumbbells with their name in a cartouche on the end. On a recent visit to Egypt, I questioned the duty archaeologist at the Cairo Museum about these objects and she didn't have a clue what they were. She checked with her University Professor and he didn't know either. I have since discovered they were called the *'Wands of Horus'* and were personalised items that a Pharaoh kept with him throughout his life. I cannot believe the Egyptian archaeologists were not aware of this. They thought the early Egyptians found it convenient to simply 'name' their statues by adding their cartouche to the hand, and never considered that they were holding a sacred and valued personal item.

These hollow, non-ferrous (mostly copper or zinc) tubes were filled with crystals or with the white powder gold and could be utilized in attaining the state of Ma`at as well as to regulate energy balance in the body something like acupuncture. Egyptians believed the cylinders attuned themselves to a particular user, so for this reason had their name in a cartouche emblazoned on the ends. Consuming white powder gold is now known to boost the immune system yet the Egyptians were able to also achieve healing by placing crystals or the powder inside the wands. Currently, experiments in Russia are having some considerable success with facsimiles of these wands, utilising them for relaxation, healing and preventative medicine. Independent studies of the Wands of Horus were carried out at the clinical bio-physics laboratory of the *Dxhanelidze First Aid Scientific Research Institute*, in St. Petersburg, Russia. Regarding these tests, Dr. M.A. Nikulin, a senior researcher with a Ph.D. in medicine stated, *"Where there are abnormalities of any kind in a person's body we observe a thermal asymmetry between the diseased parts and the healthy ones. When held in the hands, the cylinders balance out this pathological thermal asymmetry, which indicates that they actually have a therapeutic effect."*

A 50 year old woman, N. V. Vasina, was observed during E.E.G. recording and after just 5 minutes holding the wands, distinct changes were noted in the bio-electrical activity of the cerebral cortex. The alpha rhythm recorded more stably across all areas of the cerebral cortex and the 'between hemisphere' asymmetry in the occipital sections reduced noticeably as did episodes of dysrhythmia. Polymorphic beta activity, increasing in amplitude, was viewed in all areas. The Russians are now introducing these wands into alternate medicine practices.

An interesting note is that the Hebrew language certainly developed from Egyptian and it is recorded in Hebrew Talmudic writings that *'Shemen ha Mishchah'* was the anointing oil of the High Priests and Messiahs. *'Mishchah'* refers to *'anointing'* and *'shemen ha'* bears an uncanny resemblance to the Egyptian *'shem-an-na'* conical cakes we mentioned earlier that contained the *'mfkzt'* powder. [145] The Egyptians claimed that their Pharaohs gained their divinity from the *'Milk of Hathor'*, exactly as the Babylonian Kings were said to feed on the *'Milk of Ishtar'*. Doctors today tell us that mother's milk contains a substance called telomerase, the *'enzyme of immortality'* and it seems the Egyptian *'mfkzt'* or *'shem-an-na'* promoted the production of this same enzyme. [146]

Mercury was actually called 'Virgin's Milk' *(lac Virginis)* by the alchemists. The great Fulcanelli highlighted the link between alchemy and the 'Mother Goddess' religion, where barley cakes made with sacrificial blood were consumed at the end of the twelve nights of Saturnalia Gala festivals. [147] The word *'Gala'* in Greek actually means 'milk'. It appears that the attaining of Ma`at was ultimately desirable over all else and warranted the employment of whatever means it took. The success gained with the Wands of Horus in Russia would further point out that the Egyptians were privy to devices that would assist their happiness and well being; devices we are just beginning to re-discover now.

Human Sacrifice in the Christian Bible

The word of the Lord is supposedly the same yesterday, today and tomorrow and this prompted Hiel of Bethel to sacrifice his first born son in the foundations of the City of Jericho. Blood sacrifice was a fairly common practice in those times, in order to dedicate a City or new building or temple to the Lord. Hiel then sacrificed his youngest son by walling him up in the City gate posts:

- ***1 Kings 16 : 34 'In his days did Hiel the Bethelite build Jericho: he laid the foundation thereof in Abiram his firstborn, and set up the gates thereof in his youngest son Segub, according to the word of the Lord, which he spake by Joshua the son of Nun'.***

Definitely not the sort of father I would want! Can you begin to imagine the turmoil within the mind of a person sacrificing their own child? In the land of Canaan, the Irish archaeologist Robert Macalister (1870 – 1950), found hundreds of bodies of sacrificed babies, mostly fewer than eight days old, inserted upside down in huge pottery jars that had been sealed. [148] These were found in every strata level (indicating very long tenure of this ghastly practice). They were discovered to be the result of Jewish ritualistic, mass human sacrifice of supposed *'first born'*. This practice they believed was a requirement of the Lord YHWH in line with their Holy Book's sickly passages. The Christian Bible follows the same theme as the Jewish Tanaka:

- ***Exodus 22 : 29-31 'Thou shalt not delay to offer the first of thy ripe fruits, and of thy liquors: the firstborn of thy sons shalt thou give unto me. Likewise shalt thou do with thine oxen, and with thy sheep: seven days it shall be with his dam; on the eighth day thou shalt give it me. And ye shall be Holy men unto me.'***

- ***Numbers 8 : 17-18 'For all the firstborn of the children of Israel are mine, both man and beast; on the day that I smote every firstborn in the land of Egypt, I sanctified them for myself and I have taken the Levites for all the firstborn of the children of Israel.'***

Just what is the purpose of all this ritual murder?

- ***Ezekiel 20 : 26 'I let them become defiled through their gifts - the sacrifice of every firstborn - that I might fill them with horror so they would know that I am the Lord.'***

You don't have to believe me, you can read it for yourselves; the Bible confirms that there is no purpose to the killing at all.

- ***Hebrews 10 : 11 'Day after day every priest stands and performs his religious duties; again and again he offers the same sacrifices, which can never take away sins.'***

In case you missed that, we have it a second time!

- ***Joshua 24 : 19 'He will not forgive your transgressions or your sins.'***

The ancients practiced Regent sacrifice (kill the king) rituals and this could constitute part of a fertility ritual or agricultural harvest rite. In fact, the Jewish feast of Purim was loosely modeled on the Sumerian *Festival of Sacaea*, where an ordinary citizen was dressed in royal robes and after reigning for five days (in which time he was allowed to enjoy the Kings fine food and even sample his concubines) was summarily stripped, scourged and killed. [(149)] Nice gig, but unfortunately they wouldn't accept your resignation after a few days trial.

Of course the sacrifice of Jesus follows this identical theme. We can read in the KJV Bible about King Saul's seven sons and grandsons, all being ritually killed and hanged as part of the barley harvest sacrifice ritual. To the chagrin of the Church, this horrific story is still recorded in today's Bible. We can read of many planting, harvest and rain sacrifice rituals from pagan times and the ultimate sacrifice that involved killing the most prestigious members of the community, the offspring of the regent and quite often the king himself:

- ***2 Samuel 21 : 8-10 But the king took the two sons of Rizpah the daughter of Aiah, whom she bare unto Saul, Armoni and Ephibosheth; and the five sons of Michal the daughter of Saul, (married to David) whom***

she brought up for Adriel the son of Barzillai the Meholathite: and he delivered them into the hands of the Gibeonites, and they hanged them in the hill before the Lord: and they fell all seven together, and were put to death in the days of harvest, in the first days, in the beginning of barley harvest. And Rizpah the daughter of Aiah took sackcloth, and spread it for her upon the rock, from the beginning of harvest until water dropped upon them out of heaven, and suffered neither the birds of the air to rest on them by day, nor the beasts of the field by night.

Stories of ritualistic sacrifice are filtering out of America and Britain today but often they are effectively hushed up. In time sanity must prevail on this Planet, over all the intellectual passivity towards religious situations that are plainly wrong. Even now intelligent scholars are climbing the academic barriers to do battle with inane dogma within the Church. Every form of blood sacrifice, human or animal, is abhorrent. I can accept apocalyptic doomsday cult members 'topping' themselves if the decision is of their own free will but when the life of an innocent child is snuffed out by these monsters in the name of their bloodthirsty God, that is first degree murder. This is a barbaric practice and we cannot argue away its presence in the Bible. We are hearing it from a God who by his own admission, savors the smell of burning flesh. A God who is supposedly the same, yesterday, today and forever and this can't be good!

The Sphinx

Wallis Budge, an early *'Keeper of Egyptian Antiquities'* at the British Museum in London, recorded that the Sphinx was much older than suggested by orthodoxy. This was a huge departure from academic protocol at the time and certainly caused some heartburn and media coverage. Ancient Egyptian writings tell us that when cleared of sand in 500 B.C.E., the Sphinx had brass claws on its paws and carved stone wings folded along its back. Frederick Lewis Norden (1708-1741), a Danish naval captain and explorer of Egypt, made sketches of the Sphinx in 1737, showing that these were still in place at this time. Despite this, the *Probert Encyclopedia of Egyptian Mythology* claims that the Greek styled Sphinx has wings but the Egyptian style does not. Looks like someone might have it wrong. [150]

How 'Green' is the Bible

Another area where the Church is out of touch with modern thinking is in caring for our planet. In our Bibles we read:

- ***Genesis 1 : 28 'And God blessed them, and God said unto them, be fruitful, and multiply, and replenish the Earth, and subdue it: and have dominion over the fish of the sea, and over the fowls of the air, and over every living thing that moveth upon the Earth'.***

We noted before that this commands man to *'replenish the earth'*, which would indicate that this may not be the first time around for man. Next, for those who view the Earth as a living entity that should be treated with respect, being harmonious with Nature and the Universe, it is hard to swallow God's command to, *'subdue it'*. Nevertheless, the Earth citizens, of the past two millennia, have certainly followed this instruction to the letter and have done just that.

There is something of a related paradox contained in this passage. The *'Sefed Zohar'* (or Book of Splendor), is a Kabalistic mystical work of Judaism. The introduction includes a richly metaphorical discourse given by Rabbi Chizkiyah explaining that the spiritual forces that protect and watch over us are called the *'13 Attributes of Mercy'* and correspond to the first 13 words of the Torah. The Attributes of Mercy personify sharing, and it is explained that this embodies the positive energy within our world. Followers of Judaism believe that meditatively browsing the Hebrew or Aramaic wording actually awakens our desire to share and arouses a spiritual light that effectively removes chaos from our lives. The Zohar introduces a mother goddess known as *Shechinah* (radiance) who was really a feminine side of YHWH, a living animating force that ensures all living things of planet Earth are harmonious and nurtured. *Shechinah* also refers to the (feminine) misty presence of God between the cherubim on the 'ark of the covenant'.

Where the paradox comes in, is that the rabbinic and doctrinal teachings warn man not to be lured in any way by the beauty of the material world. It calls them short-lived achievements, which are based on egocentric drives and ambitions. Strangely, they hold that attunement with Nature amounts to idolatry. [(151)]

The Creation

Most followers of the Christian religion claim to find enlightenment, love and peace within the pages of the Bible. Of course we all find favorite passages that serve us best but this should not be to the exclusion of all others. We can have a bit of fun with the Biblical creation but it does of course have a serious side and is taken quite seriously by Christians. Here we will look at some very odd passages that don't show the creation in the vein we learned in Sunday School. Starting right at the beginning:

- ***Genesis 1 : 1 'In the beginning God created the Heavens and the Earth.'***

... Not a whole lot of detail there!

- ***Genesis 1 : 2 'And the Earth was without form and void; and darkness was upon the face of the deep.'***
- ***Genesis 1 : 3 'And God said, Let there be light: and there was light.'***

We must appreciate that this means God started work, made all the planets and did all this initial creating of the World - *in the dark*. This introduces a problem...God is God right? So he can do anything he likes but we have to read all the way down to *Genesis 1 : 16* before he makes the Sun for there to be any light! There are some problems in between too:

- ***Genesis 1 : 11-12 Trees were created;***
- ***Genesis 1 : 26-27 followed by man.***
- ***Genesis 2 : 7-9 Man was created before the trees.***

- ***Genesis 1 : 20-21 God created birds;***
- ***Genesis 1 : 26-27 followed by man.***
- ***Genesis 2 : 7 God created man;***
- ***Genesis 2 : 19 followed by birds.***

- ***Genesis 1 : 24-25 Animals were created;***
- ***Genesis 1 : 26 before man.***
- ***Genesis 2 : 7 Man was created;***
- ***Genesis 2 :19 before animals.***

- ***Genesis 1 : 31 God's creations were good.***
- ***Genesis 6 : 5-6 God's creations were not good.***

The Bible does not start off well so let's sneak a look at how the whole thing turns out in the end. OK, we can read in the Bible, a prediction of what will occur in the last days before Jesus comes again:

- ***Matthew 24 : 29 'Immediately after the distress of those days, the sun will be darkened, and the moon will not give its light; the stars will fall from the sky, and the heavenly bodies will be shaken.'***

How do we explain this? Well, Einstein told us it is all relative so for an observer on the Earth to see the stars fall from the sky, an enormous 'black hole' would need to suck the Earth upwards. So the Sun has gone out, the Moon is not giving any (reflected) light; the Stars have all fallen from the sky! So it is pitch black.

What happens next? We are told about the end time in Matthew 26 : 64:

- ***'And every eye will see the Son of Man sitting at the right hand of the Mighty One and coming on the clouds of Heaven.'***

He will need to be very radiant and I'll tell you what; this whole thing will need to be *quick*, because 9 minutes after the Sun goes out we will all commence to join the Woolly Mammoths. We'll all be frozen solid!!!

Gambling Chips in Las Vegas Churches

This may come as a surprise to those of you who have never visited Las Vegas, where, I can confirm, they do have poker machines in MacDonald's. (I have seen them!) Believe it or not, in this city there are still more Catholic churches than casinos and it would come as no surprise that many worshippers at Sunday services will drop casino chips in the collection plate rather than cash. Since they get chips from many different casinos, the churches have devised a novel method to cash in the offerings. The multitude of churches send all their collected chips to a nearby Franciscan monastery for sorting and then the chips are taken to the casinos of origin and cashed in.

This is handled by the 'chip-monks'. Sorry, I bet you didn't see that one coming!!

CHAPTER THIRTEEN

MISSING SHIPS

'Facts do not cease to exist because they are ignored.'

Aldous Huxley

Forbidden Archaeology

With the pre-Cook expeditions outlined previously, it is a certainty that early explorers vessels were wrecked around the Australian coast, particularly that of Western Australia where the 'Roaring Forties" would drive a sailing vessel towards the rocky coast. Scuba adventurer Ben Cropp produced a TV special on the myriad of wrecks, some quite ancient that infest the dangerous waters of Torres Straight. Queensland's Barrier Reef is also hazardous to shipping as Captain Cook discovered. Some amazing relics of ancient shipwrecks have been located and many more are still no doubt awaiting discovery.

- Many sightings have been made of the 'Spanish Galleon' in the 18 Mile Swamp on North Stradbroke Island off the Queensland coast.
- Wollongong apparently is notable for the wreckage of an ancient wooden ship off its coast.
- Two ancient ships have been located in swampland near Perth, and are believed to be Egyptian.
- Skin-divers claimed years ago to have retrieved a number of 16th-century Spanish coins and other relics from the remains of an old wooden shipwreck off Tweed Heads (NSW).
- From a shipwreck at Suffolk Park about 5km south of Byron Bay, two wooden pegs were subjected to dating processes in 1993 that

returned a timeframe between 1450 and1500. The shipwreck was uncovered by sand mining in 1965 but is now buried under 4m to 10m of sand. In the 1950s people could still recall the remains of three masts protruding 3m from the sand at an angle of 45 degrees. Sand mining operations later bulldozed the masts out of the way. Much earlier, residents could recall portions of the hull protruding above the sand. When the rudder was unearthed in 1965, it was 4.2 m (14 feet) in length, suggesting the ship it steered could have been 50 to 75 metres (167 to 250 feet) long. It is suspected to be Portuguese. Aboriginal legends tell of a massacre of sailors in retaliation for the rape of Aboriginal women. [152]

Spanish Galleon on North Stradbroke Island

As a young man in 1968 and 1969 I was employed by Consolidated Rutile as a bulldozer driver in the mineral sands on North Stradbroke Island off the Queensland coast not far from bayside Brisbane. I lived in the caravan park at Dunwich and clearly recall the day three of the fellows who worked with me returned from a fishing expedition near the 18 Mile Swamp, to say they had sighted the legendry Spanish Galleon.

In Australia, there appears to be considerable reluctance in the academic community to accept or even investigate any maritime artefact that could possibly pre-date the voyage of Captain James Cook. Any earlier discovery would apparently mess with our heritage, so despite a considerable number of sightings of this shipwreck it is firmly categorized as mythical. I accept that a non-professional may be hard pressed to delineate the wreck of a pre-Cook, 'Spanish Galleon' from the wreck of any other old ship. Based on eye witness accounts, the one on Stradbroke Island actually seems too short to be a galleon and is more likely to be a caravel or carrack. That changes very little, because the ancient Spanish artefacts and coins found near this particular location and the dating of 1597on at least one coin, are particularly difficult to overlook. This would make it probable that the ship was sunk in the 16th or early 17th century.

One story in circulation claims that the University of Queensland investigated this wreck a few decades ago and a drill brought up a fragment of munz metal (an alloy of zinc and copper) which of course was not invented in the time of Spanish galleons. They are said to have used this detail to neatly scuttle the validity and antiquity of the wreck. Nevertheless, it does not begin to explain where the ancient Spanish artefacts are coming from. There is a significant body of anecdotal material that links the Galleon with members of the Aboriginal population of Stradbroke Island in times long past. In pre-European days there were two separate tribes of Aborigines on Stradbroke Island. One tribe inhabited the north end and the other the southern area around Swan Bay and Jumpinpin. Apparently, these two tribes were significantly different and spoke completely different languages. It appears that after white settlement at Amity Point and Dunwich the two tribes moved into a satellite position around the white settlements and eventually amalgamated; a blending that appears to have resulted in the end of the two separate tribal entities. There are also numerous stories which state that the Stradbroke Island Aborigines have had Spanish gold coins in their possession as well as holding other artefacts from the 'Spanish Galleon'. Some stories even state that certain Stradbroke Island Aborigines are custodians of the galleon's hidden treasure and that this knowledge is passed down carefully through the generations.

If not from the Galleon, where did the Stradbroke Island Aborigines obtain this example and other Spanish coins?

The first well-documented search for the shipwreck in the swamp was in about 1894 by the Hon J. George Appel, the Queensland Colonial Secretary. Appel heard about it from his friend Mathew Heeb an Island resident who accidentally came upon the wreck while out in the bush looking for good timber. He described it as having a *'high poop and forecastle'*. Heeb retrieved about 50 kilos of copper plate and fittings from the shipwreck (effectively putting paid to the University's munz metal story) and later showed this copper trove to his friend the Hon. George Appel. Immediately, Appel showed great interest in this mysterious shipwreck so Heeb took him by boat to the 'Stockyards' near Slipping Sands where they walked overland to a hill from which they could see the so-called galleon. A noted local historian, Isabel Hannah, accompanied them and documented the find and location. It seems they located the Stradbroke Island shipwreck soon after a fire had burnt through the swamp but were not able to get close to it due to heavy rains which immediately followed the fire and flooded the swamp. Later, when they returned better equipped to deal with the flooded swamp, they could not find the wreck due to the regrowth of reeds in the swamp and the shifting sands.

- In the early 1920's Jim Bryce went with Southport boat builder Tony Street in order to strip timber off the remains of the shipwreck in the 18 Mile Swamp near Swan Bay. It was not stated but from the report it appears it would have been the Stradbroke Island Galleon.
- In 1934 Dr. George 'Boy' Young, with a group of Rover Scouts, found the Stradbroke Island Galleon after a fire had swept through the 18 Mile Swamp. He and his friends all took things off the shipwreck. Doctor Young took a sailor's dirk, the other scouts took such things as coins and other items. A photograph of the dirk found by Dr. Young still exists today.
- In the same year, 1934, Jim Walker found the wreck on his third expedition into the swamp on Stradbroke Island. He retrieved an iron 'roved' bolt and some timber from the ancient shipwreck.
- A sighting of the shipwreck in the 18 Mile Swamp during World War II was reported by Cyril Broome, a R.A.A.F. pilot trainer.
- My workmates from Consolidated Rutile definitely sited the wreck in 1968 as stated.

Archeologist Greg Jefferys has been searching for the shipwreck since 1989 and led an expedition in 2007 after finding a silver coin dated from 1597. A number of artefacts have been re-discovered in recent years that were originally taken from the shipwreck. These include a brass walking stick handle and a ship's bell as well as the above mentioned dirk. [(153)]

Several Spanish coins have turned up over the years mainly in the hands of local aboriginals. I recall meeting people who had seen them when I lived on the Island in 1968 and 1969. The coin found by Greg Jefferys is silver though much corroded. About the size of an Australian ten cent coin, it is being checked by experts but appears to be a Spanish one re`al coin, although a coin dealer stated from the photograph that it looked like an old English silver coin. The dealer added, *"If it is the genuine object it does suggest a late 17th century wreck. It's pre-Captain Cook by a long way."* An English pre-Cook shipwreck would be more amazing than one of Spanish origin.

The Mahogany Ship at Warrnambool

The Mahogany Ship refers to a putative, ancient shipwreck that is purported to lie beneath the sand approximately six miles west of Warrnambool in south-west Victoria, Australia. In most accounts it is supposed to be a Portuguese caravel but some reports say a Chinese Junk. While there is no conclusive evidence today that such a wreck exists, many accounts of the relic persist, from supposedly reliable witnesses over a long tenure. Early reports relating to the ship touch upon two cardinal characteristics: it was described as being constructed of panels and its timbers were said to be of a dark wood, described as either mahogany or cedar. In terms of these criteria, the vessel did not resemble ships built in northern Europe in the 18th or 19th centuries.

The most popular theory suggests that the vessel is the missing ship of Portuguese sea captain Cristóvão de Mendonça, who set out from Malacca in the Spice Islands specifically to look for the Great South Land in 1521. Another theory links the ship to Portuguese sea captain Gomez de Sequeira, lost in 1525, however, historically de Mendonça would seem the more likely. Of the three caravels under the command of de Mendonça, at least one never returned. A theory has been put forward that on this voyage a map was made of the East Coast of Australia. We discussed earlier the French world maps (the Dieppe maps) and some believe that Mendonça's information was added since these maps depict Australia's southern coastline as far as Armstrong Bay - only six kilometres west of Warrnambool. This is precisely where the wreck is said to lie. The notion that this map also depicts the East Coast of Australia is the subject of some historical debate even though it appears authentic. [(154)]

It is believed that Admiral Hong Bao with three ships, serving under Chinese Admiral Cheng Ho (Zheng He), explored Australia in 1421 and made landfall at Bunbury, south of Perth. From there he supposedly sailed a short distance northwards to explore the Swan River and is believed to have re-stocked provisions and made repairs to his ships. It is theorized that Hong

Bao used Western Australian Jarrah (a beautiful, hard red timber that is plentiful in that area) before proceeding on his mission to explore the southern coast of 'Greater Java'. Apparently all three ships were lost, explaining why records of this voyage are scant. A further hypothesis is that the Jarrah, previously unknown in shipbuilding, is the timber mistaken for Mahogany and the Warrnambool wreck is actually a Chinese Junk. [155]

If the existence of this ship was substantiated, it would cast a very different light on the earliest phases of exploration of Australia by both Asians and Europeans, some 250 years before Cook. Based on information from those who recalled having seen the ship, extensive searches were conducted in late 1999 and again in 2004. Heavy drilling equipment that penetrated to a depth of 10 metres was utilized and the probes yielded unidentified old wood fragments. [156] Des Williams and Phil Latimer of Ballarat submitted samples to the CSIRO, who identified the timber as oak. This is not considered conclusive evidence for or against the 'Mahogany Ship'. It is quite possible that the hull could be constructed of Mahogany or Jarrah, whilst the decking or fittings were of oak. During another 'dig' in 2004 a drill was said to have brought up from a depth of 10 metres, about twenty *"lumps of wood of a deep burgundy'.* Nothing more seems to have been done but one would expect that if this was considered to be timber from an ancient ship, then excavations would have been commenced.

Researchers are thwarted somewhat by the lack of records which could also be due to the national secrecy of the time. The mariners would not have publicized their clandestine operations if they were entering waters deemed Spanish under the Treaty of Tordesillas. This treaty signed in 1494 allocated specific meridians to the Portuguese and Spanish mariners to the exclusion of all others. Maps and documents of such a voyage would have been kept locked away to avoid antagonizing Spain and to keep the discoveries from other nations. The incident of this shipwreck would never have come to light except that some 30 individuals have recorded accounts of the wreck. These reports stress that it is a dark colour like mahogany and include descriptions of an unusual ship's hull, possibly similar to that of a Portuguese caravel or of a large Chinese Junk.

- The first sightings of an old wreck between Warrnambool and Port Fairy were recorded in 1836. [157] On 18th January 1836, a party of three whalers from Port Fairy, Gibbs, Smith & Wilson, traveled to the mouth of the Hopkins River in search of seals. Their whaleboat was overturned and one man drowned. The two survivors walked back to Port Fairy along the coast. Approximately halfway back, near Tower Hill, the men discovered a ship wreck, 300 yards inland amongst the sand dunes. [158]
- They reported their find immediately to Captain John Mills, in charge of the Whaling Station, on their return to Port Fairy. He visited the wreck and described 'hard dark timber - like mahogany'. [159]
- Mills specifically remarked on the hardness of the timber and stated that the construction was unlike any Portuguese or Spanish ship of his knowledge. This further supports that it may have been a Chinese Junk.
- In the mid 1800s a local woman, Mrs. T. Manifold, described the ship in detail. Instead of familiar planks, it had wooden panels, which is actually how caravels were constructed. [160] Nevertheless, Mrs. Manifold and 24 others closely examined the ship and concluded (for reasons best known to themselves) that it was in fact a Junk from Hong Bao's missing ships. They could be correct because a local Yangery Aboriginal legend tells of *'yellow men'* who came from the wreck to live with the natives. This is supported by the distinctive colour and facial features of the Yangery tribe. [161]
- John Mason of Belfast near Warrnambool described his encounter with the wreck in the *'Melbourne Argus'* published 1st April 1876. It is unfortunate that this was the April Fool's day edition because it detracts from the genuineness of his report, obviously filed earlier. Mason states that the wreck was enormous, exceeding 100 tons, very weather beaten with much of the decking gone and the hull filled with sand. He further documents that the local Natives claimed it had been there since their tribes earliest recollection.
- Author, Henry Kingsley referred to this wreck in his book, *'Geoffery Hamlyn'*, having a character advising the English on the folly of sneer-

ing at the Dutch or Spanish since they were here in Australia before you.

- The site where drilling brought up wood samples, was consistent with the first European sightings of an old shipwreck made in 1836. More than 30 other accounts of the wreck were received by the 1880s. It is quite possible that this is from the wreck of the legendary 'Mahogany Ship' (162)
- Another eyewitness account was presented by the former editor of the *'Warrnambool Examiner'*, local historian Richard Osburne, who wrote about the wreck in his book, *'History of Warrnambool'* (pub lished 1877): *"In connection with this wreck, the author remembers to have noticed a wreck in the hummocks between Belfast and Warrnambool, in 1847 or 1848; but it was much nearer Warrnambool than Belfast - in fact, it was only two or three miles from the former place, to the west of the big hummock which was supposed to fill Warrnambool Bay with drift sand washed by the Merri River until the cutting was made."* On 25th June 1890, Osburne followed up with a letter to the Port Fairy Gazette, during a period of heightened interest in the wreck, although he was unsure of the provenance of the ship and specifically stated that there was little to suggest it was of Portuguese origin.

Australian waters are like a great maritime museum holding silently the records of the various nationalities of seamen who searched for the Great South Land and those who gave their lives in the attempt. In time more and more secrets will be given up that will in some cases clarify our past and in others simply present more mysteries.

CHAPTER FOURTEEN

COLONY IN CENTRAL AUSTRALIA

'... whoever controls the past, controls the future.'
George Orwell

Discovering the Dutch Colony

An interesting article appeared in the 'Leeds Mercury'; 25th January 1834, *'Discovery of a White Colony on the North Shore of New Holland.'* The article told of a secret English expedition led by Lieutenant Nixon that ventured into central Australia in 1832, and discovered a small group of 300 white descendants of a Dutch shipwreck. The story was later reported again in the *'Perth Gazette'* of 1837. The original *Leeds Mercury* article stated that; *"A Correspondent living near Halifax has favoured us with the following interesting communication".* This correspondent has now been identified as T. J. Maslen, a retired Army Lieutenant of the British East India Company and his motives just may prove to be less than pure. The article went:

"To the editors of the Leeds Mercury.
Gentlemen,

-- A friend of mine lately arrived from Singapore, via India overland, having been one of a party who landed at Raffles Bay, on the north coast of New Holland, on the 10th of April, 1832, and made a two months' excursion into the interior, has permitted me to copy the following extract out of his private journal, which I think contains some particulars of a highly interesting nature, and not generally known.

The exploring party was promoted by a Scientific Society at Singapore, aided and patronized by the Local Government, and its object was both commercial and geographical; but it was got up with the greatest secrecy, and remained secret to all except the parties concerned. (For what good purpose it is impossible to conceive); Extract from an unpublished manuscript Journal of an exploring party in Northern Australia, by Lieutenant Nixon.

'15th May 1832.- On reaching the summit of the hill, no words can express the astonishment, delight, and wonder I felt at the magical change of scenery, after having traveled for so many days over nothing but barren hills and rocks, and sands and parching plains, without seeing a single tribe of aborigines excepting those on the sea coast, and having to dig for water every day.

"Looking to the southwards, I saw below me, at the distance of about three or four miles, a low and level country, laid out as it were in plantations, with straight rows of trees, through which a broad sheet of smooth water extended in nearly a direct line from east to west, as far as the eye could reach to the westward, but apparently sweeping to the southward at its eastern extremity like a river; and near its banks, at one particular spot on the south side, there appeared to be a group of habitations, embosomed in a grove of tall trees like palms. The water I guessed to be about half a mile wide, and although the stream was clearly open for two thirds of the distance from the southern bank, the remainder of it was studded by thousands of little islands stretching along its northern shores: and what fixed me to the spot with indescribable sensations of rapture and admiration was the number of small boats or canoes with one or two persons in each, gliding along the narrow channels between the little islands in every direction, some of which appeared to be fishing or drawing nets. None of them had a sail, but one that was floating down the body of the stream without wind, which seemed to denote that a current ran from east to west. It seemed as if enchantment had brought me into a civilized country, and I could scarcely resolve to leave the spot I stood upon, had it not been for the overpowering rays of a mid day sun, affecting my bowels, as it frequently had done, during all the journey.

On reaching the bottom of the hill in my return to our party at the tents, I was just turning round a low rock, when I came suddenly upon a human being whose face was so fair and dress so white, that I was for a moment staggered with terror, and thought that I was looking upon an apparition. I had naturally expected to meet an Indian as black or brown as the rest of the natives, and not a white man in these unexplored regions. Still quaking with doubts about the integrity of my eyes, I proceeded on, and saw the apparition advancing upon me with the most perfect indifference: in another minute he was quite near, and I now perceived that he had not yet seen me, for he was walking slowly and pensively with his eyes fixed on the ground, and he appeared to be a young man of a handsome and interesting countenance. We were got within four paces of each other when he heaved a deep and tremulous sigh, raised his eyes, and in an instant uttered a loud exclamation and fell insensible on the ground. My fears had now given place to sympathy, and I hastened to assist the unknown, who, I felt convinced, had been struck with the idea of seeing a supernatural being. It was a considerable time before he recovered and was assured of my mortality; and from a few expressions in old Dutch, which he uttered, I was luckily enabled to hold some conversation with him; for I had been at school in Holland in my youth and not quite forgotten the language. Badly as he spoke Dutch, yet I gathered from him a few particulars of a most extraordinary nature; namely, that he belonged to a small community, all as white as himself, he said about three hundred; that they lived in houses enclosed all together within a great wall to defend them from black men; that their fathers came there about one hundred and seventy years ago, as they said, from a distant land across the great sea; and that their ship broke, and eighty men and ten of their sisters (female passengers?) with many things were saved on shore. I prevailed on him to accompany me to my party, who I knew would be glad to be introduced to his friends before we set out on our return to our ship at Port Raffles, from which place we were now distant nearly five hundred miles, and our time was limited to a fixed period so as to enable the ship to carry us back to Singapore before the change of the monsoon. The young man's dress consisted of a round jacket and large breeches, both made of skins, divested of the hair and bleached as white as linen; and on his head he wore a tall white skin cap with a brim covered over with white down or the small feathers of the white cockatoo. The latitude of this mountain was eighteen degrees thirty minutes fourteen seconds south; and longitude one hundred and thirty-two degrees twenty-five minutes thirty seconds east. It was christened Mount Singapore, after the name and in honour of the settlement to which the expedition belonged."

A subsequent part of the journal states further, *"...that on our party visiting the white village, the joy of the simple inhabitants was quite extravagant. The descendant of an officer is looked up to as chief, and with him (whose name is Van Baerle), the party remained eight days."*

This name *Van Baerle* gives us something concrete to research. He was said to be descended from an officer on the ship that was wrecked. A letter from the Government of Batavia has been located stating; *"With this ship [Concordia] we send home the assistant, Constantijn van Baerle, out of service"*. So it seems a fair assumption that this was the original Captain van Baerle, so let's check what happened to the ship *Concordia*? According to the Leeds Mercury article the Dutch ship had been a great vessel, and after she foundered... *"...eighty men and ten of their sisters with many things were saved on shore." Concordia* was indeed a big ship, of just on 900 tons and left Batavia with two other vessels, *Zuiderburg* and *Mercurius* on 15th January 1708, bound for the Cape and then the Netherlands. She disappeared with 130 people on board, including some women. Only *Mercurius* reached the Cape of Good Hope so we believe the Dutch colonists were survivors from the *Concordia* and perhaps the *Zuiderburg* wrecked in February 1708. (163)

The *Leeds Mercury* newspaper article continues:

"Their traditional history is, that their fathers were compelled by famine, after the loss of their great vessel, to travel towards the rising sun, (east) carrying with them as much of the stores as they could, during which many died; and by the wise advice of their ten sisters they crossed a ridge of land, and meeting with a rivulet on the other side, followed its course and were led to the spot they now inhabit, where they have continued ever since. They have no animals of the domestic kind, either cows, sheep, pigs or anything else; their plantations consist only of maize and yams, and these with fresh and dried fish constitute their principal food, which is changed occasionally for Kangaroo and other game; but it appears that they frequently experience a scarcity and shortness of provisions, most probably owing to ignorance and mismanagement; and had little or nothing to offer us now except skins. They are nominal Christians: their marriages are performed without any ceremony: all the elders sit in council to manage their affairs; all the young, from ten up to a certain age, are considered a standing militia, and are armed with long pikes; they have no books or paper, nor any schools; they retain a certain observ-

ance of the Sabbath by refraining from their daily labours, and perform a short superstitious ceremony on that day all together; and they may be considered almost a new race of beings." (164)

Around the time of this expedition early settlements were being founded on the coast of the Northern Territory at Port Essington, at Fort Dundas on Melville Island and also at Fort Wellington at Raffles Bay. Remember the explorer Ludwig Leichhardt travelled from Jimbour station to Port Essington in 1844. Raffles Bay was named by the explorer Phillip Parker King in 1818 after the famous Sir Thomas Stamford Raffles, the Lieutenant Governor of Java and founder of the colony of Singapore. On 17th June 1827 Captain James Stirling arrived at the location, from Sydney to establish an outpost to be known as Fort Wellington. The crew consisted of some convicts and some members of the 39th Regiment. They arrived at Raffles Bay and the settlement was built on the eastern side of the bay. The settlement suffered the inevitable problems of monsoonal weather, voracious wildlife, very unfriendly local Aborigines, disease, pestilence, tropical lethargy and extremely remote isolation and as a result was eventually closed down in 1829. If the party in the Leeds Mercury story entered Australia and returned to Raffles Bay as stated, in May 1832, the settlement would not have been in operation and this would mean entering Australia under extreme secrecy. Port Essington (or Victoria as it was named) was the site of three settlement attempts and it was also abandoned at the time of the Singapore groups supposed landing.

The Lost Race

Many years ago, I caught by accident, an ABC program, *'The Dutch Settlement'*, where Les Hiddens, *The Bush Tucker Man*, investigated this report of a shipwreck in Western Australia and the Dutch party traveling east to form a colony in this location in the Northern Territory. The problem was that though precise bearings were given in the article, *(The latitude of this mountain was eighteen degrees thirty minutes fourteen seconds south; and longitude one hundred and thirty-two degrees twenty-five minutes thirty seconds east. It was christened Mount Singapore...)*, no mountain or body of water fitting the article's description was located at these bearings. Les Hiddens explained how inexperienced usage of a sextant can give a phantom reading and calculated where they would have been if this had occurred. Again nothing like the scenery described by the party from Singapore was found. It would seem the secrecy of the mission, led them to distort the bearings and several other facts. Les was able to establish certain matches with a Dutch ship (the Concordia), wrecked on the Western Australian coast and believed the ship left Batavia (Jakarta in Indonesia) and research and investigations were conducted there. There is not much more I remember about this intriguing tale. Research has been conducted by the Australian Map Circle meeting in Cairns under the title, *'The secret agenda of Western Australian explorer, Robert Dale'*. This group acknowledges the assistance and collaboration of Les Hiddins and Andrew S. Cook. [(165)]

Based on research reported to the *'Society for the History of Discoveries'* in 2000, this group believe that it is possible that Governor Sterling sent a man called Robert Dale on a secret expedition to the centre of Australia during March-May 1832, purportedly to look for grain said to be growing there (Cook, 1999). The whole Singapore thing appears to be a fabrication and it seems the expedition party may have actually left from Fremantle and landed at Fowler's Bay on the south coast of Australia. From there, they would have marched due north to an area near Alice Springs before finally returning to the coast. If so, their expedition entered territory that then belonged to New South Wales. Sterling would certainly have wanted to keep secret this trespass into the territory of a 'rival' colony run by Governor Darling. If this is true (and it seems likely that it is), the Singapore connection is a wholly fabricated smokescreen. In addition the *Scientific Society at Singapore*, who promoted the expedition according to the newspaper article, has proved to be non-existent. This makes it most likely that it is the Dale expedition that is being discussed. It is unlikely though, that the experienced Dale would take incorrect Sextant readings so we must assume that the location was deliberately confused.

Finding Some Proof

Tom Ammerlaan is a Dutch-Australian who recently researched the lost Dutch Colony and concluded for various reasons that the settlement and the site of Mt Singapore was in fact Palm Valley in central Australia. He also identified the man called Thomas Maslen who he believed submitted the article to the

Leeds Mercury. Ammerlaan tells us that the Lutheran Church established its Hermannsburg Mission in this location with three ministers, Kempe, Schwartz and Schultze. In 1876 Pastor J. Kempe submitted a paper to the Royal Geographic Society (South Australia branch) documenting the establishment of the mission and some of the tribal customs of the local Aboriginal people he had observed. He noted that many local Aboriginals had lighter hair than was usual and in the opening paragraphs of the paper, Kempe made the following observation; *"It is quite certain that many of the women had Jewish names such as Judith, Paula and Mirjam, before they ever saw a white man".* [(166)] Regarding these comments, Tom Ammerlaan discovered; *"These names were all from the Old Testament, and according to Dr. Femme Gaastra in Holland, were in popular use in the Netherlands in the early 1700s. Certainly, names like Judith, Paula and Mirjam, are extremely unlikely to have been adopted by Aboriginal people in Central Australia as a result of the British settlement at New South Wales or South Australia."* He also located Aboriginal legends of Godlike light haired people settling in the area. [(167)]

If the *Leeds Mercury* story is true, and if Thomas Maslen provided it, which seems almost certain, then who gave him the details of the secret expedition in the first place and how come the whole story has been dormant for so many years? If young Robert Dale and his party did put ashore at Fowlers Bay, and then headed due north, they would eventually arrive precisely at Palm Valley, 480 miles in from the south coast, or as the Leeds Mercury article states, nearly 500 miles. Palm Valley sits at precisely the longitude documented in the article and the latitude has been deliberately altered to indicate a location some 500 miles south of Raffles Bay. I recall Les Hiddens was looking on the right longitude 480 miles south of Raffles Bay whereas we now believe it should have been 480 miles north of Fowler Bay. And what if it was Robert Dale who stumbled across that strange-looking bloke in his cockatoo feather hat and bleached white leather clothes? It unequivocally places a Dutch colony in Australia in February 1708, eighty years before the English. It also shows that our politicians were playing games of subterfuge, right from the formation of the colony.

Macassans & Baiini

The Aboriginals of Arnemland, in the Northern Territory, used the word *'Macassans'* to refer to the Indonesian (Sulawesi) trepang fishermen-traders, with whom they came in contact well before Australia's recorded history. Some 450 Yolngu Aboriginal words have their origin in the Macassan/Indonesian language, such as *rupiah* for money and *balanda* (Hollander) for white person. This indicates a definite mingling of the cultures at some early stage.

Local Aboriginals also tell of the *'Baiini'* people who came to the coast even before the Macassans in *'lolperu'* (sailing ships). They came as families, men women and children, and on the shores of Arnhem Land, built houses made of stone and ironbark. The women were beautiful, with lighter skin than the Aboriginals and wore coloured sarongs of many patterns. They planted rice in both Warramiri country and Gumaidj country. The womenfolk were often seen weaving at their looms which they brought with them. Their clothes were woven with yarn dyed with beautiful colours, in large pots. The old Baiini name for this cloth was *'jalajal'*, while the Macassans called it *'liba'* and Europeans know it as *'dumala'*. The Baiini women are spoken of in many Yirritja songs, planting rice, cooking, weaving, dyeing, fishing, making armbands and necklets, stitching the sails for their boats and caring for their families. The men fished and hunted with harpoons and traps as Aboriginals do today, but are not remembered as well as the womenfolk. [(168)]

Just who the Baiini people were is pretty much unknown with no record of them in history. *'The La Trobe Journal - God's One Country'* at the State Library of Victoria claims, *"The eunuch-explorer* (Chinese Admiral Cheng Ho) *Zheng He may have traveled to Australia early in the fifteenth century,* (see Chapter 2; about the Chinese artefact found in Darwin) *and it is entirely possible that the Baiini - to whom the Aboriginal peoples of Arnhem Land refer - were Chinese travelers who came each year to gather trepang. At least it can be said that contact between China and Australia has a much longer history than the appearance of Chinese characters in our literature.* [(169)] This is a believable scenario, because trepang was particularly prized by the Chinese as an aphrodisiac and was most plentiful in northern Australian waters. The huge money the catch would bring back in China would justify long voyages and difficult conditions for the seafarers. Traces of the Baiini remain along the coast of north-eastern

Arnhem Land and the islands nearby, from Blue Mud Bay to Elcho Island. At Guramura in Arnhem Bay, the remains of a large Baiini settlement still exist with later superimposed Macassan and Japanese influence, where gardens were planted with rice. [170]

The Lost City of Burrungu

A story is being circulated that Australian aborigines claim a white man's ancient city called Burrungu, (the *'city of taboos'*) exists hidden in the remote hinterlands of northern Australia. They say that legends of the aborigines tell of white men living in the city many thousands (hundreds?) of years ago. *'They were so tall they needed very big buildings', the natives claimed. 'The city is taboo. It was once a place of much activity'. The story goes on: 'Could this have been a prehistoric outpost in the boondocks of Australia for some race of aliens from other worlds? The thinly populated continent would have been perfect for such a base.'* [171] If we allow a lot of latitude for exaggeration and 'science fiction' reporting of these particular writers, it is just possible that this could match the above community of 300 Dutch souls or even possibly the *'Macassan'* or the *'Baiini'* settlements. It is further claimed in their story that the *'Australian Weekend News'* reported that three men made it through the remote outback to visit the ruins of this alleged city, known as Burrungu. They reported ruined walls, stone houses, wide courtyards, and stately arches that look down upon statues set along tree-shaded streets. Great story … but it all sounds just a bit dodgy! Firstly there is no newspaper named precisely as above. *'The Australian'* newspaper puts out a Weekend edition called *'The Weekend Australian'*. A search of their archives revealed no such storey. A search of the www also showed no such story other than the versions recorded above. There is an Australian Aboriginal tribe called *'Burungu'* which could be the origin of the name of the City Burrungu; however, it certainly does not sound like a Dutch or Macassan name, and accordingly does not appear to match the above history.

An elderly Western Australian Professor, Carl von Brandenstein has revealed that he believes a Portuguese Colony using West African slaves was formed in the Kimberley region near Buccaneer Archipelago. The professor has located stone African style huts on High Cliffy Island and notes an Aboriginal tribe originally from Montgomery Island that spoke pure Portuguese. The Professor is considered to be a competent anthropologist and has extensively documented this scenario.

I find it hard to believe; however, that an entire stone city called Burrungu, complete with wide streets and stone statues and built for a giant race still exists in northern Australia. One would think it would have been spotted from the air by now and even if it was located in heavy undergrowth, campers and four wheel drivers cover most countryside pretty well today and certainly would have come upon it. In addition, what about the three men who supposedly visited it? Did they find this archaeological treasure trove and then remain silent about it? Did they give up the million dollar rights to their story in books, magazines and TV. No, I don't believe so. This one just has to be rubbish!

The Australian Pygmies

Today, Australians seem particularly reluctant to acknowledge the existence of the little people from the Atherton Tableland rainforest areas, inland from Cairns in Queensland. The Sydney geographer, Griffith Taylor, in his 1927 book, *'Environment and Race'*, speculated that these tribes known as *'Negritos'* or *'Barrineans'* were a unique race that settled in Australia even before the Aborigine. The first volume of Manning Clark's *'History of Australia'* gives credibility to their presence but today their existence and small stature have been effectively erased from public memory. These pygmies were measured at 4'6" (140cms.) for a fully grown male and were an entirely different race to the Australian Aborigine or Torres Strait Islander. The *"Encyclopedia of Aboriginal Australia'* (1994), published by the Australian Institute of Aboriginal and Torres Strait Islander Studies, acknowledges the existence of the tribes called the Djaduganjdji, Mbarbaram (Barbaram) and Yidinjdji (Indindji) but does not draw attention to their tiny stature. An entry under *'Rainforest Region'* documents the existence of *'small, curly-haired people with languages which have distinctive features'* but makes no mention of their pygmy attributes.

We might ask why would those involved in Aboriginal anthropology wish to airbrush from our history, the fact that Australia once had a pygmy people. It would seem that the radical Aboriginal political movement of the

Photograph of Australian Yidinjdji pygmy tribe members taken in 1893.

1960s and 70s, found the existence of this race an inconvenient counter-example to one of its central doctrines, more particularly, if they actually pre dated them.

The notion of several waves of Aboriginal settlers in Australia countered the activist's suggestions of aggressive white imperialists invading their country and disrupting a single Arcadian Aboriginal people living in harmony with their environment. As a result, these ancient indigenous Australians have been effectively expunged from history by both black and white races. In their work *'The extinction of the Australian Pygmies'*, Keith Windschuttle and Tim Gillin, (Quadrant, June 2002) state, *"The story of human habitation of this continent is not the exclusive property of anyone. It should be the concern of all of us, black and white, to ensure it is told as openly and as truthfully as possible."*

Accordingly it is imperative that the Pygmy people can be recognized and the story is shared.

Joseph Birdsell, was 186 centimetres (6'1") tall and is photographed with a twenty-four-year-old male of the Kongkandji tribe, height 140 centimetres (4'6") at Mona Mona Mission, near Kuranda, North Queensland, in 1938.

CHAPTER FIFTEEN

EGYPTIANS & PHOENICIANS IN AUSTRALIA

'Only puny secrets need protection.
Big discoveries are protected by public incredulity.'
Marshall McLuhan *'Take Today'*, 1972.

Egyptians in Australia

A book first published in London in 1923 called *'The Children of the Sun'*, by Professor W. J. Perry, is a second volume of research into the early history of civilization. In this work the learned Professor of Anthropology, documents his study of Egyptian settlement throughout Oceania. This book demonstrates with scholarly research that the Egyptians sourced gold, pearls, turquoise and obsidian throughout the Pacific region. One of these places was certainly Australia.

Very few people are aware that boomerangs were discovered in the tomb of Pharaoh Tutankhamen. Detractors try to call these artefacts 'message sticks', but I viewed these items in Cairo Museum and that is plainly implausible. This fact, when added to other evidence confirms that Egyptians must have visited Australia in pre-historic times. Scientists working with the British Museum have discovered that eucalyptus resin was employed in the embalming of the dead in Egypt. From the study of ancient mummies they believe its use in Egypt dates back to 1,000 years B.C.E. At that time, eucalyptus was found pretty much exclusively in Australia and to a lesser extent, in parts of New Guinea. Between 1905 and 1920, an exceptional early Egyptologist, G. Elliot Smith, wrote several books on Egypt and a number of specific works on

Aboriginal depictions of Wandgina Gods. Note Phoenician writing on the turban.

mummification. He stated that mummification was practiced in northern Australia and the Torres Straight Islands and noted that it was fairly apparent that these natives had been taught Egyptian methods. Other discovered artefacts such as inscriptions and gold scarabs, should convince even the hardest skeptic that Egyptians and their seafaring allies, the Phoenicians, sourced commodities in Australia in pre-historic times and made fairly frequent visits.

Rock art in the Kimberley region of northern Western Australia depicts the Wandgina God with Phoenician writing on the turban. The white face and red robe indicates Gods who were known as *'The Shining Ones'* in Hebrew scripts, or *'Shiny Brights'* by the Chinese. These are certainly the same entities called Anunnaki who brought science to the Sumerians 10,000 years ago. The Egyptians called them Neteru and Urshu (watchers) and in the Bible they are Elohim and Nephilim, with the word 'watchers' used many times. For example:

- ***Jeremiah 4 : 16 "Make ye mention to the nations; behold, publish against Jerusalem, that Watchers come from a far country, and give out their voice against the cities of Judah."***
- ***Isaiah 13 : 5 "They come from a far country, from the end of heaven ..."***

In the illustration, we can compare an Aboriginal Tjuringa (sacred) stone from the Kimberley region of Australia with the depictions of Aten worship with Pharaoh Akhenaten from around 1350 B.C.E. Coupled to the other evidence, this further indicates contact between the Australian tribes and Egypt in pre-historic times.

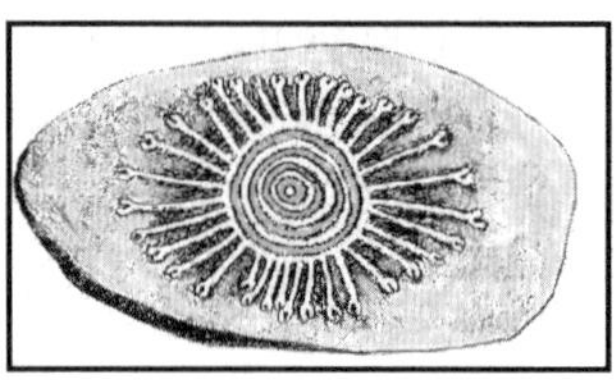

Pharaoh Akhenaten believed the power of The Aten 'encompassed all' and depictions showed little hands on the sun's rays.

The first Europeans into this region, the early missionaries, and even a Professor of Anthropology from Sydney University, were astounded to be greeted by stone age natives, with a Masonic handshake. This has also been reported from the Tolai culture in New Guinea, and it would seem that the ancient Masonic order (that apparently commenced in ancient Egypt), certainly spread its wings in ancient times. The Tolai culture is also famous for the Duk Duk, a 'witch doctor' dressed as a mysteriously feathered creature that supposedly had mystical powers. They take part in ceremonies that occur in early May. These ceremonies have an uncanny resemblance to the *Jack in the Green* ceremony, held on May day in medieval Europe.

Phoenicians in Australia

Late in the year 2000, historians in Australia were shocked by an ABC News report that a 3,000 year old mine had been located on the Queensland coast near Sarina. There was also evidence that the harbour had been utilised in ancient times to ship out ore. Local resident Val Osborne had been studying the site for 10 years and noted that Freshwater Point, once an island and now an isthmus, bore striking similarities to the ancient Phoenician port of Tyre. As well as the pre-historic mining operations, Osborne located inscriptions, ruins of ancient sea walls, wharves, graves plus other artefacts which would all suggested a Phoenician colony, dating from as early as 1000 B.C.E.

A report about these discoveries from the Sarina Shire Council states: *"Egyptian, Hebrew, Phoenician and Ogham scripts are documented from sites all over Australia along with constructions, harbours and roads"*. Probably not surprisingly, these finds have been *"ignored in the face of official Australian history and British policies"*. Why is it that officialdom feels the populous cannot handle the truth? The report states further: *"It is expected that academic controversy will occur in any future investigation"*. Val Osborne explained that the University of Queensland sent an archaeologist to the site, supposedly with instructions to come back with a report that *"there is nothing there"*! I am not about to debase the University of Queensland but if Osborne is right, this appears to be a common occurrence with the conventional orthodoxy of archaeology and anthropology. If finds challenge our nice tidy Anglo Saxon heritage, they must be fraudulent! That certainly does not explain away a bronze chariot

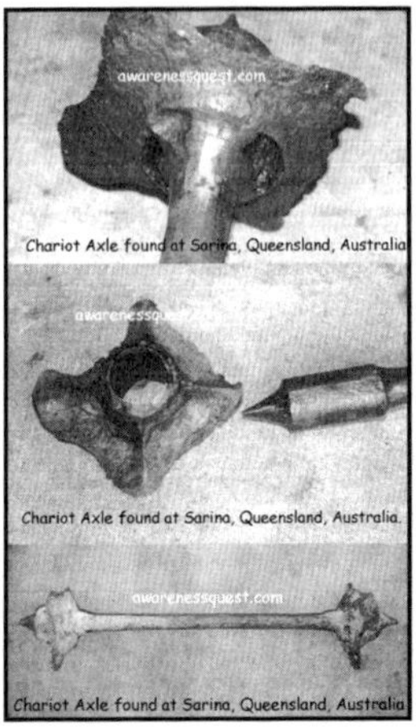

axle also recovered at Sarina. If chariots were landed here it would indicate that roads had been constructed and livestock transported. This would have to suggest a reasonably mature colony.

A bronze chariot axle discovered at Sarina.

Toowoomba

My parents were both born in Toowoomba. My grandparents and great grandparents rest in Toowoomba cemetery. My brother and sister were born in Toowoomba and I have lived and worked there over the years. It is an unassuming, thriving, provincial metropolis; the rural hub of the agricultural area known as the Darling Downs. There is nothing whatever to suggest that Toowoomba would hold any ancient archaeological interest, but that all changed back on 23rd July 1974. While digging footings for a new factory in North Street, Toowoomba, a 92 lb. basalt rock was unearthed by Andrew Nott, carved with a solar motif with hieroglyphs of serpents.

This exciting find was featured in the *Toowoomba Chronicle* for some time and attracted the interest of Marilyn Pye, an amateur archaeologist who gained a lot of press at the time. Marilyn visited the site, bought the artefact and flew it to Hawaii and then New York where it was supposedly identified as belonging to the most ancient Meso-American culture - the pre-Mayan *La Tolita*, estimated to date from 2000 B.C.E. We are told Marilyn became aware of the supposed *'Hopi Prophecies'* concerning the return of the icon, from an Iroquois Indian called John Hill, in Manhattan. The story goes that the Hopi distributed a number of these symbols to the far corners of the earth and when they are all found and returned, the *'great purification'* can begin.

Marilyn reported that the rock was finally returned to the Hopi Indians, and the elder 'Grandfather David' Monyonga became very excited and said: *"This is what we have been waiting for … there are three more to come"*. This sounds just a bit implausible to me and Marilyn Pye's further 'archaeological adventurers' in far North Queensland don't in any way alleviate my concerns. It was reported that in this location she is seeking a Golden Pyramid and traces of the 'Garden of Eden'. She has identified a scarab artefact as having belonged to Moses who lost it whilst wandering for forty years in the wilderness (of Australia). As the reader would have noticed, I am not averse to challenging establishment thinking and appear to consider several variant ideologies, but this idea from Ms. Pye is a bit too 'way-out' for me - way, way-out!

The sun-motif rock appears genuine and I don't wish to sound cynical; however, a story from my time in the Northern Territory will help explain my concern with this entire Hopi legend. Following the devastation of Darwin by Cyclone Tracy at Christmas in 1974, the Government shipped in much needed supplies and since they were landed at the R.A.A.F. base, the Air Force handled the distribution. Now amongst the items handed out were a truckload of generators, since the city was flattened and of course had no power supply for quite some time. In his haste to get the supplies to the most needy areas, the particular officer gave out the generators (which were valuable units) without recording the recipients. After some three or four months when power was restored, a rather large advertising campaign was mounted suggesting those with generators should bring them to a collection point. Of the hundreds given out, I think it was about three that came back. On a fishing trip on the East Alligator River soon after, I took particular note that every camp on the river had a portable generator driving everything from fridges and florescent lighting to microwaves and hi-fi music.

Accordingly, the legend of distributing these sun motif engraved rocks to the far corners of the Earth in the hope that 3,000 years hence they would all be found and returned to the Hopi, is outside human nature and outside common sense. In addition, researchers in the US have not been able to find any trace of the almost blind, archetypal Hopi chief, 'Grandfather David' (Monyonga) or his successor, and as a result, I personally believe the *'great purification'* might have to wait for quite a while yet.

Doug's Rock

An ancient artefact depicting the Hindu Elephant-headed God, *Ganesha*, was found near Toowoomba and we can only wonder how it got there. Ganesha is the *'remover of obstacles'* and the *'God of beginnings'* and revered since ancient times in India. A group of seventeen granite stones with Phoenician inscri-

Equally baffling, a statue of the Indian God Ganesha.

ptions were also found in this location. Some of the inscriptions have been translated and purportedly read, *'Guard the shrine of Yahweh's message'* and *'God of Gods'*. Another inscription supposedly reads, *'This is a place of worship of Ra'* and *'Assemble here to worship the sun'*. Ra was of course, the Egyptian sun God and to see both Ra and the Jewish Yahweh side by side in supposed Phoenician inscriptions, gives me just a bit of heartburn. I would want to re-check that particular translation. Nevertheless, someone - quite possibly Phoenicians - visited Toowoomba in ancient times.

A Toowoomba newspaper report on the Phoenician rock inscriptions.

I have in my possession a rock given to me by a friend called Doug that carries similar inscriptions. Doug resides just outside Toowoomba and located the broken part of this rock in a load of gravel delivered to his home. I have had to outline the inscriptions in chalk as they do not show up well in photographs but are quite apparently carved inscriptions. These are not yet translated but I am hoping for an ancient prophesy that states words to the effect: *'Ian Ross Vayro will win Gold Lotto and his books will all be best sellers!'* Hey, I can hope!

The Gympie Pyramid

The story of the Gympie Pyramid is best covered in an e-book researched, written, compiled and released by Brett Green who has expended vast amounts of time and energy on interviewing long time residents and relentlessly digging for the truth. The first European to locate the pyramid in modern times was in fact Brett's great-grandfather, John Green. His son, James Green, left us much information about the local Aboriginal people and the original record of the Gympie Pyramid. John Green commenced compiling records of the local history in 1863. He documented considerable early journal evidence of the terraced hill and the nearby rock stepped pyramid as well as an insight into his discussions with the local Ka'bi natives. There is now so much misinformation being sprouted by incompetent researchers that the true stories are simply being distorted and discounted. Amidst a lot of controversy, there are three main points of confusion. [172]

1. A terraced hill exists on the outskirts of Gympie and originally had stone structures on it, said to be from a time prior to modern European settlement. In recent times, it has been shrouded in mystery and controversy. There are theories that a community of Italian Winemakers grew grapes on these terraces (Moorwood, 1976) and the story has been re-hashed so often it is now considered fact by some. I find this highly implausible as Gympie is certainly not a grape growing area due to the acidity of the soil and quite unlikely to be the location of commercial cropping. The terraced hill appears to me to be entirely unsuitable for agriculture and particularly unsuitable for grape growing. This conclusion was also reached by archaeologist Greg Jeffrey (c.1989) who noted that the electoral roll, land deeds and cemetery records for Gympie gave no indication of an Italian community. He further discussed the lack of production records of table grapes or wine production from the Gympie region. [173] This terraced hill is sometimes claimed to be the pyramid but that is absolute nonsense.
2. The Gympie pyramid was a nearby but entirely separate structure in the form of a step pyramid made of huge blocks of stone. It was around 100 feet high, about 150-200 feet long, and contained at least 13 'steps'. A wall made from irregular, freshly quarried stone surrounds Gympie's Surface Hill Uniting Church in Channon Street. This massive wall has an old section from the 1880s and a newer section from the 1930s. While it is probable that pyramid rock was utilized in the old section, claims that the entire wall was constructed utilizing stone from the pyramid are not correct. It is thought that stone from the pyramid was likely used to fill in the open mining shafts to allow the Uniting church to be built over them. The Gympie Catholic Church is another controversial story yet to be proven. Their connection with pyramid stone was discovered around 1990 during renovations but of course they want no connection with a 'pagan'

edifice, and vehemently deny what was found. The pyramid sandstone blocks continued to disappear around the1890s when locals found them an irresistible source of material to build houses, walls, fireplaces and community buildings.

3. There is evidence that another pyramid also existed at Rainbow Beach and it was bulldozed onto a barge and dumped at sea off Frazer Island. This destruction was carried out by the Australian Army around 1950 when they built Camp Kerr Military Training area. The dozer driver, truck drivers and other laborers (12 in total) had to sign declarations of secrecy when they were engaged for the task. All are now dead ... the dozer driver apparently committed suicide or was murdered, about 8 years ago, just 5 hours before Brett Green and his associates were appointed to interview him. They were subsequently questioned by police and the death was never reported in the press and no police file on the matter is on record.

The Ancient Step Pyramid at Gympie.

Many ancient Egyptian artefacts have been located in the Gympie region and there seems no doubt that someone mined gold there over several decades in ancient times. When the new railway cutting was constructed just outside Gympie, a strange tunnel was encountered that led into the pyramid site. It was dynamited, sealed, and covered over so that it would not affect the safety of the rail line. I have also heard unconfirmed reports that Egyptian tombs were discovered during construction of the rail cutting, and that Joh Bjelke-Petersen (the then Premier of Queensland) visited the site and personally evoked the National Secrets Act.

A gold scarab is said to have been found at nearby Mothar Mountain along with inscriptions on a large rock in the same area. A stone statue referred to as the 'Gympie Ape' mirrors depictions of the Egyptian God, Thoth, and was found in the bush near Gympie. A jade Ankh was found near Murgon along with some stone ruins which were reportedly discovered in dense bush land some years ago. An Egyptian stone calendar was dug up near Rockhampton in 1969. A later Egyptian colony (200 - 300 B.C.E.) had been deduced for the Cairns area from coins, a scarab and inscriptions located in that area. Other pyramids have been located at Gosford along with accompanying artefacts. There seems no question that Egyptians visited Australia over many years and sourced gold and other commodities here.

The mis-information regarding the Gympie pyramids continues to grow on the internet and I have deliberately dismissed the esoteric stuff from this report. I believe the most responsible researcher on the subject is Brett J. Green, who has devoted his book *"The Gympie Pyramid Mysteries"* to the long standing regional stories of ancient stone ruins, old photographs, pioneering family interviews, artefacts found, pioneer sketch drawings and hand copies of pictographs witnessed on the sandstone blocks found in the Gympie and Cooloola regions of southeast Queensland. Green has endeavored to present a generalized overview of the facts, fictions and fantasies concerning claims of ancient visitations and settlements by Phoenicians, Egyptians and whoever else was supposed to have ventured into Australian waters in ancient times.' [(174)] Regarding the reluctance of Academia to acknowledge these enigmatic finds and in fact its serious attempts to denigrate or eradicate them, it becomes fairly apparent to any researcher that our history is being manipulated at a fairly elevated level.

CHAPTER SIXTEEN

STRANGE CREATURES

'Be Skeptical of the Skeptics.'

Bernard Haisch, *'UFOs and Mainstream Science'.*

Beast of Bodmin Moor

A large black cat, reportedly seen around Cornwall, England, and associated with livestock deaths is known locally as the Beast of Bodmin Moor. The animal is believed to be an escaped puma, panther, or leopard that has gone native. Although the story has extremely long tenure of over two decades, it is unlikely that the animal has found a mate and bred. Large feline skulls have been reported in the location but without the rest of a skeleton. This would suggest that these are most likely from thrown out feline rugs or wall trophies. One of these skulls was examined by the Natural History Museum of London, which used forensic entomology to prove it had died elsewhere.

Reports of the Beast began circulating in the 1980s and 1990s, and several similar sightings have popped up all over England. Known as Alien Big Cats or ABCs, over 300 sightings were reported in 1996 alone. They are sometimes called Ghost Cats. This prompted Britain's Ministry of Agriculture, Fisheries and Food to conduct an official inquiry into ABCs, and arrive at the insipid conclusion that although there was *"no verifiable evidence"* of ABCs in Britain, *"the investigation could not prove that a 'big cat' is not present."* Whatever the truth of the matter, it is not prudent to relegate the Big Cats to the folklore dustbin because in Scotland the similar 'Kella' Cat has now been shot and examined, proving its disputed existence once and for all.

Ghost Cats

The name of Ghost Cats reminds me of an incident in my youth that I will relate as it happened. At the time I shared an apartment in Brisbane with a Texan lady called Valerie, who worked with me. Our company opened a branch on the Gold Coast and we were both requested to relocate and run that branch. Valerie found a magnificent newly built apartment at Surfers Paradise that featured a fan shaped lounge looking over the ocean with a bedroom either side - so we wouldn't disturb each other. It was a beautiful apartment block and in fact Jack Brabham, the world champion racing driver, owned the top story penthouse. After an exhausting Saturday involving moving three trailer loads of belongings to this apartment, I couldn't face the return trip to Brisbane and decided to sleep on a mattress on the floor of the new unit. After something to eat, I chose a bedroom at random and crashed out.

Sometime about 2.30am., I awakened to see a large black cat walk soundlessly through the bedroom and into the ensuite. It was like a chubby black lion cub, far bigger and stockier than a domestic cat. Although the unit was on the seventh floor, enough light filtered in from outside to show it quite clearly. I got up and turned on the lights, but it had completely disappeared. It didn't seem scary or sinister in any way and I actually laughed at the concept of a Ghost Cat on the 7th floor of a newly built Gold Coast apartment. Nevertheless, I had no explanation for what I had so clearly seen. Next morning Valerie arrived and chose the bedroom where I had slept. I moved into the other and did not say one word about the previous night's anomaly. After a day of locating furniture, moving in and cleaning up we retired for the night. Over breakfast next morning we looked at the magnificent view and I said to Valerie, *"This is a really nice apartment."* Valerie agreed and straight faced said, *"... but you know its haunted."* I asked what she meant and Valerie related how she had awakened between 2 and 3am, to see a huge black cat walk through her room. The bristles stood up on the back of my neck. I then related precisely what I had seen the previous night. The experiences were identical. We stayed in that apartment for over a year and never saw the Ghost Cat again or had another similar experience. I can offer no explanation.

Megalania

Fossil finds in Queensland, Australia, indicate that the giant Komodo Dragon reptile of Indonesia, once in the prehistoric past, had an even larger cousin, *Megalania prisca*, living in Australia. The fact that these creatures are long extinct is not believed by a number of folk who have encountered living giant crocodile sized lizards. There have been numerous eyewitness reports and rumors of living Megalania still in Australia, and occasionally New Guinea, but the only physical evidence that Megalania might still be alive today are plaster casts of possible Megalania footprints made in 1979.

Tasmanian Tiger

It is widely believed that the carnivorous marsupial, Tasmanian Tiger (or Thylacine) has been extinct since the 1930s, losing a battle in the food chain to the Australian Dingo. Once frequenting most parts of Australia, the wolf-like Thylacine eventually held a small ecological niche only in Tasmania, and finally disappeared altogether. Over the past few decades, however, isolated sightings in Tasmania and a few in eastern Victoria plus recordings of the howl of these creatures would suggest that there is still a miniscule population remaining. The fact that it is a nocturnal creature would assist in its remaining largely undetected.

Several people will confirm that the Tasmanian Tiger is not extinct.

New Zealand Birds

New Zealand has been the home of two very unusual birds, the Kiwi and the Moa. Early this century Australian research discovered through DNA testing that the Kiwi was actually a mutated Emu. The New Zealanders responded that at least it had the brains to get out of Australia. This fact was hard to believe for some

Is it possible that giant Moa birds still survive?

since the emu is a large and fast-running flightless bird with a wide straight beak, whereas the kiwi is a small nocturnal bird with a curved thin beak.

The giant 3 metre tall moa was universally thought to have been hunted to extinction by the Maoris but in recent years reliable sightings have continued, so it seems that some birds still survive. For those who think it unlikely that such a large and obvious bird could remain undetected on a populated island like New Zealand for several centuries, this is precisely what happened with the petrel of Bermuda that was lost for 300 years.

Ancient Coelacanth

In 1938, fishermen in the Indian Ocean off the south east coast of Africa brought up a very strange metallic-blue fish measuring almost 2 metres in length. Fortunately, when the fish was brought ashore it was noticed by Dr. Marjorie Courtenay-Latimer, the then curator of the East London Museum. She sent a quick sketch and description to Professor J. L. B. Smith at Rhodes University. From the sketch alone, the professor was able to positively identify a long extinct Coelacanth, known only from fossils found in 400 million year old rocks. With hearts more primitive than those of any other vertebrate and very tiny brains the Coelacanth belongs to an ancient era when the world was young. It was simply impossible to believe that this ancient fish species with such primitive organs could survive for 400 million years. Professor Smith commented, *"My surprise would have been no greater if I had seen a dinosaur walking down the street."* Smith was not overstating the case. This was the first known living example of a fish that existed 200 million years before the dinosaurs. Since then, others have been caught, and the species is now named Latimeria chalumnae after the observant Museum curator.

The Megatherium

A handy thing to know for your next Scrabble game is that a three toed Sloth is actually called an Ai. The modern day tree sloth of South America is a relatively small, reclusive animal of notoriously lazy demeanor. It belongs to the sole surviving strain of a diversity of sloths that inhabited a vast area of this planet at the end of the last glacial period, some 12,000 years ago. These creatures ranged in size from the one we know today, up to a distant cousin the size of an elephant. The giant Megatherium (simply meaning large mammal) has been constructed from a skeleton discovered in 1789. Standing on its hind legs the creature could rear to over 16 feet in height and it is now believed from emerging evidence that the species could still be extant. This cause was championed by Argentinean paleontologist, Professor Florentino Ameghino, who claimed 'concrete proof' that a smaller ox sized relative of the Megatherium was still living in South America. (175)

The Iemisch

A monster regarded with absolute terror is the man-killing Iemisch or Hymche. It is reported to resemble a tiger but has webbed feet to accommodate its aquatic lifestyle. In 1897, Carlos Ameghino sent some bones, said to come from an Iemisch to his brother, Professor Florentino Ameghin (who we saw above). His accompanying explanation stated:

> ***"This animal is of nocturnal habits and it is said to be so strong that it can seize horses with its claws and drag them to the bottom of the water. According to the description I have been given, it has a short head, big canine teeth and no external ears. Its feet are short and plantigrade, with three toes on the forefeet and four on the hind. These toes are joined with a membrane for swimming and are armed with formidable claws. Its tail is long flat and prehensile. Its body is covered with short hair, coarse and stiff of a uniform bay colour. In size it is said to be larger than a puma but its paws are shorter and its body thicker."***

The professor believed this was another species of the giant sloth, Megatherium, even though it is not believed to be a fierce man killer as described. Crypto zoologists prefer to think it is some unknown species of giant otter. (176)

Yowie

In the modern context, the Yowie is the generic (and somewhat affectionate) term for an unidentified and foul smelling hominid reputed to lurk in the Australian wilderness, analogous to the Himalayan Abominable Snowman, the Yeti and the North American Bigfoot or Sasquash. It has been suggested that wading in swamps in search of food caused apes to discover that this endeavor was less difficult in an upright position. The ancient ape-men that we have found as fossils may have eventually evolved into a little changed 'modern ape-man'. My bank manager is a prime example. There is some evidence for this today, particularly from remote parts of the Himalayas, China, Australia, the Solomon Islands and Northern U.S.A. It is hard to discount the thousands of reports of Big Foot, Sasquash, Skunk-Ape, Yowie or The Yeti (*metoh kanqmi* - Abominable Snowman), since these sightings are numerous and global. This creature has sufficient credibility to have been given a name by most civilizations on most continents.

Mokele Mbembe

Since the 18th century, white men have heard tales about a putative African monster generically referred to as Mokele Mbembe by various native tribes. It was said to frequent the swamps of Central Africa. Expeditions were mounted in 1980 and 1981, led by Roy P. Mackal to finally track down this beast. He received fairly consistent descriptions of a creature 33 feet long of a brownish colour with a long neck accounting for at least a third of its length. Mackall came to believe he was searching for a reptilian beast, akin to a small brontosaurus. Mackall arranged some flip cards with known animals like an elephant, giraffe, lion etc and included a picture of a brontosaurus on one card.

Each village he came to the natives gathered around to chant the native name of the animal shown on each card. When he flashed the brontosaurus, he was amazed to hear the natives without hesitation chant *'Mokele Mbembe'* with every indication that this creature was just as well known to them, and just as real as the others shown.

Today, natives claim that although becoming rare this creature is still seen. The only conclusion we can draw is that somehow this long extinct dinosaur still exists in the swamps of Central Africa where it is known as Mokele Mbembe! [177]

The Mythical Sirrush

The Sirrush was known to the Babylonians as the *Mushhushshu* and any knowledge of this beast was only re-discovered in 1902 with the excavation of the 'Gate of Ishtar' in the ancient city of Babylon situated in present day Iraq. Many beasts are beautifully depicted on this gate way and the stylish Sirrush

Why would just this one of the animals depicted, be mythical?

appears to be a majestic 'dragon-like' beast with a curved horn, a reptilian head featuring a long forked tongue and four legs showing front paws and rear talons. It seems an impossible mixture and this would usually indicate a mythical portmanteau creature as shown in similar depictions around the world. We should be cautioned, because all the many creatures depicted around the Sirrush, are far from mythical. Indeed one was at first believed to be mythical until the Urus (a now extinct variety of wild cow) was discovered to be real. With the depiction of every other beast, a now known species, we must consider that the amazing Sirrush just maybe was a creature known in ancient times. Willy Ley (1906-1969), a crypto-zoologist and science writer, suggested this may be some kind of dinosaur and pointed out that the Bible mentions the Babylonians possessed a dragon-like animal. Perhaps this is a depiction of that creature. (178)

Quoll Sighting

A few years ago, I was working in Toowoomba and camping at night in a cabin on Stringybark Mountain, near Helidon in my home state of Queensland. Coming home tired, late one night, I was amazed to see a strange creature in the car headlights, running across the road. It looked a lot like the mongoose (plural) we often saw run across the roads in Fiji. It moved in a similar way. In all my years in the Australian bush I had never seen anything like it. Next day I called on Doug, an old bushman, who had been around a bit and I asked what he thought. He smiled at the idea but agreed it may have been a ferret that got loose or something like that. I suspect he thought it was tiredness because I was working very long hours at the time.

A couple of days later on the way to work, I again saw that creature cross the road, this time in broad daylight. I phoned Doug on my cell phone and he sounded just a bit astonished. Anyway he invited me to dinner that night and I looked forward to it as Margie is the best cook in the district. After a day's work I turned up with ready appetite at Doug and Margie's place, and the first thing he said was, *"It was a quoll you saw!"*

"A what?" I replied never having heard of this creature.

"A quoll", Doug repeated. He took me to his extensive library and we read up on the quoll. We also went on the web and checked it out and yes, that was the creature I saw. Doug explained that years ago a bloke in the district came out one morning to find all his hens dead; close to a dozen, I think. They had been killed by a quoll that had sucked all the blood out of them, vampire style, without eating any part. The striking thing was that the combs of the hens were no longer red because all the blood was gone. They were kind of colourless.

Research showed us that the Eastern Quoll *(Dasyurus viverrinus)* is a carnivorous marsupial and is supposedly extinct on the mainland and extant only in Tasmania. Looking something like a ferret or mongoose, the eastern quoll hunts at night on insects, small rodents and fruit, but is known to break into hen houses after eggs and chickens. The home of the eastern quoll is usually in hollow logs or in caves. These creatures are under tight legislation in Tasmania as a threatened species. I am probably blessed that I actually got to see one, both at night and in the daytime.

CHAPTER SEVENTEEN

CHAOS OF THE CULTS

'The difference between a Church and a Cult is the amount of real estate they own.'

Frank Zappa

Religions, Cults and Sects

Many of today's 'respectable' religious denominations commenced as 'cults' in the nineteenth century. The word 'cult' has today taken on a fairly derogatory connotation because one immediately associates cults with the media portrayal of leaders such as Jim Jones of the People's Temple at Guyana or David Koresh of the Branch Davidians. The media loves promoting an image of Cults being immersed in esoteric things including devil worship, mind control, bloodshed and death, whereas Religions are supposedly orthodox receptacles of the ineffable Word of God, emanating spirituality, wholesomeness and love. Splinter groups from the mainstream religions, on the other hand, are often referred to as Sects. These groups often disagree with the mainstream religion on relatively minor points but are generally shown as fairly intense and troublesome as opposed to the 'respectable' mainstream Church whose flock question very little. The act of breaking away usually indicates a dynamic and likely charismatic new leader with new ideas on an existing mystery or a different slant on some part of the religious dogma. Wherever there has been orthodoxy, the holders of mysteries have usually been classed as heretics. Accordingly, the term 'Sects' along with 'Cults' usually has a derogatory connotation.

Orthodoxy

To differentiate between a Religion, a Cult and a Sect, we must look back to the formation of the World's three Abrahamic religions, Judaism, Christianity and Islam. Judaism was a product of the Levite scribes who came out of Egypt and their (Old Testament) scriptures were formulated and written during and soon after their captivity in Babylon, encompassing parts of the Sumerian classic literature for their genesis. Stories of the creation and of Noah's ark, for example, are straight out of the ancient Sumerian *Enuma elish*.

Soon after, the Christian religion was compiled within the Roman Church under the watchful eye of the Byzantine Emperor, Flavius Constantine. The original Jewish religion was effectively hijacked and extensively modified, a New Testament was added and the scriptures handpicked for the message Constantine wanted included in the Christian Bible to promote stability in his Byzantine Empire. All other scripture was confiscated and burned. The Roman Church classed their resultant 'manufactured' doctrine as the one true orthodox religion whilst at the same time, rather ludicrously, the original Hebrew message was classified as heretical. The Roman Church effectively eliminated the competition and enforced its orthodoxy from an unbending power base.

It didn't stop there. This new religion (and the later Islam) also hijacked the Jewish patriarchs, such as Adam, Seth, Noah, Abraham, Jacob, Moses, King David, Solomon and John the Baptist as their own, set them in their own historical timeframe and with an anti-Semitic zeal undertook to wipe out the Jewish religion. They classified anyone with differing views as heretics and quite effectively removed any alternate thought with copious amounts of bloodshed. Hundreds of thousands of innocent people died in the various purges and inquisitions because of differing beliefs. From this time until around 1500 A.D., the Catholics specifically targeted not only the pagan religions (that they would have called cults or sects) but also Manicheans, Cathars, Bogomils and also Knights Templar, Masons, Jews (particularly Desposyni), Muslims and Gypsies. They came down on science, heresy, magic and learning. Women were thoroughly disenfranchised and apart from Miriam-Mary, the mother of Jesus, Biblical women were classed as harlots and whores. Everyone developed phobias towards sex. The joys of a normal loving heterosexual relationship were seen as men *defiling themselves* with these *brazen seductresses.* The Roman Church removed from the Bible things that might empower the individual, such as astrology, karma and re-incarnation. [179] They replaced them with fraudulent introduced threats, such as Hell-fire, Purgatory and the Devil to ensure a confused and denigrated congregation eternally subservient to (and reliant on) the clergy. The Roman Church is now considered the ultimate in orthodoxy.

Actually, we humans display incredibly short memories. Religions such as the Mormons and the Jehovah's Witnesses today hold an aura of respectability, yet not so very long ago were considered 'Cults' by the worst definitions possible. Fritz Sprigmeier and David Icke have exposed the founding of many religious groups including the Church of Jesus Christ of Latter Day Saints (Mormons) and the Watchtower Society (Jehovah's Witnesses) by showing that the founding leaders were in most cases 33rd degree Masons, and initial funding and control came specifically from Illuminati families and individuals (Rothschild, Rockefeller et al). These documents are available for scrutiny and they will scare you witless. Now why do you think the Illuminati families would do this when their agenda has always been gaining control and reaping huge profits? [180]

The Danish theologian, Søren Kierkegaard (1813-1855) suggested that religion has now become escapism and entertainment for a congregation seeking magic *without*, rather than seeking things of God *within*. Otherwise intelligent people have been coerced to form into denominational groups in a herd mentality, each one entirely sure that they alone have the right group and all others are erroneous and quite likely wicked. If one could just stand back and look at the control mechanisms, they would see that they are all being manipulated and quite possibly none of them is right.

'The Book of Abraham' is claimed by the *'Church of Jesus Christ of the Latter Day Saints'* to have been translated by (the totally unqualified) Joseph Smith - from a papyrus in his possession, penned by the patriarch Abraham, himself. This should immediately prick up the ears, as no such papyrus has ever been examined and accepted by academics. According to Joseph Smith's translation (assisted by Almighty God), Noah's son Ham, had a wife called *'Egyptus'*, who also named their first daughter Egyptus. They suggest that some

descendants of Noah then settled Egypt. Ironically, the Mormons also claim Ham's daughter, Egyptus, named her first son *'Pharaoh'* and he became the first pharaoh of Egypt. [(181)] The problem with this reasoning is that the earlier rulers of Egypt were called 'Kings' and it was much later that the title 'Pharaoh' came about. In addition, we now know of the Maadi people who predated the early Egyptian dynasties and accordingly, any Pharaoh of Egypt. Most Egyptologists believe the original *'Per-aa'* meaning *'the illustrious house'* was the title from which *'pharao'* and eventually *'Pharaoh'*, derived. The image of the Pharaoh as the *'Great House'* is similar to the early Persian meaning of *'Freemason'* which, in that country, means *'Master of the House'*. [(182)]

Joseph Smith also discovered in this 'scripture' that the sun gets its light from God's home planet, a world he called *'Kolob'*. Leading Egyptologists, Professor Lutz and Professor Lesko of the University of California, agree that the original papyrus claimed by Joseph Smith to be the *'Book of Abraham'* was in fact an Egyptian funerary text called *'The Book of Breathings'* and has absolutely nothing whatsoever to do with the patriarch Abraham. It makes no mention whatever of Egyptus, of Pharaoh, or of a planet called Kolob. [(183)] Obviously, this makes it hard to support the Mormon doctrine.

Subjectivity

We must realize how subjective our selection of the religion we choose to follow really is. To be honest, our 'choice' is usually that of our parents. For example, the follower of Islam has trouble believing that the Christians worship a dead man on a cross. The Christian Bible actually spells out that if a follower of YHWH sins, they need to then sacrifice a lamb or a dove or a goat to compensate and in fact at the highest level of this doctrine they killed Jesus, the Son of God, so his blood could wash them all clean forever. If one attempted to explain that doctrine, the Moslem would be aghast. Our Christian Bible is full of animal and human sacrifice and a direct commandment states that all the 'first born' of animals and human babies are to be sacrificed to the Lord; but of course although it is Biblical doctrine and a commandment of YHWH God, that supposedly lives forever, we don't do that anymore.

Exodus 22 : 29-31 'Thou shalt not delay to offer the first of thy ripe fruits, and of thy liquors: the firstborn of thy sons shalt thou give unto me. Like-

> ***wise shalt thou do with thine oxen, and with thy sheep: seven days it shall be with his dam; on the eighth day thou shalt give it me. And ye shall be Holy men unto me.'***

Just try to explain to the Moslem the purpose of all this ritual murder? The Moslem would think you are crazy and that you had been 'taken in' by the worst cult on the planet. A Christian believes their Bible until this unpalatable stuff comes up and then retires to the 'nice' passages about love and everlasting life, which are more amenable to today's Christian walk. In similar fashion, it is made very easy for a Christian to form an opinion on the Moslem religion of Islam after watching just a couple of stories on CNN, and holding no other information about the doctrine. We really need to be more tolerant and more objective.

Raise Your Consciousness

Richard Dawkins states repeatedly that there is no such thing as a Christian child or a Muslim child. He makes this heartfelt plea: *'Please, please raise your consciousness about this, and raise the roof whenever you hear it happening. A child is not a Christian child, not a Muslim child, but a child of Christian parents or a child of Muslim parents'.* [(184)] Dawkins goes on to explain that this is an excellent piece of consciousness raising for the child as well. They will ultimately appreciate the respect shown to them and come to understand that at an appropriate future time, they have the right to evaluate and choose for themselves what to accept and what to reject, with their own growing maturity. It would be hugely beneficial if they could actually choose freely without the threat of condemnation.[(185)] We cannot possibly cover all cults and sects here but should look at a cross section of some of the more notable ones.

Tuesday Lobsang Rampa

Just before the 'youth rebellion' of the 1960s when the Beatles and Rolling Stones revolutionized popular music, there was a global interest in Eastern mysticism and religion. In 1956 an interesting book purporting to tell of Tibetan mysticism was released, that went on to become a best seller during the 1960s. It was a strange and powerful book called *'The Third Eye'*; the autobiography of an equally strange Tibetan monk called Tuesday Lobsang

Rampa. I bought this book and over time, a number of the 18 follow up titles including, *'You Forever'*, *'Doctor from Lhasa'*, *'The Rampa Story'* and *'The Cave of the Ancients'*. All were best sellers.

Genuine scholars of Tibetan Buddhism had some serious concerns about Rampa's works and some openly accused him of being a fraud. Completely by accident, I noticed that this book was registered as FICTION and was documented as fiction in the front notes of my copy. I drew the attention of my friends to this fact but no one seemed to notice or care. The books continued to enjoy a credibility that was simply not warranted or deserved.

With some research, I discovered that the Lama, *Tuesday Lobsang Rampa* was in fact an English plumber's mate called *Cyril Henry Hoskins*, who had never set a foot in Tibet. When Cyril first developed an interest in the occult, he shaved his head, grew a long beard and went by the name *Dr. Kuan-so*. After reading the story of some soldiers who had journeyed through Tibet, he changed his name to Lobsang Rampa and affixed the day of the week on which he was born which happened to be a Tuesday. (Perhaps I should ask here, would you buy a book by Thursday Vayro?) When he was finally challenged, Cyril claimed Rampa's spirit had chosen to re-incarnate in his body so he really was Rampa and his wife really was *Mama san RA-AB Rampa*. How convenient! Cyril Henry Hoskins a.k.a. Dr. Kuan-so a.k.a. Tuesday Lobsang Rampa, died in 1981 and his spurious books still enjoy modest sales today.

Father Devine

One of the first modern era 'Cults' was that formed in the Deep South by a negro preacher, George Baker Jnr., who as *Father Devine* formed the *'International Peace Mission'* movement in 1907. As self-appointed *Reverend General Father Jealous Divine*, he initially became *'the Messenger'* to a small and predominantly black congregation with assistance from Samuel Morris (a.k.a. Father Jehovia) and John A. Hickerson (aka Reverend Bishop Saint John the Vine). After 1912, Baker parted company with his former associates and claimed to be 'God' to a multi-racial and international church.

He was seen by many contemporaries as a charlatan; however, he was a gifted speaker and did promote racial equality and made contributions towards economic independence for his people. In 1914, Father Devine moved his Church to New York City where his movement underwent sustained growth and began attracting many white followers as well as black. Father Divine courted controversy with his promoted communal living and by flaunting his new found affluence by driving a new Cadillac. He also fed the poor and held free weekly banquets and helped newcomers find jobs. After a time in New York, Father Devine and 78 followers were sensationally arrested for 'disturbing the peace', an event reported to be the single most famous moment of Father Divine's life. Many followers incurred a $5 fine which Father Divine, ever the showman, paid with a $500 bill. The court was embarrassingly unable to make change and the resulting publicity propelled Divine's popularity. By 1932 he was speaking to over 10,000 people at his services in Harlem's Rockland Palace, a spacious converted former casino.

Father Devine was eventually arrested again on a charge of 'disturbing the peace' and at his trial in Nassau County before Justice Lewis J. Smith, the Jury found him guilty. Justice Smith lectured on how Father Divine was a fraud and a 'menace to society' before issuing the maximum sentence, one year in prison and a $500 fine. Amazingly, Justice Smith aged just 55 died of a heart attack a few days later. Father Divine milked the *'divine retribution'* for all it was worth and was widely reported to have commented on the untimely death, *'I hated to do it. I did not desire Judge Smith to die. ... I desired only that my spirit would touch his heart and change his mind that he might repent and believe and be saved from the grave.'*

The press had a field day and failed to report Smith's prior heart problems and implied that his death was more sudden and unexpected than it really was. In time, Father Divine took on a more political orientation but failed to change with the times until the more consumer oriented population finally lost interest in the aging Father and his outdated message. The 'modern' press began treating him as a joke and did irreparable damage to his mission. In 1953, a follower called John Devout donated his 'Woodmont' 72-acre hilltop estate in Gladwyne, Pennsylvania to the movement. This French Gothic manor served as Devine's home and primary site of his increasingly infrequent banquets until his death. On 10th September 1965, Father Divine died of natural causes at this Woodmont estate. For a short time his widow, Mrs. S. A. Divine, became spiritual leader of the movement. In 1972 she fought an attempt by cult leader Jim Jones to take over the movement's dwindling devotees.

Jim Jones – People's Temple

American, James Warren Jones became a preacher in the 1950's but was not ordained as a minister until 1964. Jones' church supported the struggle for racial equality and social justice and he authored a booklet called *'The Letter Killeth'*, pointing out what he felt were the contradictions, absurdities, and atrocities in the Bible but also stating that the Bible also contained great truths. He was particularly fascinated with his ability to manipulate people and gradually moved increasingly further away from the mainstream. He claimed at various times to be a re-incarnation of Jesus, Pharaoh Akhenaten (Moses), Buddha and even Lenin and he performed supposed miracle healings to attract new members. Finally in 1972, Jones took over what was left of the Father Devine followers and adopted some of the doctrines of the *International Peace Mission* movement into his *'People's Temple'*. At this point he even purported to be the reincarnation of Father Divine.

After an investigation into his group for tax evasion in 1977, Jones and most of the members of the People's Temple moved from San Francisco to an isolated agricultural community located in Guyana that they named Jonestown. People who left the organization prior to its move from San Francisco, told the authorities of brutal beatings, murders and of Jones' mass suicide plan. In time, U.S. Congressman Leo Ryan led a fact-finding mission to the Jonestown settlement in Guyana but only after many allegations of human rights abuses came to light. Ryan's delegation arrived in Jonestown on 15th November and spent three days interviewing residents.

The delegation left hurriedly on the morning of Saturday 18th November after Ryan was attacked by a Jones supporter armed with a knife. Congressman Ryan and his people took with them fifteen People's Temple members who had expressed an urgent desire to leave the commune. This apparently infuriated Jones and as the delegation members were boarding two planes at the airstrip, a truckload of Jones' armed guards arrived and began indiscriminately shooting, killing Congressman Ryan and five others. Back at the Jonestown settlement, 908 of the remaining inhabitants, 276 of them children, died from cyanide poisoning, in what was termed a group suicide; however, some feel that mass murder is a more accurate description. An autopsy of Jones' body showed high levels of barbiturates that could have been lethal to all but a seasoned user. His drug taking, including LSD and marijuana experimentation, was confirmed by Jones' son, Stephan, and his former doctor in San Francisco.

It is now claimed that Jim Jones was in fact a CIA operative, experimenting with mind control on his followers. Admiral Stanfield Turner, the Director of America's Central Intelligence Agency, admitted publicly in 1977 that millions of dollars had been spent by the CIA studying voodoo and witchcraft for the purpose of utilizing these rituals in their operation. At a Senate hearing on 3rd Aug 1977, Turner admitted that the CIA had been mind controlling countless people without their consent or knowledge. (186)

To gain some inkling of the scale of these manipulative covert operations David Icke makes the claim:

> ***'MKUltra has involved at least 185 scientists, 80 U.S. institutions, among them, prisons, pharmaceutical companies, hospitals and 44 medical colleges and universities. Some 700 drugs are used by the 'Brotherhood's mad professors in their mind control projects to create human robots. This is why so many drugs were found at the Jonestown Compound in Guyana in 1978 when 'cult' members were murdered in their hundreds. The People's Temple cult' was created by CIA operative, Jim Jones. It was not a new religion as portrayed in the media; it was a mind control experiment.'*** (187)

If Icke is correct and Jim Jones was indeed a CIA operative, then the shocking waste of life at Jonestown can be fairly sheeted home to their mind control experiment. Perhaps Jones was just a CIA patsy but by now all evidence would be shredded and lost and certainly hard to uncover. There is some evidence that MK-Ultra's cultural warfare helped create the 'new religions' cults in the first place. It seems that the *American Family Foundation* (AFF), the secretive organization founded in 1979, and advised by the veterans of the CIA and Army Intelligence's mind-control programs: MK-Ultra, BLUEBIRD, MKSEARCH, 'anti-cult' experts, were directly involved.

Martin Bryant

Most people simply don't want to know that in Australia we have certain proof that Martin Bryant had nothing to do with the shootings in the Port Arthur massacre that the media sheeted home to him. It was never reported in the media but the descriptions and hair colour of the gunman given by the witnesses did not match the striking characteristics of Bryant at all. The *'kill-to-wounded'* ratio in this massacre could only be achieved by a master gunman, not some low I.Q. patsy. Yet the media screamed that it was Martin Bryant and that's the way it is recorded in history. That's the way Mr. and Mrs. Lemming in the suburbs accepted it and they will even argue if presented with the indisputable facts.

It has been revealed that some time before the incident, Martin Bryant underwent 'counseling' at a Tavistock Institute centre, the premier psychological warfare unit of the British Crown, which could certainly condition him for his 'patsy' role and make it almost certain that the entire Port Arthur massacre was a MOSSAD/Tavistock hit. In a report called, *'Mass Murder in Australia: Tavistock's Martin Bryant'* we read: *'Great Britain is the command center for world terrorism today ... through examining the case of Martin Bryant, the dozens of mass murderers who have exploded into the world's headlines over the last decade or so, constitute a special capability within the Crown's arsenal.'*[188] On 22nd Nov 1996, Bryant was sentenced to 35 terms of life imprisonment and to 21 years each on 37 other charges, the terms to run consecutively, and without parole. Yet authors, Allen Douglas and Michael J. Sharp, tell us:

> ***"He originally pleaded 'not guilty' to 72 counts of murder and mayhem. With a new lawyer, and under pressure, he changed that to 'guilty', which ensured that there would be no trial. Indeed, as Mullen stated at the outset of his psychiatric report for Bryant's new lawyer, 'This report is intended to clarify for the court why an insanity plea was not considered appropriate ... As one police source expostulated, "That's wild! If Bryant is not insane, who is?" However, the decision to find Bryant sane, together with his sudden change of mind to plead 'guilty' is of enormous benefit to those who want to make sure the truth never comes out. Under Australia's law, if Bryant were found insane, then he would be monitored and periodically re-evaluated, to see if he regained his sanity. Were he to do so, he would then be put on trial--and some more of Tavistock's handiwork would undoubtedly be exposed to the light of day."*** [189]

Meanwhile, Bryant rots away in jail, but who cares, he was just a weirdo anyway; the media said so! The way it was reported certainly made it easy to disarm Australia. Who has the agenda and who controls the media?

Tavistock Institute

The 11th Duke of Bedford, *(Marques of Tavistock)*, originally gave a building to the Institute in 1921 to study the effect of shellshock on British soldiers who survived World War I, with a purpose of identifying the 'breaking point' of men under stress. Sir John Rawlings-Reese commanded this project under the direction of the British Army Bureau of Psychological Warfare.

Located at 30 Tabernacle Street, London, the private and independent not-for-profit organization now seeks to combine research in the social sciences with professional practice. It undertakes the evaluation of new and experimental programs in anthropology, economics, organizational behavior, political science, psychoanalysis, psychology and sociology with new training methods alongside the regular program of group relations conferences. Tavistock's pioneer work in behavioral science of 'controlling' humans along Freudian lines established it as the orthodox 'world center' of foundation psychology. It enjoyed enormous academic clout and no one was about to step up to the plate and question the motives of this organization. Tavistock researcher, Dr. William Sargent, author of *'Battle for the Mind: A Physiology of Conversion and Brain-Washing'* (1957) stated: *'Various types of beliefs can be implanted after brain function has been sufficiently disturbed by deliberately induced fear, anger or excitement.'* [(190)]

The Churches have known about this method for years which accounts for the threats of eternal damnation accompanied by the pomp and ritual within their services. Tavistock Institute's experiments in crowd control methods have been widely used on the American public. It was Tavistock that originated the propaganda campaign to turn the American public against Germany and ultimately involve the US in World War II. It developed the mass brainwashing techniques, which were first used experimentally on American prisoners of war in Korea. This is a matter of record. Today, British intelligence, US Air Force Intelligence and State Department personal are trained along with the personnel of large corporations at Tavistock controlled institutions. Trilateral Commission, Ditchley Foundation, and the Club of Rome are conduits for instructions to the Tavistock network.

Jim Keith, the co-author of the book, *'The Octopus'*, about a writer who died mysteriously investigating an international conspiracy, himself died in 1999 under mysterious circumstances. He didn't come out of Washoe Medical Hospital after going in for relatively simple knee surgery. Rumors suggest that he was killed after revealing the name of the physician who disclosed that Princess Diana was pregnant at the time of her death. The web news service where Keith named the source also became instantly inaccessible. (Surprise! Surprise!) Keith also revealed: *'The Kennedy assassination was a British Intelligence, i.e. Tavistock hit, and its purpose was to shock the American consciousness into a near-comatose state for reprogramming, the standard Tavistock modus operandi.'* (191)

Keith also claimed that the same can be said for the assassinations of Martin Luther King and Robert Kennedy. In the book *'Mind Control - World Control'* (1997) Jim Keith tells us that German psychiatrist Kurt Lewin, who became director of the elite-sponsored Tavistock Institute in 1932, was the man who developed the precise thinking behind 9 -11. Jim Keith stated:

> ***'Lewin is credited with much of the original Tavistock research into mass brainwashing applying the results of repeated trauma and torture [of individuals] in mind control to society at large. If terror can be induced on a widespread basis into a society, Lewin has stated, then society reverts to a tabula rasa, a blank slate, a situation where control can easily be instituted from an external point. Put another way: By the creation of controlled chaos, the populace can be brought to the point where it willingly submits to greater control. Lewin maintained that society must be driven into a state equivalent to an 'early childhood situation'. He termed this 'societal chaos fluidity'.'*** (192)

Keith goes on to document CIA connections to the creation of mind control cults used to create 'controlled chaos'. These include the Symbionese Liberation Army, Jim Jones, Charles Manson, Scientology, the Unification Church, Son of Sam and Heaven's Gate. The assassination of John Lennon is also said to tie in. (193)

The Branch Davidians

Not widely understood is that this group was a breakaway from the Seventh

Day Adventist Church in 1955 and a member named Vernon Hall took over the splinter group in 1990, changing his name to David Koresh (David after the supposed King of the Jews and Koresh which they believed was God's surname). The compound in Waco, Texas was besieged by the FBI for 51 days before on 19th April 1993 the entire compound burst into flames in front of the World's TV cameras and 74 people were burned to death.

The FBI claims that Koresh followers started the fire but the 9 survivors vehemently deny this saying the fire started in the FBI attack. Few people realize that on 28th February 1993 when U.S. Bureau of Alcohol, Tobacco and Firearms (BATF) agents in National Guard helicopters zoomed in on the Mount Carmel Center, they did so with guns blazing. Despite David Koresh's pledge to surrender upon completion of his written explanation of the meaning of the Seven Seals, the FBI and the Army attacked. At dawn on 19th April 1993, and throughout the morning, tanks rammed holes in the main building and pumped (in the FBI's own words) 'massive amounts' of CS gas into the building, despite knowing that inside were more than a dozen children. The tanks demolished parts of the compound and created tunnels for the wind to blow through. The buildings at this point were saturated with inflammable CS gas and spilled kerosene. It is suggested that FBI agents deliberately sabotaged negotiations with the Davidians to prevent their exiting Mount Carmel. Their goal was to destroy the building and its damaging evidence, even if that meant the massacre of dozens of men, women and children, all witnesses to the brutal attack. Around midday two U.S. military pyrotechnic devices were fired into the main building, igniting a fire which spread rapidly through the complex which became an inferno. There is no question about this; they are quite apparent on the video.

So what was it all about? Good question but no one has bothered to ask! Survivors stated that the Branch Davidians had discovered that the CIA's *'Buffalo Airlines'* were daily transferring Cocaine, laundered money, special operations agents and arms from an old World War Two runway that bordered the Branch Davidian Village. Two of the Branch Davidian members were keeping records of this and had been able to hack into the Pentagon/CIA/FBI Black Ops databases, to confirm what was going on within the corrupt American Government. They claimed the attack was in retaliation, since the

Davidians were carrying out surveillance of the Government's spurious activities. They said the entire village knew about the CIA's activities that tied directly to George Bush Snr. and his direct involvement with the CIA, the Mafia and the global elite's intelligence operations, banking operations, drug transfers, arms transfers and global money laundering network and the CIA's, 'Guns for Drugs' transfers that were going on daily. [(194)]

Sacrifice of Children

We saw earlier the report of the Irish archaeologist Robert Macalister (1870 – 1950), who found the bodies of babies sacrificed to the Jewish God YHWH. This practice was a requirement of the Lord in line with their Holy Book's sickly passages in *Exodus 22 : 29-31* and *Numbers 8 : 17-18*. The Christian Bible also tells us about the sacrifice of children to Molech, the God of fire. A huge fire was lit within the metal Molech idol and parents threw their babies and children into the red-hot metal arms of this abomination:

> ***2 Kings 23 : 10 'And he defiled Topheth, which is in the valley of the children of Hinnom, that no man might make his son or his daughter to pass through the fire to Molech.'***
>
> ***Ezekiel 16 : 21 That thou hast slain my children, and delivered them to cause them to pass through the fire for them?***
>
> ***2 Chronicles 33 : 6 And he caused his children to pass through the fire in the valley of the son of Hinnom: also he observed times, and used enchantments, and used witchcraft, and dealt with a familiar spirit, and with wizards: he wrought much evil in the sight of the Lord, to provoke him to anger.***

This practice is also mentioned in; Leviticus 18 : 21; Leviticus 20 : 2-5 and Jeremiah 32 : 35. The Carthaginians following the rituals of the Canaanites and Jews, rolled children into a fiery pit dug in the shape of the image of Molech.

19th April – Satanic ritual

Today the Satanic ritual day still honouring the fire God, Molech is 19th April and this proves to be very significant. As shown above, the compound and Church at Waco, Texas was besieged by the FBI for 51 days before culminating in the burning to death of 74 Christians on *19th April 1993*, including

12 children younger than five years of age. You won't believe this next bit but it is nevertheless quite true. There is simply no question that a Satan worshipping group within the American Government demanded this attack and destruction with fire. Just two years later, the 'fire-god' demanded more sacrifices of children in line with this Satanic ritual, and Timothy McVeigh supposedly perpetrated the horrific Oklahoma City bombing that claimed 168 lives including 17 children at a child care centre in the building and left over 800 burned and injured. Of course you won't believe this - and that is precisely why they get away with it!

It would seem that McVeigh was a mind controlled patsy. He said he knew 19th April to be the date in 1775 that the Battle of Lexington occurred, marking the beginning of the armed uprising by colonialists against British control but it would seem he knew nothing of the Satanic relevance of the date. David Icke confirms that the events at Waco and Oklahoma City were ritualistic mass murders perpetrated by a group within the American Government. Look at the facts; a pattern is quite apparent: both took place on 19th April and both events claimed the lives of innocent people, many being young children! Look at a map and you will see that Waco and Oklahoma City are aligned directly north and south of each other, with Dallas aligned in the middle. Dallas was of course, the scene of yet another 'ritual' killing that remains highly controversial to this day; that of President John F. Kennedy. David Icke stated; *'Remember, these rituals and 'gods' are the same as those performed and worshipped by the Satanists and the Brotherhood today. This is why the children of Waco were allowed to burn to death in an inferno caused entirely by the Satanist controlled FBI and the Bureau of Alcohol, Tobacco and Firearms on 19th April 1993. These were the same deeply sick people who blew up the James P. Murrah building in Oklahoma on 19th April 1995, in which so many children died. 19th April is a Satanic ritual day relating to fire…'* [(195)]

Perhaps coincidentally on the same day as the Waco massacre, 19th April 1993, an unexplained fire in a psychiatric institute in South Korea killed another 40 people, including a number of children. There also seems to be a propensity to perform Nuclear tests on this 'day of fire'.

- 19th April 1989, Gun turret explodes on USS Iowa, killing 47 sailors in the flames,

- 19th April 1987, U.S.S.R. performs underground nuclear test,
- 19th April 1985, U.S.S.R. performs nuclear test at Eastern Kazakh Semipalitinsk U.S.S.R.,
- 19th April 1983, France performs nuclear test,
- 19th April 1973, U.S.S.R. performs nuclear test at Eastern Kazakh Semipalitinsk U.S.S.R.,
- 19th April 1972, U.S. performs nuclear test at Nevada Test Site,
- 19th April 1937, U.S.S.R. performs underground nuclear test.

The Moonies – The Unification Church

Headed by the Reverend Sun Moon who was born in North Korea in 1920, this cult utilizes a book called *The Devine Principle* that reinterprets the Biblical Old and New Testaments. Although started in 1954, this group only became prominent in 1970 when Moon moved to the United States and began organizing his religious rallies. The Unification Church is particularly well known for its mass weddings where Moon and his staff match up couples, often of different ages and nationalities. Two thousand or more couples can be married at these ceremonies. The cult went from followers selling flowers, sweets and candles to new wholly owned businesses such as the Washington Times Newspaper, hotel chains, factories and even a ballet company. These have proved to be hugely profitable and there have been ongoing claims of tax evasion against the group. Moon claims 4.5 million devotees worldwide.

The Church of Scientology

Firstly we must note that *Scientology* is not to be confused with *Christian Science*, which is an entirely separate sect founded in Boston in 1879. Its founder, Mary Baker Eddy, wrote an interesting book called *'Science and Health with Key to the Scriptures'* after she cured herself of an incurable disease via prayer and 'positive thinking' principles. With the following she received from this publicity, she formed the *Church of Christ – Scientist (Christian Science)* with doctrine encompassing the efficacy of spiritual healing according to the interpretation of the Bible.

Scientology is an entirely separate cult founded in 1954 by Lafayette Ron Hubbard. It claims around 8 million members worldwide, although a figure of 750,000 is considered more realistic. In 1950 Hubbard published a book, *'Dianetics: The Modern Science of Mental Health'*, that proved hugely popular. The idea of Dianetics was that people stored mental images *(engrams)* of unpleasant experiences that can be triggered by association and become a barrier to achieving their full potential. It seems that people are prepared to spend vast fortunes on removing these 'limiting factors' and achieve elevated personal growth. As a result, Scientology is probably the wealthiest and most powerful of today's cults. It is also by far the most classically terrorist and the most litigious. In 1993 after nearly 40 years of court battles, Scientology was able to achieve tax exemption as a religious institution, which I guess would now make it a Church.

During the 1970s, the Church of Scientology cast off its more 'crackpot' doctrine (about space aliens dwelling in a volcano) and sought a more conservative image. To achieve this they had to destroy every single record of their former beliefs, particularly from Government Departments. Apparently, the Church of Scientology managed to perform the largest infiltration of the United States Government in history to avoid the incriminating records coming to light at some future time to 'blow the whistle' on their former 'crackpot' beliefs. Somewhere around 5,000 of Scientology's crack commandos wiretapped and burglarized various agencies; they stole hundreds of documents, mainly from the IRS. No possible critic was spared, and in the end 136 organizations, agencies and foreign embassies were infiltrated. [(196)] When all of this hit the fan, the Church of course denied it all. They hi-jacked and kidnapped one of their own operatives who had been arrested for stealing documents, to prevent him from testifying. These days, the Church of Scientology generally refuses to talk about this *'Operation Snow White'*, except to say that they *'purged'* those who were involved. It seems a bit more purging may be in order as they still hold high ranking offices within the Church. [(197)]

There are many celebrities in the cult including Hollywood actors, John Travolta, Kirsty Alley, Sharon Stone, Demi Moore, Tom Cruise and Katie Holmes. In fact it has been disclosed that Tom Cruise is part of the hierarchy of this cult and the toddler Suri is a special Scientology baby. Tom is on a mission to recruit David and Victoria Beckham and troubled younger stars such as Brittany Spears to use as 'bait' in recruiting a young (rich) following to ensure continued capital growth for his Church. The Church markets its *'Dianetics packages'* to its followers in order to remove limiting factors from their lives and actually operates as a hugely profitable multi-level marketing program, similar to the old 'pyramid selling' schemes. It is required that new recruits involve themselves in these purging courses, at ridiculously inflated prices. This means the millions of dollars 'donated' to Scientology by the stars, are in fact investments which will return them immense capital gains. Australia's richest man, James Packer, and his new bride, Erica Baxter, are also members of Scientology. James Packer is a ruthless businessman and has huge holdings in casinos. It is quite believable that he would only invest his time and money in something that would offer huge returns. This would certainly explain the massive 'donations' from Media personalities we hear about.

Hare Krishna – ISKCON

ISKCON (International Society for Krishna Consciousness), best known as the Hare Krishna group, is based on one of the world's oldest religious philosophical traditions of Hinduism. Other 'New Religious Movements' with similarly based Hindu ideals include, Brahma Kumaris (Raja Yoga); Rajneeshism (Orange People, Osho); Elan Vital (Divine Light Mission); and the Maharishi Foundation (known for Transcendental Meditation). The Ananda Marga (Tantric Yoga) group adheres to similar philosophy, but in Australia still carries baggage after being blamed for the Hilton bombing in Sydney. Also encompassed in Hinduism are Zen Buddhism and relaxation techniques such as Tai Chi and Yoga.

The Hare Krishna movement was founded in the U.S. in 1966 by Indian born A.C. Bhaktivedanta Swami Prabhupada, and used the Hindu Bhagavad-Gita as its central scripture. It received a following amongst the hippies who were drawn to the simple, peaceful lifestyle offered by the movement. Former Beatle, the late George Harrison recorded the Hare Krishna mantra *('My Sweet Lord')* which was hugely popular in 1968 and donated a mansion in Hertfordshire, England, which remains the UK headquarters of the group. In the year 2002, twelve ISKCON temples in the U.S. were driven into bankruptcy over extensive child abuse claims pertaining to ISKCON boarding schools of the 1970s and 1980s. As a result, all ISKCON schools have now closed.

Rajneeshism (Orange People)

Bhagwan Swami-narayan (1781 - 1830) is the central figure of the Swami-narayan faith of Hinduism and was regarded as an incarnation of the Indian God. The title *Bhagwan* means 'blessed one' and in the 1960s & 1970s, *Bhagwan Shree Rajneesh* established meditation centers (Jivan Jagruti Kendras) in India. In 1968, he scandalized Hindu leaders by calling for freer acceptance of sex, and then at the Second World Hindu Conference in 1969 he further enraged Hindus by criticizing all organized religion and the very institution of priesthood. From humble beginnings in Mumbai (Bombay), Bhagwan moved inland to the cooler climate of Pune, and taught at his Ashram there, from 1974 to 1981. Followers called themselves *Sannyasins* (disciples) and this commitment usually entailed wearing the traditional orange dress of ascetic Hindu holy men. Bhagwan relaxed many rules and in time exempted his Sannyasins from the required ascetic lifestyle which he personally did not follow.

In mid-1981, Bhagwan moved the operation to the United States where his followers bought him a 64,000-acre ranch in Oregon to establish Rajneeshpuram. Sannyasins also provided a number of Rolls-Royces (said to have eventually exceeded 40 in number). The "Orange People's" doctrine was criticized for confusing love, religion and sex. Bhagwan's statement on live TV that Mother Theresa *"should go and jump in the lake"* infuriated parents of followers everywhere. In addition, who can forget Bhagwan's personal secretary and commune manager *Ma Anand Sheela* and her inappropriate comment of *'tough titties'* to media questions? She was certainly not a good role model for the group and was said to display questionable morals with young followers.

Bhagwan driving one of over 40 Rolls-Royces.

After multiple squabbles with neighbours, the position of the Oregon commune became untenable. Things went from bad to worse with a bioterrorism attack using salmonella on the citizens of The Dalles, Oregon. This was sheeted home to the commune's insane management team. Bhagwan convened a press conference and called on the authorities to undertake an investigation. This eventually led to the conviction of Sheela and several of her lieutenants. Surprisingly, Bhagwan was not directly implicated in these crimes; however, his reputation suffered tremendously and on a world speaking tour he was refused entry visas by more than twenty countries. He subsequently returned to India and in January 1987 to his old Ashram in Pune, taking on the new name Osho.

Bhagwan-Osho died in early 1990, aged 58, of heart failure and had previously expressed his belief that his rapid health decline was caused by some form of poisoning by the U.S. authorities during the twelve days he was held in various U.S. prisons. He claimed publicly that his Doctors had variously suspected the administration of thallium radioactive exposure to account for his failing health.

After a time of dwindling interest, today, Osho's books are more popular than ever, with translations in 55 different languages. Bhagwan-Osho's Ashram in Pune has now become the *Osho International Meditation Resort* and is a major tourist attraction, boasting some 200,000 visitors from all over the world each year. [(198)]

Children of God – The Family

In the 1960s, 70s and 80s many teenagers and young people in their twenties were recruited into the Family to the alarm of their parents. The movement commenced in 1960 when minister David Brandt Berg formed an evangelical group called *'Teens for Christ'* and began working with Californian hippies, telling them about Jesus. As youngsters, actors River Phoenix and his brother Joaquim (leaf) were Children of God members.

Devotees mostly dressed in white robes and saw David Berg as a modern day prophet (they called him Mo as a diminutive of Moses) and believed he would play a part in the final apocalypse. Berg adopted the 'free love' of the hippy movement into his doctrine, using *Matthew 22 : 39 'Love thy neighbour as thyself'* and took it to the limit of its context within sexual relationships.

Sexually transmitted diseases and specifically AIDS finally necessitated a change to this doctrine. In 1972 a group of concerned parents formed *FREECOG* (Free our children from the Children of God) to help rescue their children. The Children of God group has now distanced itself from David Berg and particularly his writings on sexual matters although the *'Law of Love'* is still fundamental to the movement.

Aum Shinrikyo

The name means *'Universal Truth Society'* and the beliefs of this Japanese group encompass an unusual mix. Their doctrine is based on Buddhism with more than a touch of apocalyptic Christianity, worshipping a God of Creation and Destruction that aligns with the Hindu God, Shiva. Led from its foundation in 1984 by the controversial messianic leader, Shoko Asahara, this dangerous cult burst into recognition with a series of killings. The cult started attracting controversy in the late 1980s with accusations of deception of recruits, and of holding cult members against their will. There were charges of forcing members to donate money and the murder of a cult member who tried to leave the cult is known to have taken place in February 1989.

Tsutsumi Sakamoto, an anti-cult lawyer, threatened a lawsuit against the cult in 1989. Sakamoto recorded an interview for a talk show on the Japanese TV channel TBS, which was secretly revealed to the cult. Cult members pressured TBS to drop the broadcast and soon after Sakamoto, his wife and child all went missing from their home in Yokohama. Police were unable to resolve the case at the time, and it was not until several years later that they were known to have been murdered and their bodies dumped by cult members. The Aum Shinrikyo cult members were then responsible for a toxic gas attack on the Tokyo Underground in 1995.

An offshoot now known as Aleph disassociates itself from Aum Shinrikyo and its former leader and has established a code of conduct to ensure its devotees stay within the law.

Raëlian Movement

The former champion racing driver, Claude Vorilhon, was born in Vichy, France to an unwed farm girl just 15 years old. At the end of his driving career, Vorilhon formed the Raëlian Movement and had his followers call him Raël. He taught that life on Earth was created scientifically by visiting extra-terrestrials called the Elohim. Their take on man's creation is positioned somewhere between the Sumerian Intervention Theory (that has extra-terrestrials intervening by manipulating existing Earth life forms into man) and the Biblical Creation by the Elohim (Gods). There is a lot of evidence to support the intervention hypothesis and the Raëlian doctrine is actually quite plausible in line with the Bible and other ancient documents. It holds more scientific credibility than most other religious doctrine. The Raëlian Movement members believe that the survival of mankind will depend on successful cloning. Their hope is that the Aliens will return and rescue them. I admire their sincerity and certainly hope the Aliens know about this!

Heaven's Gate

Sometimes compared to the Raëlians, Heaven's Gate devotees believed that they were divine spirits trapped in Earthly human bodies. (Aren't we all?) Their leader, Marshall Herff Applewhite, taught that they must seek the next level of development where they would cast off their Human shells before the destruction of the Earth. When comet Hale-Bopp passed the Earth in 1997 one published photograph showed a white dot in its wake. Convinced that this was an Alien craft come to rescue them, all thirty-nine members engaged in a mass suicide. Good-bye and good luck!

Order of the Solar Temple

This archetypal apocalyptic cult believed the World would end in 1994. Their leader, Joseph di Mambro, was supposedly a re-incarnated Templar Knight from the Crusades of the Middle Ages and would somehow lead them through death complete with new Solar bodies to live happily ever after on the planet Sirius. In Canada, France and Switzerland, more than 70 members committed suicide in an attempt to achieve their goal. I am just amazed that di Mambro was able to find 70 followers. Hope they were not disappointed!

Personal Choice

More than 400 children were taken from a polygamist compound in San

Angelo, Texas in April 2008 and placed in state custody as authorities continued their investigations into underage marriages within the group. The compound, headed by Warren Jeffs, was said to be a fundamentalist break-away group from the Mormon Church. Authorities claimed to have uncovered the equivalent of a small town on the 1,700-acre property. They allowed 133 women to leave the compound with their children but an unknown number of men were forced to remain at the property while investigations continued. For some reason when people band together in similar groups they appear to lose the ability to cognitively evaluate that situations they exist in are plainly not normal. The Bible predicted persecution and ridicule for God's elite and these folks appear to deliberately attract this alienation in acts of self-fulfilling prophecy.

We have just seen evidence of manipulation, mind control and sacrifice amongst the cults and unfortunately the more apocalyptic ones often result in the deaths of many innocent, though misguided followers. Recent books by this author and others disclose how even mainstream religions have been infiltrated by forces that cannot be considered good, yet the parishioners don't seem to twig that all is not well. I believe there is only one Truth and it can operate for anyone who chooses to embrace it. It is not difficult to work in harmony with the manifested pure energy of Nature, and the pay-off is massively rewarding. There is unquestionably a Creative intelligence in the Universe and modern Quantum Science is coming to the indisputable conclusion that the universal mind is a reality. We may worship this force in a myriad of ways, hopefully more altruistically than many of the religions we have just seen. As we move forward, we may continue to call this force 'God' if we choose to; however, with the plethora of severely limiting Gods that this world has already endured, I would see that as conditioned and unwise thinking.

CHAPTER EIGHTEEN

GIANTS

'There were Giants in the Earth in those days.'

Genesis 6 : 4, Holy Bible

Records of Giants

Both the Sumerian Tablets and the Ancient Egyptian records give us stories of Giants on the Earth in ancient times. We can no more explain away records of Giants and Sky-Gods (Anunnaki Watchers, Elohim and Nephilim) in our Bibles today. It wasn't heavily promoted, but amongst the Dead Sea Scrolls was found both *'The Book of Giants'* and *'The Book of the Watchers'*. The latter is contained within the Gnostic *'Book of Enoch'* with considerable mention of Nephilim and Giants. The Book of Enoch was believed to have been written around 150-125 B.C.E. and was a highly valued and well used scripture for at least 400 years, until the time it was refused entry into the Bible corpus. The discovery, in 1947, of no less than nine copies with the Dead Sea Scrolls confirmed its antiquity and its popularity. The Hebrew books of *Jubilees* and *Jasher*, mentioned in *Joshua 10 : 13* and *2 Samuel 1 : 18* in the Bible, both also contain Giant stories.

We all remember Goliath from the Disneyesque Sunday School epic; however, these additional giants and the supporting documentation make it pretty eye-opening reading. It seems apparent that Giants were reasonably common and totally accepted as fact, in those times prior to 100 B.C.E. The Sumerians documented that the Anunnaki Sky-Gods initially selected and educated their kings and leaders and this becomes interesting when we note that the title given to ancient Sumerian Kings was '*Lugal*' and this word actually means '*man of huge stature*' or in a word, '*giant*'.

Nephilim & Elohim

There is no way we can pass these documented beings off as just big men. The Bible and a considerable amount of contemporary literature makes it clear that they were huge and that they were of a different race. The Bible confirms that they were the result of Nephilim (sons of the Gods) mating with Earth women and to appreciate their size, we go to the Bible:

> ***Numbers 13 : 33 '... and there we saw the Nephilim, sons of Anak, of the Giants; and we are in our own eyes as grasshoppers; and so we were in their eyes.'***
>
> ***Jeremiah 4 : 16 "Watchers come from a far country, and give out their voice against the cities of Judah."***

It would seem that the Biblical 'Holy Ones', 'Watchers', 'Sons of the Gods,' 'Anakim' and 'Nephilim' were one and the same beings and the above passage confirms that the Nephilim are the Giants. The concept of a race of God-men, like the Anunnaki, Nephilim or Elohim, is both global and enduring throughout history, in the same way as the various myths of Giants and heroes. In addition to the Sumerian and Biblical records of these giant beings, we find records of the Greek *Prometheus* and they are found recorded in Arabic as *Jabaariyen* meaning 'The Mighty Ones.' There are similar beings documented in Islam as *Allahuma* and in Muslim literature as *Malaaikat*. We should also consider the Finnish *Wainamoinen*, the Zulu *Unkulunkulu* and the first beings formed by *Prajapati* in the Sanskrit texts. Some Indian-Hindu records call the Watchers, *Nagas*, a race also claimed by James Churchward, to have inhabited the ancient mythical land of Lemuria. In more traditional Indian literature, these beings were called *Aryans* (meaning 'Noble Ones') and they were said to have brought the Sanskrit language. There are also primitive myths amongst the African Dogon people that refer to the *Nommos* and the being *Oannes* who landed in the Red Sea. The Chinook Indians of Oregon believed in the semi-divine people called *Ulhaipa*, who preceded humanity; and similar beings were named *Sehuiab* by the Lummies. Australian Aborigines have a tradition of the *Nurrumbunguttias*, who were the original demi-Gods from the sky who created man and were identical; it seems, to the Sumerian Anunnaki and their Watchers. Aboriginals believe that many were drowned in a great flood, while others returned to the sky. This shows amazing consistency and this subject is a full time study in itself. Amazing too is that there was a name for these entities on every land mass and yet today we treat them as juvenile mythical reporting from the ancients.

This gives us a timely reminder that the Bible is but one source. In the Biblical story, however, things are a little confused; for example:

- **Genesis 6 : 4** Tells us that there were Nephilim before the Flood.
- **Genesis 7 : 21 - 23** is adamant that all living things other than Noah and his family were annihilated by the Flood.
- **Numbers 13 : 33** tells how spies sent by Moses saw Nephilim, the descendants of Anak (hence Anakim) who came from the Giants, after the Flood.

This has to mean that, at least, some Nephilim were able to escape the flood. There is further supporting information:

- **Deuteronomy 9 : 2** records: 'A people great and tall, the descendants of the Anakim whom you know and of whom you heard it said, "Who can stand before the descendants of Anak?"
- **Deuteronomy 1 : 28** confirms that the sons of the Anakim, a race of Giants descended from Anak of the Nephilim, dwelt in the Promised Land. (Well after the flood.)

Supporting the loss of all giants in the flood, we find the traditional version of The Apocalypse of Peter, which differs from the version of the same name found at Nag Hammadi; '*... and cast them down straightway and bring forth to judgment all the sorrowful forms, yea, of the ghosts of the ancient Titans and of the Giants and all whom the flood overtook.*' (199) It is only fair to caution that the original word used and translated in the Bible as 'Giants' is the same word used by the historian, Flavius Josephus, to depict *'big, strong men as the mighty Titans.'* The actual translation to 'giants' is not entirely accurate, although these beings are elsewhere described as being close to three metres tall. Note also that in Greek mythology there are two types of Giants called *'Gigantes'* and *'Megistanes'*. The Megistanes were documented as a bigger species of Giant and ironically 'Megistanes' in Greek also means 'Titans'. (200)

Goliath & Other Biblical Giants

To most of us, Goliath was simply a Sunday School story about a brave shepherd boy triumphing over the nasty Giant by using only his slingshot. It was a prototype of the *'Jack and the Beanstalk'* theme. Let's revisit that story:

> ***1 Samuel 17 : 4 'And there went out a champion out of the camp of the Philistines, named Goliath of Gath, whose height was six cubits and a span.'***
>
> ***1 Samuel 17 : 49 'And David put his hand in his bag and took thence a stone and slang it and smote the Philistine in his forehead, that the stone sunk into his forehead; and he fell upon his face to the earth.'***

We are told Goliath's height in cubits, which holds little meaning today. A standard Biblical cubit, the length from a man's elbow to his fingertip, is standardized at 17.5 inches, or 44.4 centimetres. By this reckoning, Goliath was 9 feet 5.75 inches, or just under 3 metres tall. The Bible also records other Giants that we should examine. Let's start with Goliath's family and read about the Giants of Gath.

- Joshua 11 : 21 & 22 tells how Joshua cut off the Anakim (giants) from the mountains and destroyed them, leaving Anakim living only in Gaza, Gath and Ashdod.

Gath is important here. Why? Because in 1 Samuel 17 : 4 & 23 Goliath is referred to as the 'Philistine of Gath'.

- In 2 Samuel 21 : 22 it states that four brothers of Goliath were all born in Gath.
- 1 Chronicles 20 : 5 (also 2 Samuel 21 : 16-17) tells of the father giant and four brothers of Goliath called:
  (i) Ishbi-benob, killed by Abishai, son of Zeruiah
  (ii) Saph (or Sippai), killed by Sibbechai, the Hushathite
  (iii) Lahmi, brother of Goliath, killed by Elhanan, son of Jaare-oregim of Bethlehem.
  (iv) Unnamed son of the giant of Gath with six fingers on each hand and six toes on each foot, killed by Jonathan, son of Shimea.

Unfortunately, the Bible story has been altered, but the alteration is easily detected. In fact number (iii) was not called Lahmi at all. In the early Bibles this was the story of the killing of Goliath, not by David, but by Elhanan. This was changed to *'Lahmi, brother of Goliath'* for later Bibles. It appears that to justify David's rising from a shepherd boy to become king, the killing of Goliath was attributed to him and accordingly, Elhanan was credited with dismissing 'the brother of Goliath.' Quite probably, the unnamed giant in (iv) was originally named Lahmi, but this is not covered. Study of an early Bible will show that the concept of attributing the demise of Goliath to David was certainly fabricated in later Bibles. (201) When we check the involvement of King Saul, we find another discrepancy:

- 1 Samuel 16 : 19-23 Saul knew David well before the latter's encounter with Goliath.
- 1 Samuel 17 : 55-58 Saul did not know David at the time of his encounter with Goliath and had to ask about David's identity.

It appears that the David and Goliath story was pretty much fabrication but it could be based on a much older story that we should look at. There is an ancient record, written by an Egyptian political refugee called *Sinuhe*. He documents that he was a courtier who inadvertently overheard state secrets at the death of Pharaoh Amenemhe I. In fear for his life, in March, 1960 B.C.E., Sinuhe left Egypt for the land of Canaan and traveled to Byblos, then on to Southern Syria, where he became a military adviser. He describes his boldest adventure when he had to fight a Giant, the supreme warrior of all Canaan, in single combat. In fact, the Giant hurled javelins at him, which Sinuhe was able to avoid and he was able to dispatch him with his own battle-axe, after firing an arrow into his neck. Sinuhe was enticed back home to Egypt by Princess Nefru, who offered him an elevated position, complete with a formal funeral with mummification, on his death. This was hugely attractive, as it would 'guarantee' eternal life. (202)

Now, King David was said to rule for forty years, from 1001 B.C.E., to 961 B.C.E. and accordingly, his supposed battle with Goliath would have been some years before he was made king in 1001 B.C.E. This means the Sinuhe story would predate it by almost 1000 years and is quite possibly the template on which the David story was based. It seems that many other Giants were used as mercenaries and were recruited by various Biblical armies. Size and reputation, as well as bravado, were extremely important and obviously affected the going hire out rate. Each army appears to have boasted a champion who built up a reputation, somewhat like the gunslingers with notched 45s in the old American West. Later, King David had a group of '30 Mighty Men', mentioned in 1 Chronicles 11 : 10-15. Their three giant leaders were named:

- Jashobeam, a Hachmonite, who supposedly killed 300 men in one battle with his spear.
- Eleazar, the son of Dodo the Ahohite, who was one of the 'Mighties'
- Abishai, the brother of Joab who, it seems, in verse 20, also killed 300 with his spear in one battle.

We are also told of Benaiah, the son of Jehoiada, the son of a valiant man of Kabzeel, who had slain two 'Lion-like' men of Moab and he also slew another giant. He was also a member of David's 'Mighties', but it seems he did not quite make the top three:

> ***1 Chronicles 11 : 23 - 26 'And he slew an Egyptian, a man of great stature, five cubits high (2.5 Metres); and in the Egyptian's hand was a spear like a weaver's beam; and he went down to him with a staff and plucked the spear out of the Egyptian's hand and slew him with his own spear. These things did Benaiah the son of Jehoiada and had the name among the three Mighties. Behold, he was honourable among the thirty, but attained not to the first three: and David set him over his guard.'***

To project more credibility, the Bible passage goes on to individually name all the 30 members of the 'mighties.' Additional Biblical accounts of Giants of Canaan appear:

- ***Numbers 13 : 22 'And they ascended by the south and came unto Hebron; where Ahiman, Sheshai and Talmai, the children of Anak, were.'***
- ***Numbers 13 : 28 'Nevertheless, the people be strong that dwell in the land and the cities are walled and very great: and moreover we saw the children of Anak there.'***
- ***Numbers 13 : 33 'And there we saw the giants, the sons of Anak, which come of the giants: and we were in our own sight as grasshoppers and so we were in their sight.'***
- ***Deuteronomy 3 : 11 'For only Og, king of Bashan, remained of the remnant of giants; behold, his bedstead was a bedstead of iron; is it not in Rabbath of the children of Ammon? Nine cubits (over 4m)***

was the length thereof and four cubits the breadth of it, after the cubit of a man. (The scribe adds, 'after the cubit of a man', since a giant's cubit, from elbow to fingertip, would obviously be longer).

- ***Deuteronomy 3 : 13 'And the rest of Gilead and all Bashan, being the kingdom of Og, gave I unto the half tribe of Manasseh; all the region of Argob, with all Bashan, which was called the land of giants.'***
- ***Joshua 13 : 12 'All the kingdom of Og in Bashan, which reigned in Ashtaroth and in Edrei, who remained of the remnant of the giants: for these did Moses smite and cast them out.'*** Note: Ashtaroth again.
- ***Joshua 17 : 15 'And Joshua answered them, "If thou be a great people, then get thee up to the wood country and cut down for thyself there in the land of the Perizzites and of the giants, if mount Ephraim be too narrow for thee."***

This is hard to comprehend, but a related passage makes it even more confusing:

- ***Hosea 9 : 3 'They shall not dwell in the Lord's land; but Ephraim shall return to Egypt and they shall eat unclean things in Assyria.'***

Ephraim was a tribe of Israel, named after the second son of Joseph, but its relevance here is not clear. They were shown to be worshippers of Ba`al, in Hosea 13 : 1 and did not expel the Canaanites from their allocation of the 'Promised Land', but cohabitated with them, in Joshua 16 : 12; however, their relationship to giants and why they would return to Egypt or eat unclean things escapes me. (203)

Giants (With Polydactyly)

Is it possible that modern giants, like some of the massive wrestlers and basketball stars - and even Robert Wadley, listed in the Guinness Book of Records as the tallest man who ever lived - actually carried a recessive gene of the Anunnaki offspring? Worth noting, too; in records of giants is the often present 'polydactyly', (having six fingers on each hand or six toes on each foot); sometimes, double rows of teeth are recorded and occasionally, stubs of horns on the upper forehead. (204) The syndrome of polydactyly is not uncommon and in Arizona in 1979 alone, there were 11 cases recorded just among the Native American population. Marilyn Monroe was a famous polydactyly, with six toes on each foot. The wife of Henry VIII, Anne Boleyn's execution was justified by claiming the six fingers on each hand and six toes on each foot proved she was a witch. The band, Oasis, were associated with an amazing new guitarist, Charlie Rodriguez, who's unique playing, is assisted by having six fingers on each hand. 'Hound Dog' Taylor, the American blues musician, was also born with an extra finger on each hand. Taylor, while drunk, amputated the extra digit from his right hand with a razor blade. His left hand had the extra digit for the rest of his life and contributed to his distinct electric guitar playing style. Sir Garfield Sobers also was born with extra fingers, on each hand, that were removed during childhood. UFO researchers claim that Aliens recovered from the Roswell, New Mexico crash site had six fingers on each hand and six toes on each foot. This cannot be dismissed in the instant, because the intelligentsia and those initiated into 'mystery schools' certainly saw something special in this. For example, the 'enlightened' artist *Raphael* (Sanzo Raphello, 1483-1520 A.D.) deliberately painted a very clever sixth finger on the Pope, as a pictorial cryptogram, in his painting *'Sistine Madonna'* and in case that was missed because of the way it was angled, a sixth toe on Joseph's foot in his work, *'Marriage of the Virgin'*. It seems we are rediscovering things that were known in the ancient mystery schools. The polydactyl gene, as researched by Mendel, has proved not to be recessive at all but rather is a dominant gene. In fact, in India, there is a village where one third of the population has polydactylism. [205] We can wonder; is it a throwback to past Giants and accordingly, to the Anunnaki genes utilised in the creation of man?

Traces of Giants

There are several archaeological finds to support the existence of ancient giants; however, they mostly fly in the face of everything most of us were taught to believe. Accordingly, they don't gain much attention and don't really receive the credibility of less contentious finds:

- In Great Britain, Strand magazine, in 1895, showed a photograph of a fossilized giant of 12 feet 2 inches tall (almost 4 metres) photographed against a railway carriage with an accompanying story. [206] The writer, W. G. Wood-Martin, told how the above fossilized giant

The fossilized giant with polydactyly found near Belfast, Ireland in 1875.

was found not far from Belfast, in Antrim, Ireland, by Mr. Dyer during iron-ore prospecting operations in 1875 and was transferred to the London and North-Western Railway Company's goods yard in 'Bro.S/t.' This giant also had polydactyly of hands and feet. Dyer showed the giant in Dublin, Liverpool, Manchester and arranged to display it in London. A business partnership with Mr. Kershaw turned to argument in 1876 and the fossil apparently disappeared. (207)

- On his historic round-the-world trip in 1520, *Ferdinand Magellan* had an interesting reference made in his ship's logbook. He mentioned a race of giants (Tehuelches) living on the Pacific coast of South America. Antonio Pigafetta, the chronicler of the expedition, recorded it thus:

  'One day, when no one was expecting it, we saw a giant, completely naked, by the sea. He danced and jumped and singing, spread sand and dust over his head ... He was so tall that the tallest among us reached only to his waist ... The captain named these people Pataghoni. They have no houses but huts, like the Egyptians. They live on raw meat and eat a kind of sweet root which they call 'capac'. The two giants we had on board ship ate their way through a large basket of biscuits and ate rats without skinning them. They used to drink a half bucket of water at once.'

  In this same location, *Captain James Cook* recorded that he captured one of the South American giants and tied him to his ship's mast. This giant was reported to be over nine feet tall and incredibly strong. Apparently, he freed himself from the ropes and was last seen when he dived overboard.
- Commander Byron of the French warship, *'La Patrie'*, claimed that, in 1858, he met with the highly tattooed chief of a tribe of seven feet tall giants, in Port St. Julien in Patagonia, Argentina.

- A six toed Dwarf (Deng) named Khnumhotep (Khnumhotpu), possibly from Nubia; a man with a deformed head and a hunchback, afflicted by Pott's disease, was an Egyptian court favourite put in charge of Royal Linen for Pharaoh Pepi II around 2250 B.C.E. He was sufficiently well thought of that a statue was made of him for posterity.
- A large stone bearing the perfect imprint of a human foot 14.5" (0.5M) long was shown to members of the Ohio State Academy of Science, in 1896. The stone had been taken from a hill 4 miles north of Parkersburg, West Virginia, some 20 years earlier. [208]
- A carnival of horses, bears, turkeys and six toed humans left tracks in what is now solid rock near the headwaters of the Tennessee river, a few miles South of Braystown, North Carolina. According to Josiah Priest, a 19th century writer on antiquities, the strange human tracks included one track of giant footprints 16" (.5M) long and 13" wide at the toes and 5" wide at the ball of the heel. [209]
- Ivan T. Sanderson, a well-known zoologist and frequent guest on Johnny Carson's 'Tonight Show' in the 1960s, once related a curious story about a letter he received regarding an engineer who was stationed on the Aleutian island of Shemya during World War II. While building an airstrip, his crew bulldozed a group of hills and discovered, under several sedimentary layers, what appeared to be human remains. The Alaskan mound was in fact a graveyard of gigantic human remains, consisting of crania and long leg bones. The crania measured from 22 to 24 inches from base to crown. Since an adult skull normally measures about eight inches from back to front, such a large crania would imply an immense size for a normally proportioned human. Furthermore, every skull was said to have been neatly trepanned (a process of cutting a hole in the upper portion of the skull). [210]
- In the bed of the Paluxy River, near Glen Rose, Texas, there are human footprints 18" long and 5" to 7" wide. John Green along with Jack Walper, a professor of Geology at Texas Christian University, discovered them in 1976. [211]

- Ellis White, a government trapper, in the area of Great White Sands, New Mexico, found giant tracks in 1931, seemingly of a human being. A year later, a party of four, including White and O. Fred Arthur, supervisor of Lincoln National Park, found 13 Giant prints in the foothills of the San Andres Mountains. The very clear prints are 16-22" long and 8-12" wide and about 5 feet apart. On revisits, in 1972, 1974 and 1981 more tracks were found. [(212)]
- From the publication, *'The History of Marion County'*, in Ohio, complied from past accounts, published in 1883, we read: *'In removing the gravel bluffs, which are numerous and deep, for the construction and repair of roads and in excavating cellars, hundreds of human skeletons, some of them of giant form, have been found. A citizen of Marion County estimates that there were about as many human skeletons in the knolls of Marion County as there are white inhabitants at present!'* [(213)]
- Mastodon remains are occasionally unearthed and from time to time, discoveries of the remains of Indian settlements are indicated by the appearance of gigantic human skeletons, with the high cheek bones, powerful jaws and massive frames peculiar of the red man, who left these as the only record with which to form a clue to the history of past ages. [(214)]
- An eye witness said that three giant skeletons were found at the mouth of Paw Paw Creek, while Nim (Nimrod) Satterfield was Justice of the Peace. Jim Dean and some men were digging for a bridge foundation and found these bones at the lower end of the old buffalo wallow. The witness thought it was Dr. Kidwell, of Fairmont, who examined them and said that they were very old, perhaps thousands of years old. She said that when the skeletons were exposed to the weather for a few days, their bones turned black and began to crumble, so Squire Satterfield had them buried in the Joliffe graveyard (Rivesville). All these skeletons, she said, were measured and found to be about eight feet long.' [(215)]
- Jewish Talmudic and Midrashic literature contains several references to Giants, as outlined by G. H. Williamson and quoted by Neville Spearman, *'Road in the Sky'*, UK 1959. [(216)]

- No less an historian than Tertullian (died c. 220 A.D.) recorded that a number of Giant skeletons were found in Carthage whilst he was living there. Then in 1858, a newspaper story reported that a 'sarcophagus of Giants' was found on the site of that same city, Carthage. [217]
- The Ancient Hebrew scriptural Book of Jasher tells of Giants and calls them the sons of Anun. This possibly refers to the leader of the Anunnaki, who is called *An* in Sumerian and as *Anu* in Babylonian.
- In 1757, Christian VI, The King of Denmark, commanded the Royal Society of Sciences in Copenhagen to publish a two-volume series of books called *'Travels in Egypt and Nubia'*. That volume was written by Fredrick Lewis Norden after seven years of extensive research and included this observation: *'There runs amongst the people that inhabit Egypt at present, a tradition that there were anciently in the country, Giants and that they raised, without much difficulty, the pyramids, the vast palaces and the temples, whose remains occasion at present our admiration.'* [218]
- There are confirmed reports from Professor W. B. Emery, of skulls and anatomical remains of Giant Sky-Gods from the late pre-dynastic period in the Northern part of Egypt. He spoke of *'remains of a people whose skulls were of greater size and whose bodies were larger than those of the natives, the difference being so marked that any suggestion these people derived from the earlier stock is impossible.'* [219] Throughout *'Contra Celsus'*, Book VI, Chapter I, the work of the Christian eunuch Origen, we find several mentions of the Biblical Giants and it is made apparent that earlier Giants were totally accepted as fact by learned men of that time. [220]
- In 1891, at the centre of one of the large Ohio burial mounds, excavators found the skeleton of a giant man in copper armor. On his head was a copper helmet with copper moldings encasing his jaws. On either side of the head were wooden antlers attached with copper and the mouth cavity was filled with large but decayed pearls. Around the neck was a bear teeth necklace. The remains were found at a depth of 14 feet. [221]
- A skeleton of 9 feet tall (nearly 3 M) was recovered from a stone

burial mound at Brewersville, Indiana, in 1879. A mica necklace was around the neck. Indiana archaeologists excavated the mound and scientific observers from New York, as well as from Ohio, plus a local physician, Dr. Charles Green and the property owner Mr. Robinson were involved. (222)

- A giant skull was recovered from Lovelock Cave, 22 miles South West of Lovelock, Nevada, by guano miners, in 1911. The local Paiute Indians said their legends told of a tribe of 9-10 feet, red haired giants; the Si-te-cahs, who were the enemies of the local Indians. These tribes eventually joined forces to drive the Giants out. Various artefacts, skulls and bones from Lovelock are displayed in the Humbolt Museum in Winnemucca, Nevada and also at the Nevada State Historical Society's Museum, in Reno. Despite considerable opposition, anthropologists now concede that the red headed Indians did exist in the West. (223)

Giant skulls have been found in many places on most continents.

- A recent TV documentary claimed that on 27th September 1998, several hundred citizens of Varonezh, a town 200 miles South of Moscow, witnessed the landing of a UFO craft, out of which came several 9 feet tall (3 Metre) Giants. (224)
- Peruvian tradition tells of huge giants in ancient Peru alighting from ships that sailed from the Pacific, who forced the Incas to retreat into their mountain strongholds. (225)
- There is an unusual report of a woman who worked for the New Mexico Parks Department, who made an unusual discovery and was sworn to secrecy about her find. A flash flood exposed the skeletal remains of a number of 'Giants'. They were about 8 feet tall and had six fingers and toes. They also had an unusual double row of teeth. The entire site was 'cleaned' under the supervision of the Smithsonian Institute and the FBI and nothing has been seen or heard about the

discovery since. [(226)]

- This author has also met 'George', who, whilst working for the Police Department in Greece, located an ancient graveyard of giant skeletal remains. [(227)]
- The British, American and Canadian Navies all seem to be keeping silent about the Franklin expedition, in 1845, involving 129 men and the British ships *Erebus* and *Terror.* Led by explorer Sir John Franklin, they were to chart a Northwest Passage across the Arctic from Europe to China and study Arctic anomalies. According to a discovered message left by these men, the ships are frozen in the ice off the northwest coast of King William Island but they have never been found. (A recent TV report claims the authorities are investigating sightings of these ships and will positively locate them soon.) Members of the crew were never seen alive again but their mutilated remains were found in 1929 on King William Island. In 1980, studies were done on three of the exhumed bodies and revealed signs of a bizarre autopsy. This is quite a mystery, but we should note that the local Inuit Eskimos record categorically that they saw a Giant on board one of the ships just before it became stuck fast. [(228)]
- The ancient Greek *Book of Barloch* tells of a tribe of 49,000 Giants.
- The apocryphal works, *'The Book of Judith', 'The Wisdom of Solomon'* and *'The Wisdom of Jesus, the Son of Sirach'* all mention Giants surviving the flood. The latter book is included in the Septuagint and in the Roman Catholic canon as the Old Testament book of *Ecclesiastes.*
- *The Book of Baruch*, a pseudepigraphical work written in the first century and preserved in a sixth century Syriac Vulgate Bible states, *'There were Giants famous from the beginning, that were of so great stature and so expert in war ... but they were destroyed, because they had no wisdom and perished through their own foolishness.'*
- In another part, reminiscent of the story of Enoch and the Watchers, it goes on, *'These first Giants were very highly developed, intellectually, artistically and physically; they had power over birds and animals ... they misbehaved and were abolished by God and ordinary men took their place.'* [(229)]

Twelve toed petroglyphs from Utah.

- There are six-toed footprints on Anasazi petroglyphs in the Canyon lands of Utah and six-fingered Sky Kachina in the traditions of the Laguna, Hopi and other Pueblo Indians. The Brazilian Ugha Mongulala, believe their 'Ancient Fathers', who came from the stars, had twelve fingers and twelve toes.

A very ancient Bronze Age copper mine has been discovered outside the town of Llandudno on the northern coast of Wales in the U.K. This is a massive mine, many kilometres long on 9 levels and is believed to be 3,500 years old. A suspected 1,700 tons of copper has been extracted by breaking up the ore with sledge hammers. Literally hundreds of ancient sledge hammers are still to be found in the mine but the amazing thing is that these weigh up to 30 kilograms. Seriously, who is going to work underground all day swinging a 30 kilogram sledgehammer? The sledgehammer in my tool shed is actually 12 pounds, (around 5 kilos) and more than half an hour swinging that would likely kill me. Of course, no 30 kilogram (65 pound) sledgehammer can be bought, they are not made. The mine itself is built on a massive scale and the only tenable conclusion is that the mining activities were originally conducted by a race of giants. [(230)]

Most people today would have trouble believing that a race of giants once roamed the Earth. Nevertheless, the Bible is adamant that Giants were a reality. There certainly appears to be sufficient evidence shown above, to afford them some careful consideration.

CHAPTER NINETEEN

MIRACLES & COINCIDENCE

'Science is founded on the conviction that experience, effort and reason are valid; magic on the belief that hope cannot fail nor desire deceive.'

Branislaw Malinowski, *'Magic, Science and Religion'*, 1948.

Miracles vs. Magic

After entering life by the biologically impossible feat of parthenogenesis (virgin birth), we were taught that the Biblical Jesus did supernatural 'miracles', presumably to demonstrate that he was a God and not a man. Since Jesus was not deified until 325 A.D., these are quite apparently fraudulent additions in the Bible. I say this because the repudiation of scientific principles is required to present a miracle. Man did not invent 'science'; he only discovered the principles and learned the applications. Science is based on fixed principles as unalterable and immutable as those by which the Universe itself is regulated and governed. Man can predict an eclipse - but he cannot alter it. It is only the application of pre-existing scientific principles that allows the prediction. [231]

The actual word 'miracle' only appeared in the English language from 1137 A.D. although it is derived from a very ancient Latin root. In the early texts, Jesus was in fact recorded as a doer of *'paradoxa erga'*. Now 'paradoxa' does not mean *miracle*; it means *contrary to favorable opinion* and 'erga' means *works*. Accordingly, Jesus performing *'works contrary to favorable opinion'* appears to have very little to do with the current English records of *miracles*. We must therefore question why God would bother to overcome the chaos in the beginning and set the universe in place, governed by strict rules of order and Nature, if he then permitted Biblical miracles to repudiate these same rules and thus negate God's order.

Fundamentalist Christians must somehow reckon that since God is 'pulling the levers' in the system, he can at any time manually over-ride it to present us with a miracle at any time he sees fit. This rationale notwithstanding, God is arguably unlikely or perhaps even unable to pull rank on the system of his own devising. In reality, it is pretty certain that Jesus did not do any miracles and in the Bible he states this fairly clearly. The Church actually invented the miracles and fraudulently added them to the Bible to satisfy the rabble and attract the gullible. Note the supposed words of Jesus:

> ***Mark 8 : 11-12 'And the Pharisees came forth, and began to question with him, seeking of him a sign from heaven, tempting him. And he sighed deeply in his spirit, and saith, "Why doth this generation seek after a sign? Verily I say unto you, There shall no sign be given unto this generation".***

Was Jesus lying here? Are we to believe that after stating this, he then went out and commenced performing gratuitous tricks and doing miracles that contradict his stance and in turn repudiate and violate the laws of Order, Nature and Science? Well just a few verses later in the Bible, the miracles start and continue through the book of Mark. When one understands the attitude of the clergy, it is far more believable that the miracles attributed to Jesus are fraudulent additions. Celsus accused the Church Fathers saying:

'You utter fables as if in a drunken state, producing self-induced visions and you even possess the art of making them sound likely. You have altered three, four times and oftener, the texts of your own tales in order to deny objections made to you.'[232] To that accusation a presbyter called Synesus bellowed; *'The rabble desire nothing better than to be deceived'*. The word *'rabble'* being the name given by the Church to the *'vulgar multitudes'*. [233] Bishop Eusebius agreed with Synesus that it was fair game to dupe the congregation: *'How it may be lawful and fitting to use falsehood as a medicine and for the benefit of those who want to be deceived.'*[234] The learned Catholic Father Saint Jerome who constructed the Vulgate Bible said: *'There is nothing as easy as by sheer verbosity to deceive a common crowd or an uneducated congregation'*. [235] Gerald Massey wrote in 1907: *'When the Egyptians portrayed a human impossibility - a miracle - they depicted a pair of feet walking on the water. The Christian miracles are false*

modes of explaining that which was ignorantly misappropriated.' [236]

The reality is that Nature has not once ever repudiated its own laws, yet men are tricked or tell lies every single day. There are millions of lies told every year and over the centuries this would amount to billions. If we are to rationally evaluate if a Biblical miracle ever took place, the odds against, are actually billions to one. [237]

Message from Fatima

The Church hierarchies confirm that the 'virgin' Mary has been responsible for various appearances and miracles performed across the world over several centuries. These apparitions of *'Our Lady'* mostly appear in remote Catholic villages and almost always, to children or illiterate, simple, naïve adults. The best known example, today, is probably the appearance at Fatima, Portugal, in the spring of 1917, when three shepherd children, *Lucia dos Santos*, aged 8, *Francisco Marto*, aged 7 and his sister, *Jacinta Marto*, aged just 5, spoke with the 'virgin' on a number of occasions and received several messages from her. A simple study of the facts will show the completely implausible nature of this particular 'miracle' and the inane messages that the 'virgin' actually imparted to the children. This does not instill much confidence in the 'infallible' Church that declared it a miracle. [238]

L-R, Jacinta Marto, aged 5, her brother Francisco Marto, aged 7 and Lucia dos Santos, aged 8.

A thinking person can see that the occurrence of 'happenstance' miracles would result in universal confusion, resulting in chaos within the organized 'system', attributed to God. Surely our God must dwell in harmony within the Universe and Nature. The uncertainty generated by the event of a miracle would, of necessity, fracture that bond.

It is not widely publicized that in 1916, prior to any visions of the 'Holy Virgin', Jacinta, Lucia and Francisco claimed to have met a 'luminous man' who told them he was an 'Angel of God'. He taught them to pray; *'My God, I believe in Thee, I adore Thee, I hope in Thee, I love Thee.'* It should be noted that if one truly knows God, they would not verbalize, *'I believe in Thee'* as this 'Angel' supposedly did. The very act of praying to an entity would hopefully communicate one's belief in that entity. It is not normal to announce to 'My God' that one 'believes in Him'. For example, we teach children to say, 'I believe in Santa Claus', or 'I believe in Easter Bunny' who are not real entities, yet we don't say 'I believe in Pope Benedict', or 'I believe in Queen Elizabeth II', or I believe in 'President George Bush.' This verbalism is wrong.

On a subsequent visit, this 'Angel' supposedly asked the children *'to pray for the forgiveness of sinners and offer sacrifices'.* For goodness sake, these were young peasant children who owned nothing material to sacrifice. Were the children to kill fatted lambs from their parent's flock to comply with this direction? No! It seems these were 'blood' sacrifices and the children themselves were to be sacrificed? It would be normal to ascertain what form these sacrifices were to take, however, this point is never questioned by the poor gullible souls who swallow this nonsense. How smart is it for an 'Angel' to ask young children to perform sacrifices? God would have to be getting pretty desperate! On another occasion the 'Angel of God' told the children, he was the *'Angel of Portugal'*, which would indicate that each country must have its own head angel.

Excuse my cynicism but now that the children were initiated into 'religious show-business' by this 'luminous man', they were ready for the main event with the 'virgin' Mary herself. So in due course, they met with 'Our Lady', who performed a non-scriptural version of the Eucharist with two of the children, Francisco and Jacinta. These two children were required to drink a symbolic Eucharist of the blood of Christ but did not get to 'eat of the body'. They were also asked to make reparation for the crimes of ungrateful man, in order to console God. [(239)]

They were little children, for goodness sake! The eldest, Lucia, who observed all this, although only 8 or 9 years of age at the time, made the startling revelation that all three children immediately understood that Francisco and Jacinta were to die. So we are still looking at 'human sacrifice' to console God, in the twentieth century. Why this religion believes that it requires the sacrifice of the 'innocent' to redeem the 'guilty', I cannot comprehend! Wasn't Jesus the ultimate sacrifice for the sins of mankind? Why was the death of these children now required? If one is a believer, then this is sacrilegious to the extreme and actually denigrates the atonement of Jesus. After Jesus, there was no other sacrifice required. The ultimate sacrifice had been paid, further sacrifice was superfluous. No one seems to pause for even a moment to consider that this actually defies common sense; it contravenes scripture, it is entirely illogical and particularly unfair.

Eighteen months later, these two children fell victim to influenza and passed away; whether coincidental or not, we cannot say. In addition, Jacinta suffered enormously, due to a tumor in her chest. If this is the sacrifice Our Lady spoke of, it is a sobering thought that these two children were summarily sacrificed and the third was made to suffer extreme pain. We are looking at a particularly nasty requirement of this cruel, pagan, 'Christian' doctrine. In fact, this is not a God or a doctrine I would wish to be associated with.

At a number of meetings prior to their deaths, the children continued to see the apparition, but not so the thousands who flocked to the location. Doesn't this tell us something? Lucia asked the 'virgin' for cures for many who had petitioned her and received this amazing response; *'I will cure some but not others because the Lord does not trust them.'* In other words, they believe sufficiently to undertake the arduous journey to request a cure from Almighty God, but the Lord does not trust them sufficiently to provide relief. Now, seriously, what is there not to trust? What could they do with a testimony like being miraculously healed? They could believe more, they could dedicate their lives to God or to helping others; but no, it can't happen - because the God, who knows alpha to omega, doesn't trust them. He is still going to judge them on judgment day where He can wreak revenge if required, but can't heal them because of His own lack of trust. There is something intrinsically wrong with the entire message of this particular apparition and I am amazed no one has brought it up, or considered it before.

Our Lady also showed concern for the atheism of Russia and claimed she had come to ask for that territory to be dedicated to her *'Immaculate Heart'* and the Communion of Reparation of the first Saturdays. Russia would be converted, she said and there would be peace; however, she added a rider in case her prophecy failed. If not, she said, the 'errors' of Russia would be spread throughout the Earth, preventing peace and causing persecution of the Church. Remember, this was 1917. (240)

Well, Lady, I believe this would be a big ask for the most educated global leaders and negotiators, yet you chose to pass it on to uneducated shepherd children who wouldn't even know where Russia was. What has this to do with them and what could they possibly do to help achieve your goals? Precious little, I feel. I doubt they even understood what you were talking about. Our Lady certainly picked the wrong forum to wreak change in the political world. Those poor folk of Portugal required love and comfort, good food, medicines and better living conditions in the troubled times of World War I. Instead she regurgitated unfathomable political nonsense, inane contradictory messages, anti-scriptural religious mumbo jumbo, ridiculous sacrifices and these very strange requests.

At the second meeting, when the children inquired of Our Lady about the welfare of a deceased friend, *Maria de Rosario*, they were assured that she was in God's care in Heaven. Now this, again, totally contradicts the resurrection scriptures. We can read in the Bible:

- ***Hebrews 9 : 7 'And as it is appointed unto men once to die, but after this the judgment.'***
- ***2 Timothy 4 : 1 'I charge thee therefore before God and the Lord Jesus Christ, who shall judge the quick and the dead at His appearing and His kingdom.'***
- ***1 Thessalonians 4 : 16 'For the Lord Himself shall descend from heaven with a shout, with the voice of the archangel and with the trump of God; and the dead in Christ shall rise first.'***

Our Lady also stated that another acquaintance, *Amelia*, was in 'purgatory' and would require much prayer. Again, this is contrary to scripture, which does not even mention this 'purgatory' half-way house between Earth and Heaven. The Roman Church introduced this fictitious place where departed souls could undergo cleansing and purification for their sins, by the prayer of others, before they are able to enter heaven. This, of course, proved to be quite profitable for the Church, as many wealthy parishioners were happy to pay large sums to assist loved ones out of purgatory. Since Rome teaches a system of salvation by faith as well as by works, mixing grace with human merit, purgatory fits in quite nicely. Check for yourself, however; purgatory does not appear anywhere in the Bible and was actually a device from ancient Druidic doctrine that was adopted by the Roman Church purely for reasons of profit.

Even the word translated as 'hell' in the New Testament has meanings other than a place of fire and damnation. In reality, there is not one original mention of a place like this in the Old Testament or the New Testament. Dr. Barbara Thiering even showed that the Biblical, *'fire that burned forever'* actually referred to the Jerusalem rubbish tip. Fire in those times was a symbol of purification, not of damnation within a fiery eternity. All that nonsense was adopted later.

The 8 year old child, Francisco Marto, (the apparition said), must say a lot of rosaries in order to make the Heavenly cut, again contradicting the Church's own scripture of 'belief', not 'works'. The 'Blessed Virgin' then promised an end to World War I, but warned; *'... if man doesn't cease to offend God, he would have another worse war commence.'* Now we can read:

> ***Job 35 : 6-7 'If thou sin, what shalt thou hurt him? And if thy iniquities be multiplied what shalt thou do against him?'***

The Lady sure wasn't up on scripture! Worse was to come! She warned that when you see the night sky lit up, it is a sign from God: *'That He is going to punish the world for its crimes of war and hunger and persecution of the Church and the Holy Father.'*

Hang on a bit! On the one hand, she claimed that the war was a punishment for offending God; on the other it was the crime that warranted the punishment. She surely can't have it both ways. The poor children certainly didn't understand the things that were happening; they became puppets for religious entertainment within the Church. In addition, can somebody also please explain to me how 'hunger' is a crime?

There was no miracle here! It becomes apparent that this Lady was a phony with a farcical message. Her dialogue lacks any form of structure or logic and is not in harmony with scripture and as such, would not even be considered by an intelligent, thinking person. Add to this that she required the sacrifice of innocent children to make amends for all the iniquity she describes and yet, despite the sacrifice of the children taking place, the First and Second World Wars still ran their course anyway. This 'Virgin' comes across as a total fruit cake who is ill-informed on scripture, on sacrifice, on global politics, on protocol and certainly has her wires crossed on the will of God. The poor children should have been fed and comforted, then quietly counseled about their make-believe friend. The Roman Church should be chastised for the exploitation of the innocent children and of its more gullible parishioners. This sort of practice, however, continues unabated to this day.

As a side note, Pope John Paul II was shot in the Vatican on 13th May 1981 when a young Turkish gunman fired four shots from a 9 mm pistol. Two struck the Pope in the stomach, one in his right arm and the fourth hit his little finger. It is worth noting that after he was released from the *Agostini Gemelli University Polyclinic*, where he recovered, the Pope thanked *'Our Lady of Fatima'* that none of the bullets found his heart. So here we had a 'magic bullet' steered away from the Pontiff 's heart by this same Lady of Fatima. I personally believe she was lying down on the job or the bullets wouldn't have hit him at all! (241)

Coincidence

Carl Gustav Jung, the great psychologist and philosopher, didn't believe in miracles and over time developed the idea of *'synchronicity'*. He wrote an enlightening essay on the subject called, *'An acausal connecting principle'* which cited the existence of an *active force* behind coincidence. Jung's study of coincidence also identified a certain sense of humour at times, behind many coincidences. This it would seem indicates the involvement of some form of Cosmic Joker. (242) For example:

- Three Englishmen traveling on a train in Peru in the 1920's found themselves the only occupants of their carriage. Introducing themselves they discovered one was named Bingham, the second man was named Powell and the third couldn't believe it. He was Bingham Powell. (243)
- A memoir sent to Arthur Koestler in 1973 after the publication of his book, *'The Roots of Co-incidence'*, has a touch of Irish humour to it. Anthony S. Clancy of Dublin wrote; *"I was born on the seventh day of the week, seventh day of the month, seventh month of the year, seventh year of the century. I was the seventh child of a seventh child and I now*

have seven brothers; that makes seven, sevens. On my twenty-seventh birthday I was at a race track and noted that the number seven horse in the seventh race was called 'Seventh Heaven' and in addition had a handicap of seven stone. It was too good an omen to miss so I bet seven pounds for a win. It finished seventh!" (244)

- Joseph Figlock was walking down the street in Detroit in the 1930s when a baby fell on him from a high window. He broke its fall and saved its life. A year later the same baby fell on him again from the same window. Both Figlock and the baby survived. (245)
- In 1883, Henry Ziegland of Honey Grove, Texas, jilted his sweetheart who then killed herself. Her grief-stricken brother then tried to avenge her death by shooting Ziegland. The bullet grazed him and buried itself in a tree. The brother believing he had killed Ziegland then took his own life. Twenty years later Ziegland was cutting down the tree with the bullet in it and found the going tough so instead he used dynamite. The blast dislodged the bullet and sent it through Ziegland's head killing him instantly. (246)

Many times, what is a simple coincidence is claimed to be a miracle. The contrary is also true when the notion of coincidence can be stretched to the limit. Let's look at a shocking example:

James Dean's Porsche.
This was one jinxed car!

- When actor James Dean died tragically behind the wheel of his Porsche sports car in September 1953, it set off an amazing string of events associated with the car.
- When the wreck was towed from the crash site to a garage, the tow truck driver reported severe back injuries sustained whilst recovering the vehicle.
- At the garage, the Porsche's engine slipped and fell on a mechanic breaking both his legs.
- The engine was subsequently bought by a doctor for his racing car; the drive shaft was used in another racing car. In the next race both the doctor and the driver with the drive shaft were killed.
- James Dean's car was later taken to be repaired in order to put it on show but the entire workshop complex was gutted by fire.
- After another attempt the vehicle was displayed in Sacramento and fell off its mount breaking a teenager's hip.
- Later in Oregon, the vehicle was displayed on the back of a truck, which got away and crashed through a store window.
- Finally in 1959 the vehicle was mounted on steel supports but somehow fell breaking into 11 pieces. It seems that this particular car did not enjoy being on display. (247)

There are some amazing coincidences on record:

- A man riding a moped bike was killed by a taxi in Bermuda in 1975, exactly one year after his brother, whilst riding the same moped, had been killed by the same taxi with the same driver and carrying the same passenger. (248)
- Identical twin boys born in Ohio were adopted from birth into different families. In 1979 after 39 years apart they met for the first time to discover some amazing coincidences. Both had been called James and worked in Law Enforcement although they both enjoyed carpentry. Each had married a woman named Linda, had a son, one named James Allan and the other James Alan. They had both divorced and married a second wife called Betty. They both holidayed at the same beach in Petersburg, Florida and both had a dog called 'Toy'. (249)

- When King Edward VII of England was a young man and still the Prince of Wales, he was a keen fox hunter. One of his friends and frequent companions on the hunt was the actor Edward A. Sothern. As a token of esteem the Prince presented Sothern with a golden match box attached to a watch chain. Sothern greatly valued the gift and carried it everywhere with him until the day he was thrown from his horse during a hunt and try as he may, could not locate the golden match box. Sothern had a duplicate made and in time passed it on to his son.

  Lytton Sothern also became an actor and during a tour of Australia gave the trinket to a friend called Labertouche. Back in England, Lytton's brother George was riding with hounds when he met the old farmer whose land the hunt was using. When it was discovered that he was indeed the son of Edward Sothern, the farmer presented him with the original match box lost for 20 years and found only that very morning by a farm hand. Lytton and George had another brother named Edward after his father, and also an actor. Edward was on tour in America when this incident occurred and George wrote to him sharing the details of the coincidence. Edward was on a train when he finally got to read his brother's letter and was so taken by the tale that he shared it with Arthur Lawrence, another actor whom he had met just that day. He pondered out loud what might have become of the duplicate golden match box when Lawrence dangled a chain in front of his astonished face. On it hung the golden match box given to him by Mr. Labertouche.[(250)]
- There is a much repeated story in Asia, about the Great Fire of Tokyo in 1657 that is simply uncanny. A kimono successively owned in the dowry of three teenage girls, each of whom died before she had a chance to wear it, was believed to be so unlucky that it was exorcised and cremated by a Japanese village priest. As the garment was being burned, a violent gust of wind sprang up fanning the flames and spreading them out of control. The ensuing fire destroyed three quarters of Tokyo, leveling 300 temples, 50 palaces, 9,000 shops, 61 bridges and many homes. More than one hundred thousand people

died in the blaze. (251)

In 1887, green children emerged from a cave in Banjos, Spain.

Impossibilities

It is recorded that two children emerged from a cave near Banjos in Spain in August 1887. Their skin had a greenish hue and their clothes were said to be of an unknown material. Their eyes appeared oriental and they could not speak Spanish. At first they would not eat and the boy died. The girl survived and learned enough Spanish to explain that they came from a sunless land and both she and the boy had been swept up by a whirlwind and deposited in the cave. She died in 1892, her origins still unknown. (252) This story is very similar to one told about a boy and a girl who emerged from a cave in Woolpit, England in the 11th century. The girl said they came from a sunless land. (253)

There is no explanation for how a Soldier was transported from Manila to Mexico.

A Spanish Soldier reported for duty at the Palace in Mexico City. He was quite conspicuous because of his quite different uniform and he was immediately questioned by the guard's superiors. The soldier was baffled at finding himself in a strange land and told the amazing story that he was stationed in Manila, Philippine Islands and the Governor had been killed the night before. He had been ordered to report for duty at the Palace in Manila but somehow appeared at the palace in Mexico City. He could offer no explanation and his incredible tale landed him in jail. Two months later word arrived from Manila that the Governor had indeed been assassinated, precisely the night before the soldier appeared and confirmed the details of his impossible story. The soldier was allowed to return to his home in the Philippines and we are left to ponder the record of this incredible story. [(254)]

A Tall Tail?

A *Judge of Session* from Scotland, Lord Monboddo (1714-1799), was considered somewhat eccentric but very learned. While studying the works of the great taxonomist, Linnaeus, he read about a Swedish sailor called Lieutenant Koeping who had seen some amazing things during his time serving in the Far East. The Judge tracked down a copy of Koeping's book and had part of it translated from Swedish. It told how Lieutenant Koeping and his shipmates of the Dutch East India Company landed in the Nicobar Islands and encountered a fierce tribe who had tails. Before they could get away, Koeping said the natives captured and ate some of the crew. Judge Monboddo searched fanatically and discovered many reports of natives with tails. He published his conclusion in a book stating that many natives in Borneo and the Philippines and Formosa are born with 6 inch tails. He believed that midwives clandestinely removed them at birth. The learned Judge found himself the butt of a thousand bad jokes but held to his research. [(255)]

This would be just a novelty story except that I, personally, had a report this year, that sportsmen noted in the showers after a game, that the team from Africa had six inch tails. If there were not some truth in it, why would a team report something so obviously bizarre? The onlookers in the showers were said to be quite stunned by what they saw.

CHAPTER TWENTY

HOLY (CHRISTIAN) RELICS

'The rabble desire nothing better than to be deceived.'

Bellowed by a presbyter called Synesus at the Council of Nicea 325 B.C.E.

Doi Suthep

Many years ago I was touring the North of Thailand and discovered how in 1296 the magnificent town called Chiang Mai (new town) was made the capital of the ancient kingdom, replacing Chiang Rai (old town). Chiang Mai has hundreds of Buddhist temples (a temple is called a 'wat' in Thai) and these include the amazing elevated Wat Phrathat Doi Suthep, the most famous temple in the area.

Wat Phrathat Doi Suthep sits over the former mountaintop home of an old hermit.

A squabble commenced between two brothers, princes of neighbouring provinces over ownership of a collarbone relic of the Buddha, stored in a local Chedi. This prized relic was housed in a priceless coral box within a solid silver box within a solid gold box. To prevent the squabble from escalating, the accommodating relic split in two allowing the princes to each have a relic for their temples. To celebrate this miracle, the prince of Chiang Mai decided to build a new Wat and a new Golden Chedi to house the miraculous relic. He allowed providence to choose the perfect site by placing the relic of the Lord Buddha on the back of a sacred white elephant proclaiming that the animal should choose the place. In front of a huge crowd the elephant was released. It trumpeted, turned around three times then it headed for the top of a local mountain, where it trumpeted and circled again before lying down. The onlookers took this as a sign from the Buddha that this was the auspicious place to build the temple. Doi Suthep was the name of an old hermit who had lived on the top of this mountain for many years. Getting building materials to the mountain top was actually a greater miracle than had just been performed, but a magnificent Wat was constructed there in 1383 A.D. and was named *Wat Phrathat Doi Suthep* in honour of the old hermit. He was then credited with the wisdom of locating that spot even before the miraculous elephant, and was afforded a lot of respect. The temple stands to this day and its location affords superb views over the city.

Helena

It would seem that religious relics were just as accommodating in the first century after Christ. Emperor Constantine's Mother, Helena scoured the Holy Land (at taxpayers' expense), to secure relics of every kind for the newly created Christian religion. These were distributed (for a price) right across Christiandom. Among this lot was the timber of the True Cross, the severed head of John the Baptist and the heads of the three Wise Men (note the Persian literature claims there were five Magi or wise men, and the Bible does not say anywhere that there were actually three).

In 1928 the skulls of the 'three' wise men were still being displayed in the Cathedral of Cologne and six different churches in Italy had on show, the severed head of John the Baptist. There were a number of shrouds from the burial of Christ (still depicting his wounds and smelling of myrrh) even though *John 19 : 40* claimed the body of Christ was, *'bound up with bandages'.* There were any number of 'crowns of thorns' relics from the crucifixion, which somehow remained intact because it would seem all these religious relics took on incorruptibility from their contact with Jesus. Saint Gregory of Tours produced one that was still green and apparently renewed itself daily, which did little to vouchsafe the authenticity of this particular ancient relic. Also located by Helena was almost the full wardrobe of the 'virgin' Miriam-Mary and left-over powdered breast milk that suckled the Christ child, a 'Holy Nail', preserved as it had been when it penetrated the flesh of Christ, but the real prize was the bloodied *flagellum* - the Roman whip that had flogged Jesus. Other objects of veneration were the bodies of the saints, Luke, Andrew and Timothy, disinterred for re-burial in Constantinople. [(256)] For years a roaring trade was done in Saintly body parts with literally thousands being documented. Pope Gregory the Great had refused to donate the head of Saint Paul to Constantina yet despite this, another one turned up in a jeweled case in San Marco in Venice while three skulls of Saint Mary Magdalene were on view at various locations across the City.

Saint Augustine

Unscrupulous traders milked the gullibility of parishioners for all it was worth and the trade in macabre religious relics and objects of devotion became a full blown industry. The unashamed deceptions were never rebuked or prevented by Pope or Priest and the affront to the intelligence of the congregation continued unabated. The first century Saint Augustine was very much against the requirement for relics as a symbol of faith and did much to stem the flow, albeit temporarily. In his writings, he complained about *'travelling salesmen dressed as monks'*, who sold supposed relics of martyrs to the gullible. Despite this he actually praised those who carried off the remains of Saint Stephen to Tbilisi where they still continued to work miracles.

Religious Fraud

The sacred bones of Saint Rosalia (c. 1160) were put on display in Palermo in 1930, but were later proved to be from a male goat, yet still the ignorant faithful filed past in awe. For the edification and mental stultification of his flock, Abbot Martin (c. 1498) obtained for his monaste in Alsace, Lorraine, the following inestimable articles:

- A spot of blood from the Saviour
- One arm of the apostle James
- Part of the skeleton of John the Baptist
- A bottle of 'breast milk' from the 'virgin' Mary

This collection awed his parishioners but it didn't come close to that of a monastery in Jerusalem that presented the wings and tail feathers of the Holy

Ghost, from when that entity came down in the guise of a dove. Alongside it was a finger from when the Holy Ghost appeared as a man. [257] At Soissons in France the Church held a baby tooth shed by the infant Jesus. Regardless of the Soissons claim a monastery in Charroux boasted the full set. In Italy, France and Spain the tooth fairy would have had a full time job on Jesus teeth alone. There were teeth held everywhere! At nearby Leon the public were shown canisters of powdered 'breast milk' from the 'virgin' Miriam-Mary along with lockets of her hair. In 1501 in England, packets of this powdered 'breast milk' and a number of 'the virgin's' girdles were displayed to the gullible in a number of locations. Queen Elizabeth of York, procured one of the girdles and it was given as a wedding present to Catherine of Argon on her marriage to her son Henry VIII. Later, Henry VIII was able to purchase at great expense a vial of the Jordan water used by John to baptise Jesus along with a tear shed by Jesus over Lazarus, in an attempt to avert the plague of 1531. The tear had actually been stored in a phial by an accommodating Angel and kept by Mary Magdalene along with a phial containing a droplet of the sweat of Saint Michael, from the occasion when he confronted the Devil. [258] Across Spain, enough 'virgin's' milk was displayed, to feed a dozen hungry calves and enough lockets of hair to make a hundred wigs. There were enough bones of the saints to fill a good sized cemetery.

A Dutchman living in Constantinople (c. 393) purchased a leg of the donkey upon which Jesus rode into Jerusalem, for a princely sum, only to discover that four legs had previously been sold by the same Priest. When Bishop Ferund was asked to adjudicate on this particular fraud, he gravely assured the Dutchman that God could multiply and produce as many 5 legged donkeys as he chose for his chosen ones. The Dutchman left happily, believing all was well as the Bishop had stated. Two years later Bishop Ambrose displayed a 15 foot length of the true cross in his church and the gullible lined up to buy a fragment. [259] John Calvin stated around 1545 that enough 'True Crosses' had been sold to construct a ship. [260] In fact there is a record of 62 of them being presented to the public between 326 A.D. and 680 A.D. alone. It would seem that 'True Crosses" have the miraculous ability of multiplying in a similar manner to the loaves and fishes.

In 371 A.D., the Cathedral of Arras in France held some additional Manna that fell from Heaven, along with a Holy candle presented to Bishop Lambert in 1105 by the 'virgin' Miriam-Mary herself, to avert an epidemic. This candle subsequently burned continuously from 1105 until 1713. [261] In Rome a major Church displayed Christ's original manger which proved to be a 19th century packing case, and no less than seven Churches displayed his umbilical cord. A like number had his foreskin from the circumcision ceremony, preserved as a ghoulish relic by his mother. [262] It seems, Miriam-Mary was quite a hoarder and left behind enough baby teeth, locks of hair, wedding rings, shoes, stockings and shifts to fill a museum.

I think it is sad that true believers are fed this stuff by a Church that obviously feels it is necessary. If you are interested, I understand the sale of the Brooklyn Bridge is being negotiated and I can get it for you at a good price!

Phallic Worship

Early Canaanite worship utilized the display of genitals and the naked body as a significant feature of worship, and early Christian writings show deep concern at this practice. Despite this reluctance on the part of the presbyters, phallic worship certainly existed in the early Christian Church and statues of Christian saints have been found displayed in various churches, complete with oversized penises.

As another example, in Southern France women who had been denied the joys of motherhood, invoked the intervention of St Foutin, an ithyphallic saint said to be the first Bishop of Lyons, in an attempt to rectify their situation. When Protestants captured the town of Embrum in 1585 and destroyed the local church they discovered relics of the saint's phallus. Its tip was red, said to be from the many libations of red wine poured over it by childless women. Perhaps this speaks more about the particular talents of that saint during his lifetime! Professor Gregory Webb of Cambridge University and Secretary of the Royal Commission on Historical Monuments discovered that a staggering *ninety per cent* of all pre-Reformation churches in Britain hid pagan fertility symbols such as the stone image of a phallus within the Christian altar. [263] Can you believe it? Ninety per cent!

Saint Berenice?

Saint Veronica's veil is still displayed by the Pope at his Catholic Easter Mass for an adoring public. It also features in the Good Friday pageant performed each year in Malta. This particular relic carries with it just a touch of humour. It is reputed to be the cloth offered to Jesus to wipe his face as he dragged the cross *(Luke 23 : 27)* by a woman originally named Berenice. The cloth miraculously took on a very sharp image of Christ and as a result Berenice took it to Rome, where in time she became canonized as Saint Veronica. Why Saint Veronica? Well, in competing with other similar icons displayed at the time, Berenice's shawl was touted as *'vera icon'* meaning *'true image'* and this was later mistaken as the name of the saint. Thus Berenice became 'vera-icon' and to this day is known in English as Saint Veronica. The sordid debasement of human intellect by the presentation of these icons and relics by the Church for the ultimate purpose of public extortion, is way beyond orderly comment.

Shroud of Turin

Despite scripture to the contrary, the Shroud of Turin is still promoted by the Church as the shroud in which the body of Christ was laid, and miracles are still attributed to this relic today. In 1988 small pieces of this cloth were submitted to three quite separate and independent facilities in Zurich, London and Tuscon, Arizona. The dating tests were thorough and meticulous and an amazing result of impressively close agreement, showed the manufacture of the cloth was very close to 1350 A.D. (between 1260 A.D. and 1390 A.D.). The date would seem to be very accurate considering that unknown to the evaluation groups, this particular shroud was first exhibited in 1357 at a Church in Lirey, France. This newly built Church of St. Mary was inaugurated on 28th May 1356, by Henri de Poitiers, the Bishop of Troyes who was very much against its display. Geoffrey de Charny, it seems, circumvented the Bishop by dealing directly with the schismatic Pope at Avignon, who gave his permission for the church at Lirey to house and display the shroud. A Bishop of the Church claimed the shroud was exhibited, *"to attract the multitude so that money might be cunningly wrung from them, pretended miracles were worked, certain men being hired to represent themselves as healed at the moment of the exhibition of the shroud."* [264] Bishop Henri de Poitiers was incensed at this total fraud and ordered the canons to cease this money making racket. He had undertaken painstaking research on the supposed relic and had even located the original artist who had coated a statue with resin and wrapped it in a banquet-sized tablecloth, to portray the image of Christ and then painted in the wounds with red ochre. In 1389, however, the exhibition was re-commenced with Papal blessing. Henri's successor, Bishop Pierre D'Arcis, in whose diocese the Church stood, became so incensed that he threatened the canons of Lirey with excommunication if they did not withdraw the shroud from exposition. They implored the king of France and the Papal legate to intervene. The exhibition had been a huge draw card and a great income generating concern so it is not surprising that both men gave permission for the exposition to continue. When the Bishop protested further, the Pope upheld the validity of the legate's approval. Bishop D'Arcis then wrote to Pope Clement VII insisting that the canons had obtained Papal permission by underhanded methods. He declared that the shroud was a painting - a fraud exposed thirty-four years earlier by Henri de Poitiers, who had conducted a thorough investigation. The canons, he said, had kept the cloth in hiding when he had tried to secure it.

The carbon-dating of the shroud is consistent with the forger's confession to Bishop Henri de Poitiers of Troyes, and is at odds with the scripture of *John 19 : 40* (mentioned earlier) that claimed the body of Christ was, *'bound up with bandages'*. Regardless, the congregation still show reverence for this obviously fraudulent relic. The Catholic Church is well aware of the fraud and it was further perpetrated in 1498 when Giovanni de Medici (later to become Pope Leo X) commissioned Leonardo da Vinci to 'sharpen up' the images on the old cloth. [265] The cloth today still exhibits traces of the paint used by Leonardo in this undertaking. There are a number of books that claim the image on the shroud is actually a portrait of Leonardo, who is known to have used his own image in many works even including the Mona Lisa. To prove her assertions, Author, Rena F. LaCaria, duplicated the master's methods to recreate the Shroud and gives the step-by-step process she followed in her book, *'Leonardo, The Man Behind the Shroud'*. In 2002, this book was researched and endorsed by the Smithsonian Institution and a copy is now available for scholarly research and review at the Library of the Smithsonian American Art Museum, in Washington, D.C. [266]

It simply amazes me that today people still debate whether the Shroud of Turin is genuine or not. This is a testament to the power of the Vatican's propaganda machine. The shroud is and always has been a totally fraudulent, blasphemous swindle on gullible folks by a Church obsessed with power and profit.

CHAPTER TWENTY ONE

ODD FACTS, TRIVIA & PHOBIAS

'Laugh and the world laughs with you; weep and you weep alone.'

Ella Wheeler Wilcox

Phobias

This is to be a fun section not to be taken too seriously and to set the mood, here is a list of some very unusual phobias:

- *Arachibutyrophobia* - Fear of peanut butter sticking to the roof of your mouth.
- *Xanthophobia* - Fear of the color yellow or the word yellow.
- *Dutchphobia* - Fear of Dutch people.
- *Defecaloesiophobia* - Fear of painful bowels movements.
- *Ideophobia* - Fear of ideas.
- *Ouranophobia* - Fear of Heaven.
- *Pentheraphobia* - Fear of your mother-in-law. (Novercaphobia)
- *Chaetophobia* - Fear of hair.
- *Hippopotomonstrosesquippedaliophobia* - Fear of long words.
- *Afodronaphobia* - The fear of being sucked down a toilet.

Facts about Computers

- In 1954, scientists from the RAND corporation created a mock up model to show what the home computer of the future would look like. They projected 50 years ahead to 2004 but stated that even by then the required technology would not be feasible for the average

A prediction that certainly missed the mark!

home. They believed, however, that technology would advance sufficiently in 50 years to make this project possible but at huge cost. How blind they were!

- Cyberphobia, is the fear of computers or of using a computer.
- The Patron Saint of computer users is Saint Isadore of Saville.
- Today's digital watch has more computing power than the 'Eagle' Lunar Module that first landed on the moon.
- In 1943, Thomas Watson (the chairman of IBM), predicted that the future market would only ever require about five computers.

I.T. Trivia (… that you didn't really need to know):

1. Google's employees get free lunch and free haircuts.
2. About 47 million laptops where shipped worldwide in 2006.
3. One in every eight married couples in the US last year, met online.
4. If myspace was a country it would be the 11th largest in the world.
5. Atari sold 400,000 VCS consoles in 1979.
6. In Sweden the @ symbol is called a *'snabel-a'* which means an 'a' with a 'trunk'.
7. Bill Gates house was partially designed using a Macintosh computer.
8. The number of text messages sent every day now exceeds the world's population.
9. Almost 30% of IBM's employees are Indians. (Don't we know it!)

10. The floppy disk was patented in 1946 by Alan Shugar.
11. The oldest surviving computer in the world is called CSIRAC and is located in Melbourne, Australia.
12. Bill Gates began programming computers at age 13.
13. Queen Elizabeth of Britain sent her first email in 1976.
14. The name Google comes from the word *'googol'*, which is a figure of 1 followed by a hundred zeros.
15. The first domain name ever registered was Symbolics.com
16. The save icon on Microsoft Word shows a floppy disk with the shutter slide on backwards.
17. Sweden has the most affordable broadband internet access in Europe.
18. In computer language, *wysiwyg* is an acronym for *'what you see is what you get'*.
19. More than 80% of home pages on the Web are in English. German has only 4.5% and Japanese 3.1%.
20. Over four million solicitation phone calls are made by telemarketers in the United States every single day.

100 bits of Useless Trivia

1. When kissing their partner, few people ever give a thought to the fact that the amount of germs and bacteria in each other's mouth is estimated to be more than the total number of 6.5 billion people in the world.
2. America likes to think it is a hi-tech country with the smartest people. In fact there are many who never graduated from high school and more than seven percent of Americans are illiterate.
3. Las Vegas is the gambling city of the world. In order to maximize profits the casinos decided to dump all of their casino clocks. It is believed that if patrons do not know the exact time, they are more likely to stay longer.
4. It is a well known fact that one out of every nine people is born left handed. It is a lesser known fact that over two and a half thousand left handed people are killed each and every year by trying to use

right handed products; particularly power tools.

5. The phrase *"I'll be there in a jiffy"* is often used; however, very few people realize that a "jiffy" is an actual unit of time. It measures one hundredth of a second.
6. While we do not know what our dreams mean and often can't remember them, an average human has approximately 1,460 dreams every year.
7. The hardest working organ in your body is the heart. It is estimated that the heart takes over one hundred thousand beats per day.
8. The ice in Antarctica averages a mile in thickness and contains some 70% of the world's fresh water. No country owns Antarctica and it is the driest part of the planet with lower rainfall than the Gobi Desert.
9. A duck's quack will not echo and scientists don't know why.
10. Yes its true! A turtle can breathe through its butt.
11. A staggering $3 billion segment, comprising 10% of the entire music industry is now held by mobile phone ringtones.
12. The full name of Los Angeles (The Angels) is *El Pueblo de Nuestra Senora la Reina de los Angeles de Porciuncula* and when called L.A. uses just 3.63% of its full title.
13. On average, thirteen Americans are killed each year by having vending machines fall on them.
14. The Dalmatian dog is from Croatia. Dalmatian dogs are born white without the spots.
15. Mars is home to the largest known volcano in the Solar System.
16. The live human brain feels no sensation when cut.
17. All lilies are poisonous to cats.
18. Each day the sun causes about one trillion tons of water to evaporate.
19. The oldest recorded age for a dog is 29 years.
20. A Blue Whale can eat 3 tonnes of food a day but can go 6 months without food.
21. The name 'Spain' means literally *'the land of rabbits'*.
22. The Earth has over 12 million species of animal; 3 million species of plant and 1 million other species.

23. Poodles were once used as hunting dogs in Europe.
24. Snails have 14,175 teeth in 135 rows on their tongue.
25. Green coconut milk has been used successfully in blood transfusions.
26. Donald Duck lives at 1313 Webfoot Walk, Duckburg, Calisota. His middle name is Fauntleroy.
27. More people are killed annually by donkeys than in plane crashes.
28. Bee stings account for more human deaths than shark attacks.
29. The most dangerous animal to man in South Africa is the Hippopotamus, accounting for far more deaths than lions and other wild beasts combined.
30. Diet sugarless candies can be toxic to dogs.
31. A swan has over 25,000 feathers.
32. Cats have over one hundred vocal sounds. Dogs only have about ten.
33. If viewed from above the Sun's north pole, all of the planets are orbiting in a counter-clockwise direction; but while most planets also rotate counter-clockwise, Venus rotates clockwise in 'retrograde' rotation. This makes many believe it is a trapped comet.
34. It is believed that cats and dogs can only see the colours blue and yellow.
35. The distance between the earth and moon is increasing by 30 cm each year.
36. A cat's urine glows under an ultraviolet 'blacklight'.
37. A cow can be led upstairs but not downstairs.
38. American Airlines saved $40,000 in 1987 by eliminating one olive from each first class salad.
39. Pearls melt in vinegar.
40. A polar bear can run at 25 miles per hour.
41. Most cases of dog bite on humans are from German Shepherds.
42. The owner of the Marlborough Company died of lung cancer.
43. A butterfly has 12,000 eyes.
44. Sir Isaac Newton invented the cat-flap door.
45. Dolphins sleep with one eye open.
46. Dogs are mentioned 14 times in the Bible.

47. The acronym IOU actually stands for *'Is Owed Unto'.*
48. Cats have a peripheral vision of about 285 degrees.
49. The 1938 *'Man of the Year'* shown in *Time Magazine* was ... Adolf Hitler.
50. In 1987, cats overtook dogs as the number one pet in America.
51. Domestic cats hate lemons or other citrus scents.
52. A dog can smell 10 million times better than a human.
53. In 1911 a dog was killed by a meteor at Nakhla, Egypt. This unlucky dog is the only creature known to have been killed by a meteor.
54. The biggest dog on record was an Old English Mastiff who weighed 343 pounds. He was 8 feet and 3 inches from nose to tail.
55. Every year the world produces more transistors than grains of rice.
56. The first hot-air balloon was launched from Versailles in 1783.
57. The unit 'foot' was originally the length of a human foot (12 inches).
58. Originally, the inch represented the width of a thumb.
59. Human hair is stronger than the same thickness of iron wire.
60. The very first Ford cars had Dodge engines.
61. The numbers on opposite sides of a dice always add up to seven.
62. The WD in WD-40 stands for Water Displacer.
63. Cotton is heavier than water.
64. Because of the rotation of the Earth, the greatest distance can be achieved if an object is thrown due West.
65. The maximum speed of Titanic was 23 knots. She was running at 22 knots when she hit the iceberg.
66. The very first production Jet engine was made by BMW.
67. Astronauts can't burp or pass wind in space. Both biological processes require gravity to separate the liquid from the gas in their stomach.
68. Sports car manufacturers, Porsche and Lamborghini, both also build tractors.
69. Developing the engines for the Boeing 747-SP ran Rolls-Royce broke in 1974. The wingspan of a Boeing 747 jet is longer than the Wright Brothers' first flight. A Boeing 767 airliner is made of 3,100,000 separate parts.

70. Alaska accounts for more than half of the coastline of the entire United States.
71. The Eiffel Tower has 1,792 steps; The Tower shrinks 6 inches in winter.
72. The Library at Indiana University sinks over an inch each year because, when it was built, engineers failed to take into account the massive weight of all the books.
73. About 1,000 tons of dust and space material enters the atmosphere each year to land on the Earth's surface.
74. The American 'Library of Congress' is the world's largest library with more than 120 million items.
75. Plastic can be made with 50% seaweed.
76. A year on Mars is almost twice as long as on Earth.
77. Vernal Bank in Utah was built from bricks sent through the mail.
78. No piece of paper can be folded more than 7 times. (try it).
79. The Space Shuttle usually travels at approximately 17,000 miles per hour; it can accelerate to this speed in 8 minutes.
80. Bologna, just like Pisa, has a leaning tower and it is called the Garisenda tower.
81. Every year the sun loses 360 million tons of matter.
82. The 16th century Escorial palace of King Phillip II of Spain had 2,673 doors.
83. Gene Cernan was the last man on the moon.
84. Of all the planets, only Mercury and Venus do not have any moons.
85. Much of the Netherlands is below sea level and it has about 800 miles of massive dikes and sea walls to hold back the ocean.
86. There are approximately ten million bricks in the Empire State Building.
87. Actress Jayne Mansfield 'accidentally' inhaled her breast right out of her dress during the telecast of the Academy Awards in 1957.
88. The Taj Mahal in India, built between 1632 and 1654, is made entirely out of marble.
89. The electric chair was invented by a dentist. An electric chair was bought by the ruler of Ethiopia before he realised they did not have

electricity. The expensive chair was then used as his throne.

90. A US gallon is 3.785 litres whereas an Imp gallon is 4.546 litres. A Boeing 747 airliner holds 57,285 U.S. gallons of fuel. Because the temperature variance is so great between an aircraft on the ground and in flight the fuel is recorded in pounds at 6.84 pounds per US gallon. On board the aircraft a debit meter accounts for the pounds of fuel left. J-2 turbine fuel is unrefined kerosene.
91. TV antennas were invented in 1898 but TV's were not invented until the year 1935.
92. Due to increased gravity, a man weighing 150 pounds at Earth's equator would weigh about 151.5 pounds at the poles. He would weigh about 2 tons on the Sun.
93. The timekeeping quartz crystal in your wristwatch vibrates 32,768 times a second. The time standard, cesium atom in an atomic clock beats over nine billion times a second.
94. Men are four times more likely to be struck by lightning than women.
95. The first bicycle made in 1817 by Baron von Drais, didn't have any pedals. People sat on it and walked it along.
96. One cubic metre of air weighs around 2 pounds at sea level.
97. Recycling just one aluminum can saves enough energy to run a TV for about three hours.
98. Most dust particles in your home are actually dead skin.
99. The King of Hearts in a deck of cards, is the only one without a moustache. The King of Spades looks to the right while the others look left.
100. An apple is more effective than caffeine at waking you up in the mornings. Nevertheless; this author still needs Coffee.

Marree Man

Marree Man is a massive geoglyph ploughed into the landscape in South Australia, that depicts an indigenous Aboriginal man, most likely of the local Pitjantjatjara tribe, hunting with a throwing stick. It is located on a plateau at Finnis Springs, 60 km west of the township of Marree in a remote part of the central South Australian desert, just outside the 200,000 square kilometer

Woomera Prohibited Area.

A remarkable 4.2 kilometre high depiction made by someone with time on their hands.

The massive figure was discovered from the air on 26th June 1998, and is 4.2 km high with an outline circumference of 15–28 km. It is the largest known geoglyph or man-made artwork in the world and is believed to have been created with a tractor and plowing implement. This is estimated to have taken between four to eight weeks to create, but despite this its origins are a mystery, with not a single witness to any part of the extensive operation and no one coming forward to claim responsibility.

The outlines of the Marree Man figure were 20–30 cm in depth at the time of discovery and up to 35 metres in width. They were made with a 2.5 metre wide, eight-tine ploughing implement which was pulled by a sizable tractor. Each of the lines needed as many as 14 passes. The tractor would have needed to travel an estimated 400 km and possibly used more than 500 litres of fuel. It can only be assumed that a satellite navigation system and a Landsat Thematic Mapper were employed and the shape virtually programmed in to achieve the superb accuracy. It has been suggested that it may have been a parting gift from an American team about to leave Woomera, but no one is sure. It seems that someone out there was prepared to invest a lot of time and money to relieve a case of acute boredom.

Superglue Saves Man

I was amazed to discover some years ago that doctors were closing facial wounds with superglue as an alternative to stitching. This process is incredibly effective and reduces scaring. From a completely different direction, a Bogoda, Sri Lankan man escaped the death penalty by using super-glue! It appears that unknown to his jailers, the man applied super-glue to the soles of his shoes immediately prior to being led from his cell. He walked carefully on the edge of his shoes to the gallows, but then pressed them down firmly onto the stool that was to be kicked from beneath his feet. It goes without saying that the stool could not be kicked from beneath him, despite a number of attempts by officials. The hanging was deemed unsuccessful under Bogodan law, and the man was freed.

Stella Awards

I believe we should initiate an annual global award for the most inane lawsuits and verdicts recorded on this planet. These awards could be named after 81-year-old American, Stella Liebeck, who spilled hot coffee on herself and successfully sued McDonald's in New Mexico where she purchased the beverage. It seems Stella took the lid off the coffee and put the container between her knees while she was driving and was amazed when she was burned. As a result the jury awarded her a payday of $2.86 million. The trial judge reduced the total award to $640,000 which should be sufficient to see Stella out in style and as a result, we all now enjoy the insipid, luke-warm concoction McDonalds serve as coffee. The stories of some other contenders follow:

- Kathleen Robertson of Austin, Texas was awarded $80,000 by a jury of her peers after breaking her ankle tripping over a toddler who was running amuck inside a furniture store. The store owners were understandably surprised by the verdict, considering the uncontrollable toddler was Kathleen's own son.
- Carl Truman of Los Angeles, California, won $74,000 plus medical expenses when his neighbor ran over his hand with a Honda Accord. Truman apparently didn't notice there was someone at the wheel of the car when he was trying to steal his neighbor's hubcaps.
- Terrence Dickson of Bristol, Pennsylvania, was leaving a house he had just burglarized by way of the garage. Unfortunately for Dickson, the automatic garage door opener malfunctioned and he could not get the garage door to open. He also couldn't re-enter the house because the door connecting the garage to the house locked when Dickson pulled it shut. Forced to exist for eight days on a case of Pepsi and a large bag of dry dog food, he sued the homeowner's insurance company claiming undue mental trauma. Amazingly, the

jury said the insurance company must pay Dickson $500,000 for his anguish.

- Jerry Williams, of Little Rock, Arkansas, was awarded $14,500 plus medical expenses after being bitten on the butt by his next door neighbor's beagle - even though the beagle was on a chain in its owner's fenced yard. Williams did not get as much as he asked for because the jury believed the beagle might have been provoked at the time of the butt bite because Williams had climbed over the fence into the yard and had repeatedly shot the dog with a pellet gun.
- A jury ordered a Philadelphia restaurant to pay Amber Carson of Lancaster, Pennsylvania, the sum of $113,500 after she slipped on a spilled soft drink and broke her tailbone. The reason the soft drink was on the floor; Ms. Carson had thrown it at her boyfriend just 30 seconds earlier during an argument. Whatever happened to people being responsible for their own actions?
- Kara Walton, of Claymont, Delaware sued the owner of a night club in a nearby city because she fell from the bathroom window to the floor, knocking out her two front teeth. At the time Ms. Walton was trying to sneak through the ladies room window to avoid paying the $3.50 cover charge. Regardless, the jury said the night club had to pay her $12,000 plus her dental expenses.
- The most bizarre of all, Mrs. Merv Grazinski, of Oklahoma City, purchased a new 32-foot Winnebago motor home. On her first trip home from an Oklahoma University football game, having driven on to the freeway, she set the cruise control at 70 mph and calmly left the driver's seat to go to the back of the Winnebago to make herself a sandwich. Not surprisingly, the motor home left the free way, crashed and overturned. Mrs. Grazinski sued Winnebago for not putting in the owner's manual that she couldn't actually leave the driver's seat while the cruise control was set. The Oklahoma jury awarded her, $1,750,000 plus a new motor home (also with cruise control). Winnebago actually changed their manuals as a result of this lawsuit, just in case Mrs. Grazinski has any relatives who might

also be in the market for a motor home.

German Emergency

Düsseldorf residents were cut off from emergency services for more than an hour recently when a caller fell in love with one of the female 000 operators. The man ran from payphone to payphone demanding the operator be put back on the line or the city would suffer the consequences. After playing cat-and-mouse with the man, police finally caught him. His reason: *"She just sounded so damn sexy"!* (267)

Why Did They Call it That?

In Australia we have many Aboriginal place names that cause tourists some trouble and provide just a modicum of humour. Some are lovely old names but some reflect the particularly direct descriptions applied by the Australian natives:

- *Kooroongarra* - Kooroon means, 'a resting place for birds' and Garra means 'water'.
- The opal mining location of *Coober Pedy* means, *'white fellows burrows in the ground'.*
- *Toowoomba* doesn't mean anything in the local Aboriginal language. It was originally called Drayton Swamp and then The Swamp. The most likely explanation for the name comes from Aboriginals trying to pronounce 'The Swamp' making it sound like TWAMPA.
- *Wagga Wagga* means. *'place of crows'.*
- The famous surfing beach at *Bondi* took its name from the Aboriginal for *'sound of waves breaking'.*
- *Coogee* is said to be taken from a local Aboriginal word *koojah* which means *'stinking place'*, a reference to the smell of decaying kelp washed up on the beach there.
- *Coonamble* means *'plenty of dirt'.*
- The town of *Tarcoola* was named after the 1893 winner of the Melbourne Cup.
- *Cape Clear* in Victoria is miles inland and one would wonder at the name. It seems a bullock team became hopelessly bogged there and

the helpful but semi literate bullocky put up temporary signs at either approach saying *'KAPE KLEAR'*.

- *Banana* is a tiny town in Queensland that has nothing to do with growing bananas. It was named after a bullock imaginatively called *Banana.*
- *Coolgardie* was originally called Fly Flat.
- *Surfers Paradise* replaced Elston.
- *Melbourne* was firstly named Batmania after the settler John Batman; the only native-born Australian to found a state capital city.
- Australia's National capital city of *Canberra* was meant to be the Aboriginal word for 'meeting place' but a committee was involved and they blew it badly. *Canberra* in the local Aboriginal dialect actually means *'women's breasts'*. I'm going to leave that one alone!

Unlucky Cop?

This is precisely what was reported in an American newspaper:

A young policeman on a Saturday night patrol on the outskirts of (a small rural town in America), spotted an object in the middle of the road. He investigated and found it to be a golden dance shoe. The smart patrolman knew the monthly county ball was being held at the local hall and headed there with the pretty shoe. Witnesses say the young cop was quite a romantic. Anyway, he sat all the women in a line along the edge of the dance floor and kneeling down, tried the shoe in turn, on each young lady's foot. Midway along the line, he came to an extremely fat, blond woman. He tried the shoe on her foot. It was just before twelve midnight. The shoe fitted, and the woman promptly turned into a huge pumpkin, rolled off the chair, and squashed the hapless cop. Authorities are at a loss to explain this phenomenon. Mmm ... [(268)]

CHAPTER TWENTY TWO

CONSPIRACY THEORIES

'To label somebody as a 'conspiracy theorist' is to silently dismiss the idea that any of the things our research uncovers, actually ever occur in secret.'

James Christian

President John F. Kennedy

Surely, no thinking person on the planet still actually believes that Lee Harvey Oswald shot President John F. Kennedy with a 'magic bullet'. Of course, the patsy Oswald was immediately silenced by Jack Ruby (who was dying of cancer), before he could blow the whistle on the conspiracy. After the murder of JFK, around forty people connected to the case died under mysterious circumstances but the perpetrators of the scam were never identified and got off scot-free. Theories have been voiced, books have been written and films have been shot that juggled the incidents in various ways but it all came to naught. The Warren Commission was an absolute joke.

Why do you think this assignation occurred? On 4 June 1963, President John F. Kennedy (the 35th President of the United States) signed *Executive Order 11110* which returned to the U.S. Government the power to issue currency, without going through the Rothschild controlled Federal Reserve. Less than 6 months later on 22 November 1963, President Kennedy was assassinated. This bore an uncanny similarity to the assassination of President Abraham Lincoln in 1865, who also wanted to print money for the American people. For those who hold any doubts that this was the reason the President was terminated, his Executive Order 11110 was rescinded by the new President Lyndon Baines Johnson on *'Air Force One'* during the flight from Dallas to Washington DC, the very same day Kennedy was assassinated. This certainly sent out a strong message. [(269)]

Diana - Princess of Wales

I never believed Princess Diana's 'stand in' chauffeur from the Ritz Hotel, Henri Paul, would have been allowed to write himself off with alcohol whilst on duty as we were told. She was Royalty as well as a valued VIP hotel customer and as such would have had a professional driver, not some boozy slob with major issues that was portrayed to us by the media. We are asked to believe that the Mercedes chauffeured car was stolen and subsequently recovered and pressed back into service without a thorough check. The heavier armored Mercedes was used as a decoy while, Dodi and Diana were transferred to the lighter model to escape the paparazzi. This is palpable nonsense!

In ancient times the 'feast' day for the ancient Goddess Diana was *13th August* and by convention, when the numbers are reversed, this becomes the 'sacrifice' day. Accordingly, sacrifices to this Goddess were conducted on the *31st August.* The Princess of Wales died in a location that in ancient times was sacred to the Goddess Diana; the name of the tunnel, *'Pont de L'Alma'* even means, *'Passage of the Moon Goddess'.* This 'accident' occurred precisely on the 31 August 1997. How incredibly convenient! Was it an accident, or was she 'taken out'? You work out the odds. Do you need a calculator?

The 'official' inquiry like so many others, heard lies and innuendo. Evidence has now come to light that the high alcohol blood sample tested (with the high carbon monoxide content), was not Henri Paul's at all, but rather that of a suicide victim laid out in the same hospital who had got drunk before gassing himself with a car exhaust. Dominique Lecomte, the errant pathologist who did the postmortem, and Dr. Gilbert Pepin who supposedly tested Paul's blood, covered up their error and continually misled the examining magistrates during the enquiry. The Monte Carlo jeweler, Alberto Repossi, claims that the *'Operation Paget'* detectives pressured him to change his story about providing a ring for the engagement of Diana and Dodi Fayed. Repossi now says that Diana and Dodi chose a £230,000 emerald and diamond ring. His evidence is hard to refute since Dodi can be clearly seen on the security cameras, purchasing it. I have seen the film. Nevertheless, the 'official' enquiry then denied it and of course that makes it gospel! [270]

We mentioned earlier that Jim Keith died in 1999 under mysterious circumstances, after revealing the name of the physician who disclosed that Princess Diana was pregnant at the time of her death. Keith didn't come out of Washoe Medical Hospital after going in for relative simple knee surgery. The same day, the web news service where Keith named the source also became instantly inaccessible.

Pope John Paul I

During the late evening of 28th September or the early morning of 29th September 1978, a healthy Pope John Paul, Albino Luciani, known as the *'Smiling Pope'*, died after only thirty-three days in office. Nobody could possibly believe that this Pope died in his sleep of natural causes - right after he discovered the Vatican's money laundering activities and announced his decision to investigate and clean them up. He had asked for a preliminary reconciliation of all the Catholic Church's assets, which the Vatican dictators were not prepared to disclose. The Vatican 'engine room' could not survive his planned scrutiny and quickly silenced him. [271] The night of his death he told his sister, *"It's not easy being Pope"*. He certainly got that one right!

The Vatican is simply an Illuminati controlled racket that has turned us (Catholic or non-Catholic) into its modern day slaves. The one glimmer of hope was when this Pope planned monumental changes to weed out the corruption and halt the money laundering activities. 'Subsequent to Luciani's murder, the following things happened:

- *Karol Wojtlya, the CIA's candidate (a Marxist but anti-Russian) was elected Pope. Wojtlya 'sat' on the banking scandal, the collapse of Banco Ambrosiano, until several European nations threatened to sue the Vatican bank for default on their money.*
- *America's Ronald Reagan then bailed out the Vatican Bank with $300 million of 'discretionary CIA funds'. (Either U.S. tax money or illicit CIA drug money). He also then signed a Concordat with the Vatican in 1983. His reward? ... The Vatican secured the 1984 election for Ronald Reagan with the 'Reagan Democrat' (i.e. 'Roman Catholic') vote.*

- *Church canon law was reversed in 1982 so that membership in the Freemasons was no longer grounds for excommunication from the Church of Rome.*
- *The intrigue of the Vatican banking scandal has woven its way into high places of the Governments of this world. The Vatican, according to Avro Manhattan, is also a major shareholder in J P Morgan Investment firm, Chase Manhattan Bank, and Bank of America.'* [(272)]

Meanwhile it is 'business as usual' for the untouchable Vatican as it continues to pillage the Earth's populous despite its mandate to assist the poor.

World Trade Centre – 9/11

Even the most patriotic American would now have trouble accepting that Osama bin Laden was responsible for the September 11th atrocities or that hi-jacked airliners actually brought down the Twin Towers. Nevertheless aircraft supposedly piloted by kamikaze *Saudi Arabian* terrorists somehow justified the U.S.A. ripping into the *Afghans* and then invading *Iraq*. At least eight of those Saudi Arabian terrorists named in the press, whose photos adorned our newspapers, are still alive today; go figure. These Arab 'terrorists' are absent from the manifests, they don't show up on boarding videos but we are asked to believe that they took over the planes with cardboard box cutters and prevented eight different pilots of four aircraft from transmitting a four-digit hijacking code, on a 'fly-by-wire' aircraft. This is simply impossible! This is the madness on which our planet currently runs!

"This is a blatant falsehood", says Brian Desborough, *"because the Boeing airliners involved were of the 'fly by wire' type ... Whenever fly by wire aircraft are hijacked and an attempt is made by the perpetrators to fly the aircraft to an alternate destination, control of the aircraft is automatically transferred to a covert Federal ground facility, thereby permitting the aircraft to be safely landed at the nearest suitable airport."* [(273)]

Of course, in this situation the controls of commercial airliners are instantly tended inoperative and there is nothing the hijackers or pilot can do to alter the situation. This is standard procedure and even without the diligent, scientific research of Desborough, serves to prove that the 'official' story is a pack of lies.

It appears, though, that I must be the crazy one who is out of step. A survey by the *New York Times / CBS News* in 2003, ascertained that 42% of the American public actually believed that *Saddam Hussein* was directly responsible for the September 11th attacks on the World Trade Centre and the Pentagon. I would struggle to comprehend this, even if they swallowed the 'official' line of *Osama bin Laden* being responsible; but no, *Saddam Hussein.* We are certainly making it easy for them. This brings to mind a favorite quote from Professor Martin Buber: *'Mundus vult decipi'* (The world wants to be deceived). [274]

It seems Americans simply can't or don't want to believe their corrupt, puppet President is lying to them. An *ABC News* poll further claimed that 55% of Americans believed that Saddam was a direct supporter of al-Qaeda. [275] In a *CNN* interview, an American teenage soldier in Iraq, referred to as 'private A.J.', told the reporter, *"I wanna get in there and get my nose dirty; I wanna take revenge for 9/11."* When the reporter patiently explained that there was nothing to link the Iraqi government with 9/11; 'A.J.' thought a moment and then stated, *"Yeah, well that stuff 's way over my head."* [276] Unlimited firepower in the hands of babes - God help us all!

I personally viewed the film taken from a Service Station security camera of the impact that punched a hole in the wall of the Pentagon. Several eyewitnesses claimed it was a missile and not an airliner that hit the wall and I must concur that this is plainly apparent in the security film. For a start there was the relatively small hole through the brickwork; then we have the situation where the crash site simply did not resemble an aircraft crash site. In a crash where the aircraft is utterly destroyed, it is normal to see wing-tips, wheels, most of the tail and sundry bits as wreckage. The monstrous tail plane, the wings and at least some seats would have been left outside the wall even if there had been a massive fire, which there was not. Not even the remnants of the huge engines were visible at this site. No wings hit the building, nor did they appear to burn up. There is no evidence that any aircraft was ever there at all. There is not even evidence of major fire; the lawn grass was not scorched except for a few feet back! The film showed the impact point, where no aircraft wreckage was visible. We were asked to believe this was an aircraft crash, with no wreckage. It also must have been coincidence that the impact point of the Pentagon was miraculously, 'closed for renovations' at the time, with all staff moved to the other side of the building.

Checking the other evidence reported in the media, such as the FBI claim that Arab terrorists left evidence in a hotel room and in rental cars, Brian Desborough was able to report: *'Strangely, this wildly suspect claim was later contradicted by FBI Director Robert Mueller. Speaking at the Commonwealth Club in San Francisco on April 19th, 2002, Mueller stated that the terrorists "left no paper trail at all". He added: "In our investigation, we have not uncovered a single piece of paper, either here in the United States, or in a treasure trove of information that has turned up in Afghanistan and elsewhere that mentioned any aspect of the September 11th plot."* [277] Desborough goes on to describe as, *'patently false'* the suggestion that burning fuel from the airliner generated sufficient heat to melt the structural steelwork and caused the eventual collapse of the towers. He discusses how the Towers were constructed around a reinforced concrete central core and bolstered with massive steel columns of four inch thick steel. There are photos on the net showing that these steel columns were cut on an angle as is standard procedure in demolition. Eyewitnesses reported hearing explosions immediately prior to the collapse of each tower which further serves to refute the official story. MIT Engineer Jeff King correctly states that the *'squibs'* seen as puffs of smoke emanating from alternate floors on the videos of the buildings collapse, clearly demonstrates signs of controlled demolition. The videos also show building rubble ejected at high speed which would also strongly indicate the use of explosives. King also questions why all evidence was destroyed and the site 'scrubbed' to prevent any form of investigation.

It is an amazing statistic that $40,000,000 was spent investigating former president Bill Clinton's peccadilloes but just $60,000 investigating the WTC disaster. The supposed collapse of the four inch thick support columns, was not explained or addressed in the report.

The Lamont-Doherty Earth Observatory, a research division of Colombia University, is located just 21 miles north of the World Trade Centre and monitors seismic activity, as well as developing scientific instrumentation for the detection of nuclear explosions. This facility actually detected a tiny seismic signal at the precise moment when each of the airliners struck the towers, then a much stronger 2.1 magnitude disturbance for the South Tower collapse and 2.3 magnitude for the North Tower. Desborough states:

> ***'Of extreme significance, very large seismic spikes were recorded at the commencement of each quake, before any of the debris hit the ground. Another important anomaly was the fact that all cell phones in the vicinity temporarily went dead, indicating that a strong electromagnetic pulse had occurred in the immediate vicinity of the World Trade Centre.'*** (278)

This led Brian Desborough to deduce that Special Atomic Demolition Munitions (SADM) 'micro-nukes' each with the explosive force of one hundred tons of high explosive, were used to bring down the towers. The seismic record and the cell phone failure bore the characteristic signature of this micro-nuke explosion making deliberate demolition the only tenable conclusion. These things cement with absolute certainty that the Twin Towers were 'pulled' by demolition explosives and were not brought down by hijacked aircraft. Many, many witnesses reported an explosion, before each tower came down and that is fully confirmed by the seismic and visual record.

Physics Professor, Stephen E. Jones of Brigham Young University published a paper in which he conclusively proved the World Trade Centre buildings could have only been brought down in the manner they were, by explosives. Professor Jones was entirely correct; however, he received no coverage in the mainstream media for his scientific and provable claims. This now goes way beyond conspiracy theory. We must evaluate just how it would be possible to plant these explosives without being observed?

The Walls Came Tumbling Down

Although Desborough was entirely correct in principle, it seems likely that it was C-4 Plastic (that causes an identical electromagnetic pulse), that was used and not micro-nukes. Some checking confirms that the *Port Authority of New York and New Jersey* owned the Twin Towers and some surrounding World Trade Center buildings. The Port Authority's Press Release Number: 68-2001 from 26th April 2001 was headed; *'Port Authority to Lease World Trade Centre to Silverstein Properties Inc. and Westfield America Inc.'* This report spelled out the richest Real Estate transaction in New York history, valued at $3.2 billion for a 99 year lease. This covered the Twin Towers and two other buildings at the WTC and was approved by the Board of Commissioners of the Port Authority. David-Wynn: Miller, a former tool and die maker from Milwaukee, makes claims that he is sufficiently familiar with advanced explosive technology to categorically ascertain precisely how the Twin Towers job was done. He believes that as part of their fit-out, these new owners generously provided each tenant with new office furniture. This furniture included some that had the appearance of solid wood grained timber, but was actually made of C4 plastic. [(279)] Somewhat strangely, no office furniture at all was recovered from the wreckage of the Twin Towers - and this suggests that the furniture itself was the explosive. Miller explains that advanced technology made it possible for this mass of C4 Plastic, strategically distributed throughout the building, in the configuration chosen by the perpetrators, to be detonated via satellite, at a time after the planes hit the 87th floor. [(280)] This type of explosion brought into play a massive electromagnetic pulse of expansion coefficient 6.3, that pulverized concrete, steel and glass (collectively called polymer) which is also (would you believe it?) coefficient 6.3. As a result a large portion of the building instantaneously turned to dust, which blanketed the fall of the buildings and was distributed up to 5 inches deep for a mile radius around the site of Zero One. Naturally all cell phones were rendered inoperable by the pulse and computer discs instantly wiped. [(281)] This all helped in covering a multitude of dubious financial transactions and other sins.

You can prove for yourself that the assessment of Brian Desborough, Professor Stephen E. Jones and David-Wynn: Miller is precisely what happened. The World Trade Centre Towers were 1,300 feet tall and 208 feet wide. Working with the height of the buildings, we can calculate that after initial acceleration of 33 feet/second/second until terminal velocity of around 125 feet/second is attained; the building in a freefall situation, should take almost 12 seconds to hit the ground from the force of gravity:

First second - 33 feet
Second second - 66 feet
Third second - 99 feet
Fourth second - 125 feet
Fifth second - 125 feet
Sixth second - 125 feet

Seventh second	- 125 feet
Eighth second	- 125 feet
Ninth second	- 125 feet
Tenth second	- 125 feet
Eleventh second	- 125 feet
Twelfth second	- 102 feet
Total of	1,300 feet

Now watch a film clip of the fall of each building and with a stop watch, time the crash … 8 seconds. It is simply not possible for 1300 feet tall buildings to crash to the ground, by gravity alone, in this timeframe. The 'pancake' effect of each floors collapse would of course, retard it further. Burning aircraft fuel won't do it either. The only way an entire building can freefall at more than the velocity of gravity is with the aid of an enormous electromagnetic pulse. Only a micro-nuke or a massive C4 Plastic blast would do this, so accordingly it becomes very difficult to entertain any other explanation.

Actually, subterfuge is even more evident because according to demolition experts, the 'pancake' effect of having to overcome the resistance of each successive floor, would retard the fall to something close to 96 seconds. The electromagnetic pulse associated with the use of C-4 would create a sonic boom and as we saw, all the windows in the surrounding buildings were taken out. Demolition experts can confirm that this would not result from the demolition of a large building using micro nukes; confirming that a larger electromagnetic shockwave pulse was involved such as occurres with C-4.

Any recovered computer hard discs, were sent to Germany, to the best technicians available in the world, yet these technicians were unable to rescue the original data. This fact, coupled with the loss of cell phone operation, confirms the C-4 explosions as the most tenable explanation, to the point of almost certainty. (282) Brian Desborough discusses the irony of a sick scenario: that most of the flags waved by patriotic Americans in the aftermath of the atrocities on September 11th were in fact manufactured in China. He discovered: *'The official Chinese news agency recently announced that the profits from the sale of the 'Stars and Stripes' since 9/11 had been so great that it has covered the cost of manufacturing four more Chinese nuclear missiles!'* (283)

It was a Bank Robbery, Folks!

Can you begin to imagine the cover up that the loss of these buildings allowed? There are massive amounts of data, the records of money transactions and massive amounts of actual gold bullion, now unaccounted for. Well let's quantify it further: the perpetrators got away with *US$30 billion* in Gold bullion plus *US$1.2 trillion* in universal postal credits and a further *US$.7 trillion* disappeared from the Treasury located in the basement. [(284)] Between the times the airliners struck the towers, and the towers came down, the Military shut down the subway and the bullion was clandestinely removed on a special train commandeered for that specific task. All other subway trains were stopped from running while this one became the 'getaway vehicle'. [(285)] President Bush told us that a videotape that surfaced in December, 2001 was a genuine confession by Osama Bin Laden, shown gloating about the success of the September 11 attacks. I personally felt that this was highly unlikely, despite Bush's continued insistence that the tape is authentic. *"It's bogus"*, says Professor Bruce Lawrence, head of Duke University's Religious Studies program and likely the world's top expert on the Bin Laden family. Overall, this was a high technology precision operation and was not run by some exile in a cave. [(286)]

The cover-ups are there to be seen, the lies are in full view and the perpetrators just have to include the Bush Cabal. But hang on! George Bush wouldn't lie, would he? He got the Christian vote, didn't he? He's a born again Christian, isn't he? Not by the following quote from a work called, *'George W. Bush is Not a Christian'*, by Robert Guffy who teaches English at California State University: *'Recently, more and more Christians are waking up to the fact that President Bush is an imposter dragging the name of their Saviour through the mud. A number of books written by Christians, have taken Bush to task for egregious duplicity, one of the latest being 'Christian Words, Un-Christian Actions' by John Stoddard Klar.'*[(287)] Guffy further mentions that Dick Cheney, when asked by a reporter from *'USA Today'* about being the prime manipulator behind the President's actions, made this amazing revelation: *'Am I the evil genius in the corner that nobody ever sees come out of his hole? It's a nice way to operate actually.'*[(288)]

A dunce and a rat! God help us all. The enemy is within our own Governments!

Horrifying U.S. Death Ray

The 9/11attrocities were supposedly perpetrated by Osama bin Laden and Saudi Arabian terrorists. So, America chooses - for reasons best known to the Bush administration - to retaliate in Afghanistan, probably because of easy access to drug poppies and also with *'Operation Iraqi Freedom'* to liberate the Iraqi people. It liberated them alright - with high impact bombing of their families and depleted uranium distribution in their neighborhoods. It will take millennia for the radioactivity to subside in Iraq but the U.S. simply doesn't care. This has now taken a new turn. It is reported that American ground forces have been using a nightmarish new U.S. super weapon during chaotic street fighting in Baghdad. The secret tank-mounted weapon resembling something from Science Fiction was witnessed in all its frightening power by Majid al-Ghazali, a seasoned Iraqi infantryman, who described the device and its gruesome effects as unlike anything he had ever encountered in his lengthy military service. Majid al-Ghazali is also a world class concert violinist who is booked for performances in the U.S. in the near future.

The disturbing revelation is yet another piece of cinematic evidence brought back from postwar Iraq by intrepid filmmaker Patrick Dillon. His film shows al-Ghazali, whose English is less than fluent, describing the weapon he saw reminiscent of a flame thrower, but immensely more powerful. In the midst of the fighting, he noticed that the Americans had called up an oddly configured tank. Then to his amazement the tank suddenly let loose a blinding stream of what seemed like fire and lightning. Searching for a description, al-Ghazali said it appeared to be shooting concentrated lightning bolts rather than just ordinary flames. Drawing on his many years as a engineer, al-Ghazali speculates that radiation of some kind probably figures in the weapon's hideous capabilities. He observed the blast from this weapon engulfing a large passenger bus and three automobiles. Within seconds the bus had become semi-molten, sagging *'like a wet rag'*. He said the bus rapidly melted under this withering blast, shrinking until it was a twisted blob about the dimensions of a small car. As if that were not bizarre enough, al-Ghazali explicitly describes seeing numerous human bodies shriveled to the size of newborn babies.

By the time local street fighting ended that day, he estimates between 500 and 600 soldiers and civilians had been cooked alive as a result of the mysterious new tank-mounted device. In a city littered everywhere with burned-out civilian and military vehicles, U.S. forces were abnormally diligent about immediately detailing bulldozers and shovel crews to the job of burying the grim wreckage. God pity humanity if that thing is a preview of what's in store for the 21st century. [(289)]

Timothy McVeigh's Execution

Was Timothy McVeigh Really Executed? No really, that is a serious question. Forget what you saw in the media; that can be proved a pack of lies. Throughout the whole Oklahoma City bombing saga the mainstream media has ignored some serious inconsistencies. For example: some of those killed in the bombing were not killed in the blast itself but died later in highly suspicious circumstances. One such person was a hero, Mike Loudenslager who was responsible for saving the lives of many children in the Murrah Building's day care centre.

In the weeks prior to the actual bombing, Loudenslager, a GSA employee, blew the whistle on some strange activities and actually filed written complaints about the large amounts of ordinance and explosives being brought into the building by the B.A.T.F. and D.E.A, who had offices there. Others had been complaining too, including the building's security director who filed a formal complaint and promptly lost his job as a result. Thereafter fire marshals were denied access to the building when they arrived to inspect some remodeling that had been done to the day care centre. Fearing the worst, Loudenslager and the day care operator began warning the children's parents not to bring their children into the building until they uncovered just what was going on. Had they not done so, the death toll would have certainly been considerably higher. [(290)]

We saw earlier that like the burning of children at Waco, Texas; the explosion in Oklahoma took place on the Satanic ritual day for the fire God, Molech, which occurs on 19th April. Shortly after the actual bombing, Loudenslager was seen by many witnesses, including police officers and rescue workers, involved in a very 'heated' confrontation with those he suspected of being the perpetrators of the debacle. Much of his anger was aimed at the B.A.T.F. and D.E.A. who he had seen bringing in the explosive materials. He was certain this was a deliberate attack and these people were responsible for the damage. To the astonishment of those who had seen him in the immediate aftermath of the bombing, it was later reported that Loudenslager was found dead at his desk, a victim of the 9:02am bombing. This was reported after he had been seen alive by numerous rescue workers. Despite this he is now on the official list of victims claimed by the blast.

His death was to play a part in the later demise of two others, Dr. Don Chumley and Terry Yeakey, both of whom were at the Murrah Building that fateful morning. At the time of their deaths each had been trying to deliver evidence that they saw Loudenslager alive after the bombing. Dr. Chumley was killed first, when his personal jet 'crashed', to prevent his delivering evidence to a multi-county task force that he believed, would establish the truth about the Oklahoma City bombing. Terry Yeakey met his demise after attempting to do the same. Meanwhile the mainstream media has ignored compelling evidence contrary to the official line that McVeigh acted alone in delivering a truck carrying a fertilizer bomb to the Murrah Building. Literally hundreds of people have attested that the bags of Ammonium Nitrate were being brought in and stored in the weeks prior to the detonation.

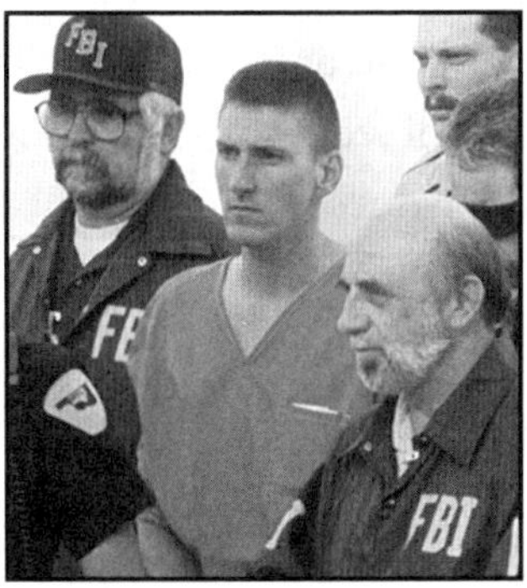

Timothy McVeigh; was he just a fall guy?

One such person is retired Air Force Brigadier-General Benton K. Partin, former head of the U.S. Air Force Armament Technology Laboratory. His request that the bombsite be preserved for further investigation was completely ignored by the U.S. Government; instead the site was covered over three weeks ahead of schedule, effectively burying the remaining forensic evidence. Moreover many eyewitnesses reported not one, but two explosions, and this is a certifiable fact which proved McVeigh did not act alone. Investigations at the Oklahoma Geological Survey at the University of Oklahoma revealed seismographic records confirming two explosions, ten seconds apart. The first occurred at 9: 02 and 13 seconds with another following at 9:02 and 23 seconds. According to Brigadier General Partin and many explosive experts, this totally rules out the explanation of a truck bomb. A more plausible explanation, they say, is a barometric bomb. This works via a process that involves not one but two explosions. The first uses an explosive known as PETN which releases a lethal cloud of chemicals, ammonium nitrate and aluminum silicate. This cloud is energized with what is described as a *"high potential electrostatic field."* A few seconds later there follows another blast using an explosive called PDTN that ignites the cloud created with a much greater force than TNT. This would account for the two blasts heard by witnesses and it would also explain the extensive damage caused by the explosion. Such a bomb is hi-tech and would certainly be beyond the scope of a supposed 'lone nut' like Timothy McVeigh. In fact, knowledge of how to construct such a device at that time was available to only a few, with the highest level of security clearance, because the barometric bomb was highly classified. In other words, only those with a high level of security clearance in the U.S. Government and security services would have access to the know-how to construct such a device. This suggests that McVeigh was not the bomber at all but purely a patsy, who was lined up to take the rap for the bombing.

And his reward? A place in the history books with a new life and a clean bill of health after his faked 'execution'. You don't believe that this was possible? Then you need to explain why, by court order, there was no autopsy and no cremation of his body after execution, despite the fact that *both are standard practice for executed prisoners in Oklahoma*. In addition, according to reporters covering the execution, McVeigh seemed remarkably calm. So there were no farewells, no last minute nerves, no clinical autopsy, no cremation and it would seem, no *body* either. In a final ironic twist McVeigh's death certificate from his 'execution' in 2001, lists his occupation as *'soldier'* and his employer as the *'U.S. Army'* despite the fact he had supposedly left the U.S. Army eight years earlier, back in 1993." [291] We are being duped here. Susan Carlson reporting for WLS Chicago on McVeigh's execution, broadcast minutes after the sentence was carried out; *"The shallow breathing continued... or what appeared to be shallow breathing ... even after they pronounced him dead."*

The above was first posted on *rumormillnews*, a forum often used by dissident US government insiders. One anonymous respondent wrote that he had personally heard McVeigh being told not to worry because: *"... we won't let you die inside."* [(292)] Susan Carlson is now also 'retracting' her report! Smart lady.

The Wrong Saddam

America invaded Iraq and of course no Weapons of Mass Destruction were ever found simply because they never existed. When the war became more unpopular, Bush was copping a pounding in the media and had to do something so he went for the big one, *'We've caught Saddam Hussein'*. A former U.S Marine Ex-Sgt. Nadim Abou Rabeh has now claimed that he participated in the fraudulent 'spider hole' capture of Saddam Hussein in December 2003. He confirms that the entire event was fabricated and the captured man was a Saddam look-alike. [(293)] Regardless, the media screamed, *'Saddam Caught'* and then after months of circus entertainment at the trial, I now ask, *'Did they hang the real Saddam?'* The answer is a resounding NO!

In the photos, it can be seen that the real Saddam had impeccable dental work with a slight regal overbite. The bearded look-alike Saddam that was hanged had very poor dental work and a noticeable under bite. The bushy eyebrows are also quite different in contour and length. Saddam's wife visited him in custody after his capture and told the world that it wasn't her husband. She was largely ignored because people chose to believe she was trying to get him acquitted. President Bush was going for full mileage out of the Saddam trial even though they quite obviously had the wrong man. An Iraqi com-

The teeth and eyebrows make it fairly apparent they hanged the wrong Saddam.

mander now swears he saw the USAF fly the real Saddam out of Baghdad and I for one believe him. (294)

With all these conspiracies and cover-ups proven to have been based on high level lies; with the myriad connections of various governments in the distribution of opium, made possible by the Afghanistan war; with the war called *'Iraqi Freedom'* destroying the oil rich country that was ancient Babylon; and with the broad daylight genocide of the Palestinian people. it's a no brainer to assume that some really evil people are running the world.

CHAPTER TWENTY THREE

SOME INTERESTING ANECDOTES

'Although small children have taboos about stepping on ants ... there has never seemed to be a taboo about pulling the wings off a fly. Most children seem to outgrow this behaviour. Those who do not, either come to a bad end or become biologists.'

Biologist, Vincent Dethier, '*To Know a Fly*', 1962.

For the Slightly Cynical

- To grant authority to a Jackass is to turn dormant stupidity into dynamic incompetence.
- Perfect health is still just the slowest way of dying.
- Team players are those who get behind a program of abysmal stupidity and then ride it all the way to financial ruin.
- Democracy is two wolves and a sheep voting on lunch. Liberty is a well-armed sheep contesting the vote.
- One of the penalties for refusing to participate in politics is that you end up being governed by your inferiors. - Plato (429-347 B.C.E.)
- Those who cast the votes decide nothing. Those who count the votes decide everything. - Josef Stalin.
- It is hardly too strong to say that the Constitution was made to guard the people against the dangers of good intentions.
- If voting could really change anything, it would be illegal.
- Inspiration is for amateurs. The rest of us just show up and work. - Chuck Close
- All relationships end badly, otherwise they wouldn't end.

- Human progress is destined to be eternally retarded by man's insatiable passion for marching in ranks behind the banner of an imbecile.
- I freed a thousand slaves. I could have freed a thousand more if only they knew they were slaves.
- You have enemies? Good. That means you've stood up for something, sometime in your life. - Winston Churchill.
- It isn't all that difficult to make a major contribution to mankind. Anyone who isn't now serving on a committee is helping immeasurably.

Worse Weather on the Weekends

This concept always suspected by fishermen, golfers and picnickers has now been proved by statistics. An analysis of weather conditions over the past 20 years confirms the following:

- Wednesday is the warmest day
- Saturday is the coolest
- There is 15% more rain on Saturday
- The next rainiest day is Sunday
- Monday has the least rain
- Tuesday has an average of 15 minutes more sun than Saturday

Researchers assume that man made emissions during the week accumulate to effect the weather on the weekend, but no one is sure.

What's in a Name

- *Grog* - Admiral Edward Vernon of the British Navy was nicknamed, *"Old Grog"* because he wore an old fashioned coarse cloak that was called a *"grogram"*. In 1740 he attempted to stamp out drunkenness in the Navy and insisted that the daily nip of rum to sailors be diluted with water. The word *Grog* became the name for a mixture of rum with water and in time the name was attributed to any alcohol.
- *Iota* – We should all recall the old saying about 'not one *iota* of difference'; That saying came about from a controversy in the Byzantine Empire when sorting out the question about the personalities within the Godhead. The problems began in Alexandria, when *Bishop Alex-*

ander and the *Priest Arius* argued over the divinity of Jesus and the relationship between Jesus and God the Father. Arius proposed that if the Father begat the Son, then the latter must have had a beginning, so there must have been a time when he did not exist and accordingly his substance was from nothing, like the rest of creation. The orthodox Catholics were told to follow Alexander and believe that God the Father incorporated, God the Son, whilst the Arian sect taught that they were separate personalities within the same Godhead. Alexander condemned these beliefs and wrote the first version of the now famous creed, proclaiming that the Son was *'one in being with the Father'*. Now the Father and Son combined in Greek is recorded as *Homo-ousion* and the Father and Son separate is *Homo-iousion* with just one Greek letter iota being the difference. The Arian doctrine was declared heretical at the *Council of Nicea* in 325 AD and the Catholic doctrine prevailed even though there was only one iota of difference.

- *Sundae* – In the late 1800s, it was illegal for milk bars to sell ice-cream sodas on a Sunday in the puritan town of Evanston, Illinois. To circumvent the ban and get around what they considered a stupid law, proprietors sold ice-cream with favoured syrup to their regular customers. With the addition of bananas and other fruit this dessert became more popular than the outlawed sodas. The different spelling was also a protest at religious objections on Sunday.
- *Granny Smith* – This internationally popular apple was named after granny Maria Ann Smith who in 1839 migrated to Sydney from Sussex in the U.K. By grafting and budding some seedlings in her garden she eventually developed the superior green apple known as a Granny Smith to this day.
- *Heavenly Host* – Throughout the Bible we find mention of the Heavenly Host. Etymology tells us that the word 'host' was a previously non-existent English word, created by the Bible translators for a Hebrew word *'Sabaoth'*. For a long time to come it was not a word in the vernacular of Bible readers. My Sunday School teachers assumed that the heavenly host must have been Angels although there was no

evidence to support this. (At other times the 'heavenly host' appear to be the stars and planets). One Bible passage states that the 'host' were 'with the angel', indicating that they were not the same beings. *Luke 2 : 13 "And suddenly there was with the angel, a multitude of the heavenly host praising God"* This stance is also supported by the learned Rabbi ben Jochai who after a lifetime of study stated that they were certainly not the same.

In fact the real English translation from the original texts that offended the translators, should have been *'heavenly army'*, not *'heavenly host'* at all, so it is unlikely angels are meant. This is confirmed when the same Hebrew word is used in the following: *Exodus 14 : 17 I will get me honour upon Pharaoh, and upon all his host, upon his chariots, and upon his horsemen.* (It is not difficult to see that this refers to Pharaoh's Army). Thus we can accept that the Heavenly Host is really an army. Now a Hebrew name of God was *Jehovah-Sabaoth* (YHWH-Sabaoth) and this confirms Almighty God as a God of war since Jehovah-Sabaoth means 'God of armies' or 'War-God'.

- *Coca-Cola* – This carbonated soft drink known the world over, was first developed as a medicine by a chemist, John Stith Pemberton, in the back of his chemist shop in Columbus, Georgia, in 1885. In the early days, the beverage was sold from his pharmacy as a patent medicine and Pemberton claimed his medicinal drink cured many diseases, including morphine addiction, dypepsia, neurasthenia, headache, and impotence. When Atlanta and Fulton County passed prohibition legislation in 1886, Pemberton responded by developing his recipe into a carbonated, non-alcoholic version of French Wine Colas that were popular at the time. The original drink was green, and at that time sold as *Pemberton's (non-alcoholic) French Wine Cola.* The name Coca-Cola is said to come from the leaves of the South American Coca shrub and an extract from the kola nut; however, Coca-Cola did once contain an estimated nine milligrams of cocaine per glass and that's quite apparently where the coca bit came from. I guess they wouldn't advertise that fact, now would they? No wonder it was refreshing! Anyway in 1903, the cocaine was removed.

Just 4 years before his death, Pemberton sold the Coca Cola rights to Asa Griggs Candler, whose marketing tactics led Coke to its dominance of the world soft drink market throughout the 20th century. It was not without some major heartburn though, because it turned out Pemberton had also sold the recipe to 4 other parties and his son had sold it to others as well. Candler formed the Coca Cola Company, the owner of Coke today and the exact formula is still a secret. Actress, Sigourney Weaver's father, Pat Weaver, is said to be one of just two people in the world who know the exact formula.

- *Chicken Marengo* – After success in the Battle of Marengo, in northern Italy, a hungry Napoleon asked for a meal. The army's supply train had not yet caught up so a foraging party went looking for food. They returned with a small hen, three eggs, four tomatoes, and six crayfish. This was cooked in a little garlic and oil and served with bread and a nip of Brandy. Napoleon was so delighted he called it Chicken Marengo and asked for this to be served after every successful battle. Today, the unchanged original recipe is enjoyed all over the world.
- *Sandwiches* – The fourth Earl of Sandwich was such a compulsive gambler that he would not leave the card table for meals. Instead he ordered a slab of cooked meat to be placed between two pieces of bread and had this as his meal. The name sandwich stuck.
- *Ampersand* – The '&' symbol that means 'and' is one of the few surviving signs from the world's first shorthand system. Invented in Rome by Marcus Tiro in 63 B.C.E., it still substitutes for the word *'and'* in several hundred languages.
- *Cigar bands* – In Cuba it was fashionable for refined ladies to smoke Havana Cigars. They wrapped narrow paper bands around their cigars to protect their delicate fingers from nicotine stains. The company that made the Havanas decided it was a good idea and adopted it to this day.
- *Manneke Pis Fountain* - The toddler son of a prominent citizen of Brussels was lost and to recruit the town's people to help him search, the father promised that if the search was successful in finding his

The Manneke Pis Fountain still surprises many tourists.

son, he would build a bronze fountain with a statue of the little boy as he looked when found. It just so happened that when found, the little boy was relieving himself and his father kept his word. Many tourists are still surprised by this fountain.

- *'Queen Mary'* – The Cunnard liner known as the 'Queen Mary' was planned to be the *'Queen Victoria'*. Before the launch in 1934, the Company chairman went to see King George V to tell him the board wanted to name the new ship after one of England's most noble queens .... Before he could finish, King George interrupted; Oh, Her majesty will be so pleased, so some quick changes had to be made and 'Queen Mary' she became.
- *White Elephant* – Albino elephants are very rare and considered sacred in many parts of Asia. The modern connotation of a 'white elephant', something that cost extravagant amounts of money but is worthless came about in the court of Siam (Thailand). The king made a proclamation that anyone who owned a white elephant must treat it as sacred and give it the very best of everything and not put it to work. This could drive the owner to penury, feeding an animal that was not income producing. If a courtier angered him, the king might suggest that he was planning to present the man with one of his own white elephants. The hapless courtier would quickly toe the line otherwise he would be forced to risk insulting the king by refusing the gift or be ruined financially with the upkeep of the white elephant.
- *Santa* - The original German Saint Nicholas was a gnome who would frighten children, then leave presents in the morning to compensate. Like the elves, Santa was originally dressed in green, until 1931, at which time he was changed to the Coca Cola colours of red and white. Santa was first utilized in a massive advertising campaign by Coca Cola from 1931, which lasted until 1964, designed to boost

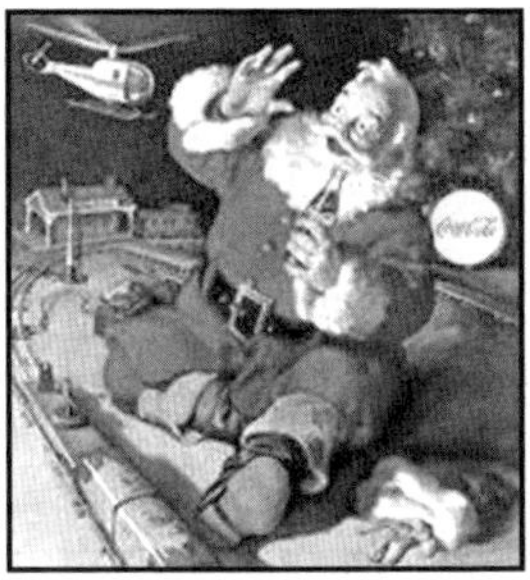

Until Coca Cola changed his dress to red and white, Santa was a green clad gnome.

sales in the American winter. The campaign Santa, was painted by Haddon Hubbard Sundblom, a native of Muskegon, Michigan and loosely based on Clement Moore's poem, *'T'was the Night Before Christmas'*, from 1922.

- *The Gregorian Calendar* – At a time when Caesar's *Julian* calendar of 365 days, had been in force for 1500 years, the accumulated error now amounted to 10 days. Pope Gregory XIII introduced his Gregorian calendar in 1582 and solved the accumulated error of the ten days by simply omitting them. In that year October 4th was followed by October 15th to get us back on track. The situation was not adequately explained to the people and there was rioting in the streets. Angry mobs paraded in the cities yelling, "Give us back our 10 days".
- *Doughnuts* – These were 'invented' by a New England schoolboy called Hanson Gregory who was tired of eating his mothers cakes that were always 'stodgy' in the middle. He persuaded her to remove the centre bit before cooking the dough and thus doughnuts were born. The idea spread and is now a favorite coffee-break snack around the world.
- *Jeep* – Popeye's pal who appears part dog and wholly fantasy gave his name to the tough little 4 wheel drive utility vehicle created in the Second World War. The vehicles exploits became as legendary as its namesake. There were Jeep models made by both Ford and Willys. The vehicle we know officially as the Jeep was a Willys (Overland Motors) MB. The M was for Military and B because it was the second production model. The first one was the MA. The MB became the definitive Jeep.

The tough all terrain vehicle of WWII took its name from a Popeye cartoon.

At London's Savoy Restaurant, Dame Nellie Melba enjoyed a sweet, that still bears her name.

- *Peach Melba* - French chef Auguste Escoffier worked at London's Savoy Restaurant and was an ardent admirer of Dame Nellie Melba, the famous Australian soprano. When she dined at the Savoy at the turn of the century, Escoffier concocted a special dessert for the singer. It consisted of a peach, poached in vanilla syrup, presented in a cup of vanilla ice-cream and covered with crushed raspberries. The Dame thoroughly enjoyed the sweet and asked its name. M. Escoffier said he would be honoured if he could call it 'Peach Melba'. The idea became the rage of London and eventually a popular dessert around the world.

Some Interesting Anagrams

DORMITORY: When you rearrange the letters: DIRTY ROOM
PRESBYTERIAN: When you rearrange the letters: BEST IN PRAYER
ASTRONOMER: When you rearrange the letters: MOON STARER
DESPERATION: When you rearrange the letters: A ROPE ENDS IT
THE EYES: When you rearrange the letters: THEY SEE
GEORGE BUSH: When you rearrange the letters: HE BUGS GORE
THE MORSE CODE: When you rearrange the letters: HERE COME DOTS
SLOT MACHINES: When you rearrange the letters: CASH LOST IN ME
ELECTION RESULTS: When you rearrange the letters: LIES - LET'S RECOUNT
SNOOZE ALARMS: When you rearrange the letters: ALAS! NO MORE Z 'S
A DECIMAL POINT: When you rearrange the letters: IM A DOT IN PLACE
ELEVEN PLUS TWO: When you rearrange the letters: TWELVE PLUS ONE
MOTHER-IN-LAW: When you rearrange the letters: WOMAN HITLER

Marker 239

Late in 1929 a new Autobahn was opened between Bremen and Bremerhaven in Germany. Within a year more than 100 vehicles had been wrecked on this highway, all at kilometre marker 239. (295) The authorities were perplexed, it was a straight section of well constructed highway. What could be causing all the problems? Survivors told Police of experiencing a surreal feeling as their vehicle was pulled off the road by a great force.

Police and construction engineers took up vantage points in an attempt to discover some explanation. That day, 7th September 1930, no fewer than 9 vehicles were wrecked at the fateful marker. A local dowser called Carl Wehrs, approached them and assured them that he could fix the problem. He was a 'water diviner' and understood much about the underground flow of water. Wehrs told them that the mysterious force was actually an enormously powerful magnetic field generated by an underground stream. To test his theory in front of the startled onlookers, Wehrs slowly advanced marker 239 with his divining rod in his hands. When he was 4 metres away the rod was wrenched from his hands by the invisible force and flung to the other side of the road, while the diviner was spun around in his tracks.

Carl Wehrs constructed and buried a copper box full of what appeared to be star shaped metal pieces right at the base of the marker. The box remained there for a week in which time not one accident occurred. Convinced they were seeing a coincidence the Police and Engineers dug up and removed the box. The next three cars along the highway were wrecked at the evil marker. The box was hastily re-buried and concreted over. No accidents have been reported there since. (296)

Returning Stones

Back in 1928, the naturalist and author, Ivan Sanderson, was visiting a rubber plantation in Sumatra, when he was witness to probably the most amazing spectacle of his life. When dinner was over, Sanderson and his colleagues were congregating on a cool verandah when small stones began to shower down on the verandah deck. In his own words, Sanderson enlarged on this experience:

"The host told us ... that these stones came all the time, particularly on certain nights and usually on still ones, but not necessarily dark ones. As everybody was amazed and skeptical, our host then told us to mark the stones in any way we liked and throw them back anywhere into the hopelessly thick tangle of vegetation beyond and around the garden or house. To mark them he found us chalk from his

desk, a file and pencils. The ladies used their lipsticks and we employed all manner of designs and devices. We all threw them back hard or lightly in every conceivable direction. Almost but not quite all the marked stones came back onto the verandah within a matter of seconds, a few some minutes later. I would say that some fifty stones at least were so marked and thrown that night … I can vouch for the fact that it would be absolutely impossible for any human … to trace, find and throw back, marked stones in that vegetation tangle, short of clearing same and sifting its entire surface." [(297)]

Open Letter to Laura

Laura Schlessinger is a U.S. radio personality who dispenses advice to people who call in to her radio show. Recently, she said that as an observant Orthodox Jew, homosexuality is an abomination according to *Leviticus 18 : 22* and cannot be condoned or tolerated in any circumstance. The following is an open letter to Dr. Laura penned by a US resident, which was posted on the Internet:

> *"Dear Dr. Laura,*
> *Thank you for doing so much to educate people regarding God's Law. I have learned a great deal from your show and I try to share that knowledge with as many people as I can. When someone tries to defend the homosexual lifestyle, for example, I simply remind them that Leviticus 18 : 22 clearly states it to be an abomination. End of debate. I do need some advice from you, however, regarding some of the other specific laws and how to follow them.*
>
> *a) When I burn a bull on the altar as a sacrifice, I know it creates a pleasing odor for the Lord (Lev. 1 : 9). The problem is my neighbors. They claim the odor is not pleasing to them. Should I smite them?*
>
> *b) I would like to sell my daughter into slavery, as sanctioned in Exodus 21 : 7. In this day and age, what do you think would be a fair price for her?*

c) I know that I am allowed no contact with a woman while she is in her period of menstrual uncleanness (Lev. 15 : 19-24). The problem is, how do I tell? I have tried asking, but most women take offence.

d) Lev. 25 : 44 states that I may indeed possess slaves, both male and female, provided they are purchased from neighboring nations. A friend of mine claims that this applies to Mexicans but not Canadians. Can you clarify? Why can't I own Canadians?

e) I have a neighbor who insists on working on the Sabbath. Exodus 35 : 2 clearly states he should be put to death. Am I morally obligated to kill him myself?

f) A friend of mine feels that even though eating shellfish is an abomination (Lev. 11:10), it is a lesser abomination than homosexuality. I don't agree. Can you settle this?

g) Lev. 21 : 20 states that I may not approach the altar of God if I have a defect in my sight. I have to admit that I wear reading glasses. Does my vision have to be 20/20, or is there some wriggle room here?

h) Most of my male friends get their hair trimmed, including the hair around their temples, even though this is expressly forbidden by Lev. 19 : 27. How should they die?

i) I know from Lev. 11 : 6-8 that touching the skin of a dead pig makes me unclean, but may I still play football if I wear gloves?

j) My uncle has a farm. He violates Lev. 19 : 19 by planting two different crops in the same field, as does his wife by wearing garments made of two different kinds of thread (cotton/polyester blend). He also tends to curse and blaspheme a lot. Is it really necessary that we go to all the trouble of getting the whole town together to stone them? (Lev. 24 : 10-16) Couldn't we just burn them to death at a private family affair like we do with people who

> *sleep with their in-laws? (Lev. 20 : 14)*
> *I know you have studied these things extensively, so I am confident you can help. Thank you again for reminding us that God's word is eternal and unchanging. Your devoted disciple and adoring fan."* (298)

I hope we can all learn from this the valuable lesson about consciousness raising, about religious tolerance, about sensible scholarship and most of all, about avoiding religious fundamentalism.

The Whale

A front page story of the *'San Francisco Chronicle'* told an amazing story about a female humpback whale who had become entangled in a spider web of crab traps and lines. She was weighted down by hundreds of pounds of traps that caused her to struggle to stay afloat. She also had hundreds of yards of line rope wrapped around her body, her tail, her torso, and a line tugging in her mouth which prevented her from eating.

A fisherman spotted her just east of the Farralone Islands (outside the Golden Gate Bridge) and radioed an environmental group for help. Within a few hours, the rescue team arrived and determined that she was so badly off, the only way to save her was to immediately dive in and untangle her ... a very dangerous proposition. One slap of the tail could kill a rescuer. Regardless, the men worked for hours with curved knives and were able to eventually free her.

The divers reported that when she was free, although exhausted and hungry, she swam in what seemed like joyous circles. She then came back to

Freeing the grateful Mother Wale.

each and every diver, one at a time, and nudged them - she thanked them. Some said it was the most incredibly beautiful experience of their lives. The guy who cut the rope out of her mouth, said her eye was following him the whole time and he will never be the same again.

THE END

REFERENCES AND END NOTES

(1) Daniel G. Hoffman, *'Paul Bunyan, Last of the Frontier Demi-Gods'* University of Pennsylvania Press, for Temple University Publications, 1952.
(2) A TAZmanian look at the World Weird Web.
(3) With thanks to The Australian Film Television & Radio School 2005.
(4) Bill Wannan, *'Crooked Mick of The Speewah'*; Melbourne, Currey O'Neill. 1985.
(5) *The English Mechanic and World of Science*, 73:260, 10th May 1901.
(6) The Stockton and Hartlepool *Mercury*, 8th April, 1865
(7) *The Unexplained: Mysteries of Mind, Space and Time*, Vol 2, Issue 24, Orbis Publishing Limited.
(8) *Scientific American*, 8:366; 30th Jul 1853.
(9) *The Unexplained: Mysteries of Mind, Space and Time*, Volume 1, Issue 8, Orbis Publishing Limited.
(10) *Ancient Man – Remains in Coal & Rock*; http://www.pathlights.com/ce_encyclopedia/Encyclopedia/13anc03.htm#Remains.
(11) *The Truth Seeker - World's Before Our Own 2*; www.thetruthseeker.co.uk/print.asp?ID=64
(12) *OOPARTS (out of place artefacts) & ANCIENT HIGH TECHNOLOGY*; http://www.s8int.com/page8.html
(13) *Ancient Man – Remains in Coal & Rock*; http://www.pathlights.com/ce_encyclopedia/Encyclopedia/13anc03.htm#Remains
(14) *Ancient Man – Remains in Coal & Rock*; http://www.pathlights.com/ce_encyclopedia/Encyclopedia/13anc03.htm#Remains
(15) *Ancient Man – Remains in Coal & Rock*; http://www.pathlights.com/ce_encyclopedia/Encyclopedia/13anc03.htm#Remains
(16) *OOPARTS (out of place artefacts) & ANCIENT HIGH TECHNOLOGY*; http://www.s8int.com/page8.html.
(17) *Guardian News & Media, Los Angeles Times.*
(18) http://www.world-mysteries.com/sar_12.htm
(19) *The Truth Seeker - World's Before Our Own 2*; www.thetruthseeker.co.uk/print.asp?ID=64.
(20) *'The American Journal of Science'*, 3:26; pages 139-140, July-December 1883.
(21) Rixon Stewart. *World's Before Our Own 2*; http://www.thetruthseeker.co.uk/print.asp?ID=64
(22) *'Mysteries of the Unexplained'*, Readers Digest General Books, 1982, page 38.
(23) Rixon Stewart. *Worlds Before Our Own 2*; http://www.thetruthseeker.co.uk/print.asp?ID=64
(24) Rixon Stewart. *Worlds Before Our Own 2*; http://www.thetruthseeker.co.uk/print.asp?ID=64
(25) Ian Ross Vayro, *'God Save Us From Religion'* Joshua Books.
(26) Richard Noone, *'Hammer and the Pendulum'*,
(27) Sources include: Rixon Stewart. *Worlds Before Our Own 2*; http://www.thetruthseeker.co.uk/print.asp?ID=64.
(28) Jimison, S. - *Scientists baffled by space spheres: Weekly World News* 27th July 1982.
(29) Jimison, S. - *Scientists baffled by space spheres: Weekly World News* 27th July 1982.

(30) Lindsay, J. F., and V. Bennett, 200. *The Late Archean Biospheric Explosion*: 37th Lunar and Planetary Science Conference, Abstract #1174, Lunar and Planetary Institute, Houston, TX.
(31) *Ancient Nano-technology* http://www.thetruthseeker.co.uk/article.asp?ID=34
(32) *OOPARTS & Ancient High Technology*; http://www.s8int.com/page6.html.
(33) *The Illustrated London News*, 9th February 1856 page 166.
(34) Berlitz, Charles. *'World of Strange Phenomena'*, New York, Fawcett Crest, 1988 and John Grant, *Great Monster Mysteries*, New Burlington Books, London, 1992.
(35) Dr. David Paterson. David.Paterson@dbce.csiro.au.
(36) *'Hidden Bits of History'*, Awareness Quest; http://www.awarenessquest.com/research.htm
(37) Dr David Paterson. David.Paterson@dbce.csiro.au
(38) Awareness Quest, *'Hidden Bits of History'*, http://www.awarenessquest.com/research.htm
(39) Awareness Quest, *'Hidden Bits of History'*, http://www.awarenessquest.com/research.htm
(40) Awareness Quest, *'Hidden Bits of History'*, http://www.awarenessquest.com/research.htm
(41) Álvaro de Mendaña from *Historia de la Marina Real Espanola* (Madrid, 1849).
(42) Rex Gilroy, *'Did Spanish Discover Us in 1558', Australasian Post*, December 31, 1988.
(43) Rex Gilroy, *'Did Spanish Discover Us in 1558', Australasian Post*, December 31, 1988.
(44) I planned to travel to the Blue Mountains to meet with Rex Gilroy and discuss this anomaly however my two emails to him remain unanswered.
(45) Rex & Heather Gilroy – *'The Temple of Nim'* - Newsletter – 2005.
(46) Rex Gilroy, *Did Spanish Discover Us in 1558, Australasian Post*, December 31, 1988.
(47) Awareness Quest, http://www.awarenessquest.com/research.htm
(48) Rex Gilroy, *Carving Out a New History, Australasian Post*, December 19, 1985
(49) Awareness Quest, *'Hidden Bits of History'*, http://www.awarenessquest.com/research.htm
(50) Awareness Quest, *'Hidden Bits of History'*, http://www.awarenessquest.com/research.htm
(51) Awareness Quest, *'Hidden Bits of History'*, http://www.awarenessquest.com/research.htm
(52) Awareness Quest, *'Hidden Bits of History'*, http://www.awarenessquest.com/research.htm
(53) Awareness Quest, *'Hidden Bits of History'*, http://www.awarenessquest.com/research.htm
(54) Awareness Quest, *'Hidden Bits of History'*, http://www.awarenessquest.com/research.htm
(55) Awareness Quest, *'Hidden Bits of History'*, http://www.awarenessquest.com/research.htm
(56) Awareness Quest, *'Hidden Bits of History'*, http://www.awarenessquest.com/research.htm
(57) Awareness Quest, *Australian Archaeological Anomalies* - www.awarenessquest.com/research2
(58) Rex & Heather Gilroy – *'The Temple of Nim'* - Newsletter – 2005.
(59) Awareness Quest, *'Hidden Bits of History'*, http://www.awarenessquest.com/research.htm
(60) Rex Gilroy, *Carving Out a New History, Australasian Post*, 19th December 1985.
(61) Rex Gilroy, *Carving Out a New History, Australasian Post*, 19th December 1985.
(62) Awareness Quest, *'Hidden Bits of History'*, http://www.awarenessquest.com/research.htm
(63) Christopher Knight & Robert Lomas, *'The Hiram Key': Pharaohs, Freemasons and the Discovery of the Secret Scrolls of Jesus.*
(64) Tore Kjeilen, Copyright 1996-2008 LookLex Ltd.
(65) R. A. Coombes, *'Naming of America'.*
(66) Andrew Sinclair, *'The Secret Scroll'* – A Chapel of The Grail, page 189.
(67) Ian Ross Vayro, *'They Lied to Us in Sunday School'*; Joshua Books.
(68) Ian Ross Vayro, *'They Lied to Us in Sunday School'*; Joshua Books.
(69) Andrew Sinclair, *'The Secret Scroll' – Sailing to the West*, page 150-1.
(70) Andrew Sinclair, *'The Secret Scroll' – Sailing to the West*, page 151.
(71) Source: Lincoln Sentinel-Republican, 12/12/1996.
(72) Source: Lincoln Sentinel-Republican, 12/12/1996,.
(73) Iamblichus Chalcidensis' account of an ancient Egyptian papyrus.
(74) Adam McLean, *Everburning Lights of Trithemius*; http://www.levity.com/alchemy/everbrn.html. This text from M. S. Ashmole 1408 page 239-

243, in Oxford, is ascribed to Johannes Trithemius (1462-1516), Abbot of Sponheim, an expert in cryptography and the occult arts.

(75) Adam McLean, *Ever burning Lights of Trithemius*; http://www.levity.com/alchemy/everbrn.html. This text from M. S. Ashmole 1408 page 239-243, in Oxford, is ascribed to Johannes Trithemius (1462-1516), Abbot of Sponheim, an expert in cryptography and the occult arts.

(76) http://www.geocities.com/athens/Olympus/6581/ancient_lights.html

(77) http://www.geocities.com/athens/Olympus/6581/ancient_lights.html

(78) *Perpetual Luminescence: The Undying Lights of the Ancients*; http://www.geocities.com/athens/Olympus/6581/ancient_lights.html quoting from; Andrew Tomas, *'We Are Not The First'.*

(79) *Perpetual Luminescence: The Undying Lights of the Ancients;* http://www.geocities.com/athens/Olympus/6581/ancient_lights.html quoting from; Andrew Tomas, *'We Are Not The First'.* This event is also covered in David Hatcher Childress, *'Technology of the Gods – The Incredible Sciences of The Ancients- The Enigma of Ancient Technology'.*

(80) *Perpetual Luminescence: The Undying Lights of the Ancients*; http://www.geocities.com/athens/Olympus/6581/ancient_lights.html quoting from; Andrew Tomas, *'We Are Not The First'.*

(81) *Lost Trails, Lost Cities*, by Colonel P. H. Fawcett. Funk & Wagnalls, New York, 1953.

(82) I am indebted to *Perpetual Luminescence: The Undying Lights of the Ancients*; http://www.geocities.com/athens/Olympus/6581/ancient_lights.html

(83) *Perpetual Luminescence: The Undying Lights of the Ancients*; http://www.geocities.com/athens/Olympus/6581/ancient_lights.html quoting from; Andrew Tomas, *'We Are Not The First'.*

(84) John Perkins, *'A Game as Old as Empire and the Web of Global Corruption'*, 2007, edited by Steven Hiatt, published by Berrett Koehler, UK. Distributed in the UK by McGraw-Hill.

(85) *'The Truth about Fisher's Ghost'*, first appeared in the famous monthly *Blackwood's Magazine* issued by the Edinburgh publishing firm William Blackwood & Sons, who published the periodical from 1817 to 1980. This version of the story was reprinted, with little change, in the book, *'The Valet's Tragedy and Other Studies'*, by Andrew Lang; published in 1903 by Longmans (London). I am indebted to *'The Truth About Fishers Ghost'*, http://simplyaustralia.net/issue6/fishers_ghost.html

(86) *'The Truth about Fisher's Ghost'*, first appeared in the famous monthly *Blackwood's Magazine* issued by the Edinburgh publishing firm William Blackwood & Sons, who published the periodical from 1817 to 1980. This version of the story was reprinted, with little change, in the book, *'The Valet's Tragedy and Other Studies'*, by Andrew Lang; published in 1903 by Longmans (London). I am indebted to *'The Truth About Fishers Ghost'*, http://simplyaustralia.net/issue6/fishers_ghost.html

(87) *'The Truth about Fisher's Ghost'*, first appeared in the famous monthly *Blackwood's Magazine* issued by the Edinburgh publishing firm William Blackwood & Sons, who published the periodical from 1817 to 1980. This version of the story was reprinted, with little change, in the book, *'The Valet's Tragedy and Other Studies'*, by Andrew Lang; published in 1903 by Longmans (London). I am indebted to *'The Truth About Fishers Ghost'*, http://simplyaustralia.net/issue6/fishers_ghost.html

(88) Ian Ross Vayro, *'God Save Us From Religion'*; page 65, Joshua Books.

(89) L. Michael Barré PhD., *'El, God of Israel —Yahweh, God of Judah'.*

(90) Ian Ross Vayro, *'God Save Us From Religion'*; page 213, Joshua Books.

(91) Ian Ross Vayro, *'God Save Us From Religion'*; pages 68 -69, Joshua Books.

(92) Ian Ross Vayro. *'Tears in Heaven'* pages 284-5 and also recorded in: *'Red Haired Mummies of Egypt' - UFO Trivia*, http://www.burlingtonnews.net/redhairedmummiesegypt.html

(93) Ian Ross Vayro. *'Tears in Heaven'* pages 284-5 and also recorded in: *'Red Haired Mummies of*

Egypt' - *UFO Trivia*, http://www.burlingtonnews.net/redhairedmummiesegypt.html

(94) Alan F. Ashford, *'When the Gods Came Down'*, Page 259.

(95) Alan F. Ashford, *'When the Gods Came Down'*, Page 259-260.

(96) Linda Moulton Howe; states that on 9 April 1983, while preparing to make a UFO documentary for HBO, she was informed by Richard Doty, a Special Agent with the Air Force Office of Special Investigations (AFOSI), at Kirtland Air Force Base in Albuquerque, that the government intended to release to her several thousand feet of film, taken between 1947 and 1964, showing crashed UFO discs and extraterrestrial bodies in historic footage to be included in the HBO documentary.
http://www.presidentialufo.com/disclosure_1980-85.htm It must be noted that Richard Doty was responsible for the cancellation of at least one episode of the proposed show when promised film footage did not arrive in time and is also held responsible by many for the emotional breakdown of Paul Bennewitz, when he released disinformation that discredited that researcher. Doty has subsequently left AFOSI and released his own book, *'Exempt From Disclosure'*, which purports to continue his disclosure of Air Force, National secrets. Many researchers note Doty's seeming exemption from the harassment suffered by other 'whistleblowers' and consider that Doty just may still be on the Air Force pay role, actively disseminating disinformation for the US Government.

(97) Copy of a letter dated 16 April 1954 from Gerald Light to Meade Layne about the events of 21-22 Feb 1954 at Muroc Field (now Edwards Air Force Base). Reported by William Cooper, *'A Covenant With Death'* http://www.alienshift.com/id40.html. Also recorded in William Cooper, *'Behold a Pale Horse'*, page 203, 1991.

(98) Dr. Richard Boylan, Ph.D., LLC, Post Office Box 22310, Sacramento, California 95822, United States of America.

(99) This information and The Apollo Astronaut conversations were mostly taken from the out-of-print book, *'Our Mysterious Spaceship Moon'* by Don Wilson (Dell, 1975). They were confirmed first hand with Amateur Radio enthusiasts who wish to remain anonymous.

(100) Source: *'Celestial Raise'* by Richard Watson and ASSK [Mt.Sashta, California] 1987 page 147 – 148. They were confirmed first hand with Amateur Radio enthusiasts who wish to remain anonymous.

(101) This information and The Apollo Astronaut conversations were mostly taken from the out-of-print book, *'Our Mysterious Spaceship Moon'* by Don Wilson, Dell Books USA 1975. They were confirmed first hand with Amateur Radio enthusiasts who wish to remain anonymous.

(102) from: http://www.holli.com/~boda/sightings.html which has now been removed from the www.

(103) Richard Andrews & Paul Schellenberger, *'The Tomb of God'*; Appendix 'E' page 451, Little, Brown & Company, Great Britain 1996.

(104) 2005 Sum mum. All Rights Reserved, *'Explore, Wonder, Discover'*. TM.

(105) 2005 Sum mum. All Rights Reserved, *'Explore, Wonder, Discover'*. TM.

(106) Ian Ross Vayro, *'Tears in Heaven'*, page 425-6; Joshua Books.

(107) Dan Brown, *'The Da Vinci Code'*, Doubleday, 2003 USA.

(108) Richard Andrews & Paul Schellenberger, *'The Tomb of God'*; Appendix 'E', page. 451, Little, Brown & Company, Great Britain 1996.

(109) Richard Andrews & Paul Schellenberger, *'The Tomb of God'*, Appendix 'E', page. 451, Little, Brown & Company, Great Britain 1996.

(110) Dan Brown, *'The Da Vinci Code'*, Doubleday, 2003 USA.

(111) Deborah R. Fowler, *'The Algorithmic Beauty of Sea Shells'* (Virtual Laboratory) in hardcover by Hans Meinhardt, Przemyslaw Prusinkiewicz.

(112) Richard Andrews & Paul Schellenberger, *'The Tomb of God'*, Appendix 'E', page 451, Little, Brown & Company, Great Britain 1996.

(113) Richard Andrews & Paul Schellenberger, *'The Tomb of God'*, Appendix 'E', page 451, Little, Brown & Company, Great Britain 1996.
(114) T, A. Davis, *'Fibonacci Numbers for Palm Foliar Spirals'*, Acta Botanica Neelandica, Vol 19, 1970, pages 236-243.
(115) Richard Andrews & Paul Schellenberger, *'The Tomb of God'*; Appendix 'E', page 451, Little, Brown & Company, Great Britain 1996.
(116) P. Prusinkiewicz, and A. Lindenmayer, *'The Algorithmic Beauty of Plants'*, published by Springer-Verlag (Second printing 1996)
(117) Richard Andrews & Paul Schellenberger, *'The Tomb of God'*, Appendix 'E', page. 451, Little, Brown & Company, Great Britain 1996.
(118) The author holds an advanced certificate as a Scientific Instrument Maker, as part of the Electronic Engineering Trades Group and has checked this concept with colleagues.
(119) Wikipedia, .wikipedia.org/wiki/Bezoar.
(120) *'Toad Venom'*, Time Magazine, 17 June 1929. http://www.time.com/time/magazine/article/0,9171,723727,00.html
(121) The author holds an advanced certificate as a Scientific Instrument Maker, as part of the Electronic Engineering Trades Group and has checked this concept with colleagues.
(122) I am indebted to Dr. Karl Kruszelnicki, *'Please Explain'*, page 207 for leading me to the site: http://www.wymsey.co.uk/wymchon/cooking.htm
(123) Professor A. Colin Renfrew, *'Before Civilisation, the Radiocarbon Revolution and Prehistoric Europe'*, 1973, London: Pimlico.
(124) Erich Zehren, *'The Crescent and the Bull'*, page 300.
(125) Ian Ross Vayro, *'They Lied to Us in Sunday School'*, Joshua Books.
(126) Isaiah's passage was recorded this way in early Bibles and this is documented by Zechariah Sitchin, *'The Twelfth Planet'*, page 145.
(127) Zechariah Sitchin, *'The Twelfth Planet'*, page 145 -147.
(128) Dr Karl Kruszelnicki, *'Please Explain'* page 211.
(129) Dr Karl Kruszelnicki, *'Please Explain'* page 211-213.
(130) Ian Ross Vayro, *'God Save Us From Religion'*, page 33-4, Joshua Books.
(131) Robert J. Gillooly, *'All About Adam & Eve'*, page 21.
(132) Robert J. Gillooly, *'All About Adam & Eve'*, page 25.
(133) Ian Ross Vayro, *'God Save Us From Religion'* page 108, Joshua Books.
(134) Karen Waryas, *'The Ancient Egyptians and the River Nile'* http://www.ems.psu.edu/academic/cause2001/waryas. The Egyptians not only depended on the Nile for their livelihoods; they also considered it to be a Deific force of the universe, to be respected and honoured if they wanted it to treat them favourably in return. Until quite recently, the rise of the Nile was celebrated on June 17, called Leylet el-Nuktah, or the *Night of the Drop*, as it was believed that on that night, a single mighty drop fell from the sky somewhere upstream to cause the Nile to rise. Though they could not control the river, they built large, complex irrigation systems to take advantage of the floods. Although fairly rare, there were times when floodwaters did not reach acceptable heights, causing mass famine and civil disturbance throughout the nation. To try to prevent this from happening, the Egyptians prayed to several Gods, including Hapi, the Nile God and Khnemu, the God of cool waters but did not involve a specific Rain God. The Egyptians respected the Nile, because to them it was considered a God that could bestow the gifts of a good flood upon them, or choose not to, if it was miffed. They understood and feared the consequences of losing the good will of the river, praising it in festivals and asking for its strength to aid them in their goals.
(135) Dr. Alvin Boyd Kuhn, Ph.D. *'The Great Myth of the Sun-Gods'*, Brian Buckner-El, Copyright: © 2007, Axum Publications. Quoted by Gerald Massey, *'Paul, the Gnostic Opponent of Peter, not an Apostle of Historic Christianity'*. 2006. See also: *'Natural Genesis'* for references to

authorities, reprinted from *The Agnostic Journal* (London), October 3, 1891.

(136) Antoine Court de Gébelin, *'Le Monde Primitif Analyse et Compare aver le Mond Morderne'* (a monumental work of Eight volumes), Paris, 1782.

(137) Gérard-Anaclet-Vincent Encausse, under his adopted name Papus; *'Le Tarot des Bohemiens: le plus Ancient livre du Monde'* (The Tarot of the Gypsies: The Most Ancient Book in the World). This has been wrongly translated and is often incorrectly known in English speaking societies as; *'The Tarot of the Bohemiens'*. This quotation also notes the Greek association of the Egyptian God Thoth, with the master alchemist Hermes Trismegistus.

(138) Samuel Roberts, *'The Gypsies': (their origin, continuance and destination.)* London 1836.

(139) Tony Bushby, *'The Secret in the Bible'*, page 185, Joshua Books.

(140) Granville C. Cunningham, *'Bacon's Secret Disclosed'*, 1911.

(141) Tony Bushby, *'The Secret in the Bible'*, pages 184-5, Joshua Books.

(142) Lewis Spence, *'Encyclopaedia of Occultism'*, 1889.

(143) Tony Bushby, *'The Secret in the Bible'*, page 187, Joshua Books.

(144) Tony Bushby, *'The Secret in the Bible'*, page 190, Joshua Books.

(145) Laurence Gardner, *'Lost Secrets of the Sacred Ark'*, page 260.

(146) Laurence Gardner, *'Lost Secrets of the Sacred Ark'*, page 19.

(147) Stuart Nettleton, *'The Alchemy Key'*, page 340.

(148) Eustace Mullins, *'Mullin's New History of the Jews'*. The International Institute of Jewish Studies, 1968. (Updated August 25, 2004) In the chapter entitled, *'Jews and Ritual Murder'*, on page 51 Mullins writes, *'There are so many thousands of well-attested examples of Jewish murder of children that we need cite only a few.'* In the book *'Excavations at Gezer'*, the archaeologist Robert Alexander Stewart Macalister (1870-1950) notes that the bodies of sacrificed young children are found in every strata of Jewish remains from earliest times. Photographs of the children's bodies are published in Macalister's book, although the book itself, like most works which attest to the criminal nature of the Jew, is now almost unattainable. It is classified as a rare book, and most rare book dealers are Jews.

(149) Stuart Nettleton, *'The Alchemy Key'*, Page 92

(150) Ian Ross Vayro, *'God Save Us From Religion'*, page 85, Joshua Books.

(151) Ian Ross Vayro, *'God Save Us From Religion'*, page 131, Joshua Books.

(152) ' *Hidden Bits of History'*, Awareness Quest; http://www.awarenessquest.com/research.htm

(153) Greg Jefferys, *'The Stradbroke Island Galleon-The Mystery of the Ship in the Swamp'*, Angus & Robertson.

(154) Stuart Duncan, *'The Discovery of Australia: The Portuguese Priority Reconsidered'*, Victorian Historical Journal, Vol. 68 no.1 April 1997, pp. 64-78)

(155) Bret Green, *'The Gympie Pyramid Mysteries'*, *The Ancient Seafarers*, page 29.

(156) Heritage Council of Victoria; http://www.heritage.vic.gov.au/page.asp?ID=121.

(157) Heritage Council of Victoria; http://www.heritage.vic.gov.au/page.asp?ID=12.

(158) Heritage Council of Victoria; http://www.heritage.vic.gov.au/page.asp?ID=12

(159) J.R. Carroll, 1989, *'Harpoons to Harvest: The story of Charles and John Mills, Pioneers of Port Fairy'*, Warrnambool Institute Press, Warrnambool, Victoria, pp.78-79) as reported by The Heritage Council of Victoria; http://www.heritage.vic.gov.au/page.asp?ID=121.

(160) *'Hidden Bits of History'*, Awareness Quest; http://www.awarenessquest.com/research.htm

(161) Bret Green, *'The Gympie Pyramid Mysteries'*, *The Ancient Seafarers*, page 29.

(162) Heritage Council of Victoria; http://www.heritage.vic.gov.au/page.asp?ID=12

(163) I am indebted to Tom Ammerlaan for his information on Dutch Australians and for his excellent research and detective work. http://www.ammerlaan.demon.nl/EARLY.HTM

(164) Leeds Mercury, 25 January 1834, *'Discovery of a white colony on the north shore of New Holland'*.

(165) Australian Map Circle, 2003;

www.accessmylibrary.com/coms2/summary_0286-9152341_ITM. This group acknowledge the assistance and collaboration of Les Hiddins and Andrew S. Cook.

(166)) I am indebted to Tom Ammerlaan for his information on Dutch Australians and for his excellent research and detective work. http://www.ammerlaan.demon.nl/EARLY.HTM

(167)) I am indebted to Tom Ammerlaan for his information on Dutch Australians and for his excellent research and detective work. http://www.ammerlaan.demon.nl/EARLY.HTM

(168) *'Australian Dreaming - 40,000 years of Aboriginal History'* by Jennifer Isaacs, Lansdowne Press, 1980.

(169) State Library of Victoria - La Trobe Journal, *'God's One Country: The Depiction of Asians by Australian Children's Authors'*; http://calisto.slv.vic.gov.au/latrobejournal/issue/latrobe-60/t1-g-t7.html.

(170) *'Australian Dreaming - 40,000 years of Aboriginal History'* by Jennifer Isaacs, Lansdowne Press, 1980.

(171) Article by Eric Norman; reproduced from: *'Gods Demons and UFO's'* by P. Warren Smith & Brad Steiger. Lancer books New York. This story is also spread by Jonathan Gray.

(172) Reference gathered from personal visits to the sites; discussions by email with Brett Green to whom I am indebted for his vast research and knowledge; *'Australia's Lost Pyramid'*, by Brett J. Green and *'In Quest of Australia's Lost Pyramids'*, by Anthony G. Wheeler.

(173) Greg Jeffrey, *'The Gympie Pyramid'* as recorded in Bret Green, *'The Gympie Pyramid Mysteries'*, An Archaeologist's Summary, page 21-22.

(174) Reference gathered from personal visits to the sites; discussions by email with Brett Green to whom I am indebted for his vast research and knowledge; *'Australia's Lost Pyramid'*, by Brett J. Green and *'In Quest of Australia's Lost Pyramids'*, by Anthony G. Wheeler.

(175) John Grant, *'Monster Mysteries'*, page 48,Quintet Publishing, New Burlington Books.

(176) John Grant, *'Monster Mysteries'*, page 49,Quintet Publishing, New Burlington Books.

(177) John Grant, *'Monster Mysteries'*, page 47,Quintet Publishing, New Burlington Books.

(178) John Grant, *'Monster Mysteries'*, page 46,Quintet Publishing, New Burlington Books.

(179) Ian Ross Vayro, *'God Save Us From Religion'*, page 19, Joshua Books.

(180) David Icke, *'The Biggest Secret'*, and this is also fully covered in both; Fritz Springmeier, *'Bloodlines of the Illuminati'* and Fritz Springmeier & Cisco Wheeler, *'The 13 Illuminati Bloodlines'*. These authors all expose the funding and 'miraculous' founding of religions such as the Mormons, Jehovah's Witnesses, etc.

(181) Book of Abraham 1 : 21-27.

(182) Rene A. Schwaller de Lubicz, *'Sacred Science - Inner Traditions'*, 1988, page 105.

(183) Ian Ross Vayro, *'They Lied to Us in Sunday School'*, page 237 & *'God Save Us From Religion'* page 84, Joshua Books.

(184) Richard Dawkins, *'The God Delusion'*, 2006, Bantam Press London, a division of Transworld Publishers.

(185) Ian Ross Vayro, *'Tears in Heaven'* page 432, Joshua Books.

(186) David Icke, *'The Biggest Secret'*, page 323, David Icke Books 1999, Bridge of Love Publications U.S.A.

(187) David Icke, *'The Biggest Secret'*, page 323, David Icke Books 1999, Bridge of Love Publications U.S.A.

(188) Allen Douglas and Michael J. Sharp, *'Mass Murder in Australia: Tavistock's Martin Bryant'*

(189) Allen Douglas and Michael J. Sharp, *'Mass murder in Australia: Tavistock's Martin Bryant'*

(190) Dr. William Sargent author of *'Battle for the Mind: A Physiology of Conversion and Brain-Washing'* (1957)

(191) Jim Keith, *'The Octopus'* page 143, as reported by Henry Makow, *'Controlled Chaos- War on Terror is Elite Mind Control'*.

(192) Jim Keith, *'Mind Control World Control'* (1997) page 44.

(193) Jim Keith, *'Mind Control World Control'* (1997) page 44, as reported by Henry Makow, *'Controlled Chaos - War on Terror is Elite Mind Control'.*
(194) The elites had to have the Branch Davidian Village eliminated because: http://www.apfn.org/apfn/elites.htm
(195) David Icke, *'The Biggest Secret'*, page 298 and 299; David Icke Books 1999. Bridge of Love Publications U.S.A.
(196) *'7 Insane Conspiracies That Actually Happened'*; http://www.cracked.com/article_15974_p2.html . Copyright © 2005 - 2007 Cracked Entertainment, Inc.
(197) *'7 Insane Conspiracies That Actually Happened'*; http://www.cracked.com/article_15974_p2.html Copyright © 2005 - 2007 Cracked Entertainment, Inc.
(198) Many thanks to Wikipedia, the free encyclopedia.
(199) Translation by M. R. James, *'The Apocalypse of Peter'*, - The Apocryphal New Testament, 1924.
(200) Ian Ross Vayro, *'They Lied to Us in Sunday School'*, page 304, Joshua Books.
(201) Ian Ross Vayro, *'God Save Us From Religion'*, page 60, Joshua Books.
(202) Ian Ross Vayro, 'They Lied to Us in Sunday School' Joshua Books.
(203) Ian Ross Vayro, *'God Save Us From Religion'*, page 73, Joshua Books.
(204) All these phenomena have been discovered on giant skeletons from the Ohio burial mounds and can be found on a web search.
(205) Ian Ross Vayro, *'God Save Us From Religion'*, page 73, Joshua Books.
(206) *Strand Magazine*, Britain, December 1895. Covered in Ian Ross Vayro, *'God Save Us From Religion'*, page 73, Joshua Books.
(207) W. G. Wood-Martin, *'Traces of the Elder Faiths of Ireland'*, London 1902.
(208) *'The American Anthropologist'*, February 1896, page 66. http://www.subversiveelement.com/FossilizedHumanFootprints.html
(209) Josiah Priest, *'American Antiquities'*, page 150. http://www.subversiveelement.com/FossilizedHumanFootprints.html
(210) Karl Shakur - *'OOPARTS (out of place artefacts) & Ancient High Technology - Giant Tales'.* http://www.s8int.com/giants6.html
(211) Frederick P. Beierle, *'Man Dinosaur and History'*, pages 22-29; Bible-Science Newsletter April 15, 1976; Pursuit, 9;83-84, Fall 1976.
(212) U.S. Army report, 1981.
(213) From the publication, *'The History of Marion County, Ohio'*.(complied from past accounts, published in 1883).
(214) From the publication, *'The History of Brown County, Ohio'*, (complied from past accounts, published in 1883).
(215) Glen Lough, *'Now and Long Ago - A History of the Marion County Area'*, (1969) This citation on West Virginia courtesy Dave Cain.
(216) Neville Spearman, *'Road in the Sky'*, UK 1959
(217) Tony Bushby, *'The Secret in the Bible'*, page 70, Joshua Books.
(218) Tony Bushby, *'The Secret in the Bible'*, page 69, Joshua Books.
(219) Professor W. B. Emery from his book *'Archaic Egypt'.*
(220) Adamantius Origen (185 - 251 A.D.) *'Contra Celsus'*, Throughout Book VI, Chapter I.
(221) *Nature*, 45:157, December 17,1891.
(222) *The Indianapolis News*, November 10, 1975.
(223) Nevada State Historical Society Quarterly 1975, pages 153 - 167, Reno Nevada.
(224) TV Documentary viewed by this author.
(225) Harold T. Wilkins, *'Mysteries of Ancient South America'*,1998. Reprint of the 1947 classic.

(226) Recorded as a first hand report
(227) Recorded as a first hand report to this author.
(228) Jeffery Blair Latta, *'The Franklin Conspiracy'*, Canada 2001.
(229) The Book of Baruch is considered to be inspired apocryphal scripture by many scholars but was classed as canonical only by the Catholic Church. It commences with the introduction, *'Baruch the son of Nerias, the son of Maasias, the son of Sedecias, the son of Asadias, the son of Chelcias, wrote in Babylon ...'*
(230) Ted Twietmeyer, *'Evidence That Giants Walked the Earth'*, Nexus magazine April-May 2008.
(231) Thomas Paine, *'The Age of Reason'*, the Library of Liberal Arts, Bobbs-Merril, 1794.
(232) Encyclopedia Britannica, 9th. Edition, Volume 10, page 783.
(233) Encyclopedia Britannica, 9th. Edition, Volume 10, page 783
(234) Documented by Irenaeus of Lyons, translated by John Keble, London 1872, quoted by Tony Bushby, *'The Crucifixion of Truth'*, page 58, Joshua Books, Australia.
(235) Eusebius, *'Ecclesiastical History'* ii.
(236) Gerald Massey, *'Ancient Egypt - The Light of The World'*, Book 12, *'The Mysteries and the Miracles'*, Original 1907, Black Classic Press.
(237) Thomas Paine, *'The Age of Reason'*, the Library of Liberal Arts, Bobbs-Merril, 1794.
(238) Ian Ross Vayro, *'God Save Us From Religion'*, page 198, Joshua Books.
(239) This was covered in Ian Ross Vayro, *'God Save Us From Religion'*, page 73, Joshua Books.
(240) This was covered in Ian Ross Vayro, *'God Save Us From Religion'*, page 73, Joshua Books.
(241) This was covered in Ian Ross Vayro, *'God Save Us From Religion'*, page 73, Joshua Books.
(242) Carl G. Jung, *'Synchronicity an acausal connecting principle'*; Routledge & Kegan Paul, 1977.
(243) A firsthand report to the editors, *'Mysteries of the Unexplained'*, Readers Digest General Books, 1982, page 47.
(244) Alan Vaughan, *'Incredible Coincidence'*, Readers Digest, August 1979, page 120.
(245) Telephone interview with Mrs. Arthur Figlock, Harper Wood, Michigan, *'Mysteries of the Unexplained'*, Readers Digest General Books, 1982, page 63.
(246) Ripley's Believe It or Not! page 133.
(247) *'The Unexplained'*, page 659, Orbis Publishing Limited, London.
(248) John Mitchell and Robert J.M. Rickard, *'Phenomena: A Book of Wonders'*, page 90.
(249) Readers Digest January 1980 page 78.
(250) Edward H. Southern, *'My Remembrance; The Melancholy Tale of "Me"'*, page 341.
(251) Noel Nouet, *'Histoire de Tokyo'* page 98.
(252) Colin Wilson, *'Enigmas & Mysteries'*, page 131.
(253) *'Mysteries of the Unexplained'*, Readers Digest General Books, 1982, page 47.
(254) Colin Wilson, *'Enigmas and Mysteries'*, page 29.
(255) John Mitchell, *'Eccentric Lives and Peculiar Notions'*, page 101.
(256) Andrew Sinclair, *'The Secret Scroll'*, Page 60-62, published by Christopher Sinclair-Stevenson, London and various works of Tony Bushby.
(257) John William Draper, (1811-1882) *'History of the Conflict Between Science and Religion'*, page 270, also documented by Tony Bushby, *'The Crucifixion of Truth'* page 142, Joshua Books.
(258) Francis Hackett, *'Henry VIII'*, page 11, 234 also documented by Tony Bushby, *'The Crucifixion of Truth'* page 143, Joshua Books.
(259) Philip Melancthon, 1497-1560, (Melanchthon is Greek for his birth name Schwarzert – black earth) a German reformer who assisted Martin Luther, *'Eclectic Review'*. also quoted by Tony Bushby, *'The Crucifixion of Truth'*, page 140-142, Joshua Books.
(260) John Calvin, *'Institutes of the Christian Religion'*; 1536.
(261) Catholic Encyclopaedia i 752.
(262) Tony Bushby, *'The Crucifixion of Truth'* page 144, Joshua Books.
(263) Stuart Nettleton, *'The Alchemy Key'*, Page 315.

(264) Bishop Robert Southerly, *'Book of the Church'*, Fourth edition, London – 1837.
(265) Tony Bushby, *'The Crucifixion of Truth'* page 148, Joshua Books.
(266) Rena F. LaCaria, *'Leonardo, The Man Behind the Shroud'*; http://www.renaflacaria.com/press-release.html
(267) http://www.morepizza.com/pages/now4.html ; a creation of bolmedia.com 2005.
(268) http://www.morepizza.com/pages/now4.html ; a creation of bolmedia.com 2005.
(269) Ian Ross Vayro. *'Tears in Heaven'* pages 91-2, Joshua Books, 2008.
(270) Ian Ross Vayro. *'Tears in Heaven'* pages 92, Joshua Books, 2008.
(271) Read the expose of how this Pope was murdered, in the classic, David Yallop, *'In God's Name'*, winner of the Gold Dagger Award for best non-fiction. Over 5,000,000 copies sold. 1984, Carroll & Graf Publishers
(272) From the Book Review, *'In God's Name - An Investigation into the Murder of Pope John Paul I'*, by David Yallop, original release 1984, Carroll & Graf Publishers; http://www.puritans.net/ bookreviewingodsname.htm
(273) Brian Desborough, *'A Blueprint For A Better World'*, page 11, 2002, TGS publishers.
(274) Professor Martin Buber, *'I and Thou'*; (Ich und Du, 1923) translated by Ronald Gregor Smith,1958 New York: Charles Scribner's Sons.
(275) Roy Arundhati, *'The Guardian'*, Weekly Newspaper U.K 2nd April 2003.
(276) Roy Arundhati, *'The Guardian'*, Weekly Newspaper U.K 2nd April 2003.
(277) Brian Desborough, *'A Blueprint For A Better World'*, page 13, 2002, TGS publishers.
(278) Brian Desborough, *'A Blueprint For A Better World'*, page 15-16, 2002, TGS publishers.
(279) From the David-Wynn: Miller DVD. It has been stated and rumored that David-Wynn: Miller is a 33rd degree Mason and until this is confirmed or rejected we should be cautious about dis-information. I would appreciate David-Wynn: Miller going public to 'scotch' this rumor, if it is false.
(280) From the David-Wynn: Miller DVD.
(281) From the David-Wynn: Miller DVD.
(282) From the David-Wynn: Miller DVD
(283) Brian Desborough, *'A Blueprint For A Better World'*, page 24, 2002, TGS publishers.
(284) From the David-Wynn: Miller DVD
(285) From the David-Wynn: Miller DVD
(286) From the David-Wynn: Miller DVD
(287) Robert Guffy, *'George W. Bush is Not a Christian'*, New Dawn Magazine, January-February 2007.
(288) Tom Engelhardt, *'Flushing Cheney'*, September 2004, www.motherjone.com/news/dailymojo/2004/02/02_500.
(289) I am indebted to Bill Dash, *'Far Shores'*, 24 Aug 2003.
(290) Rixon Stewart, *'Was Timothy McVeigh Really Executed?'* http://www.thetruthseeker.co.uk/article.asp?ID=154
(291) Rixon Stewart, *'Was Timothy McVeigh Really Executed?'* http://www.thetruthseeker.co.uk/article.asp?ID=154
(292) www.rumormillnews.net/cgi-bin/config.pl?read=10133
(293) Pentagon Denies Saddam's Capture Staged, http://www.abovetopsecret.com/forum/thread125731/pg1.
(294) *'Iraqi Commander Swears he saw USAF fly Saddam out of Baghdad'*; Bill Dash - Alamo Christian Ministries Online 10/16/2003, www.thetruthseeker.co.uk/article.asp?id=1011
(295) *'Mysteries of the Unexplained'*, Readers Digest General Books, 1982, page 173-4.
(296) *'Mysteries of the Unexplained'*, Readers Digest General Books, 1982, page 173-4.
(297) William G. Roll, *'The Poltergeist'*, page 30.
(298) This letter was written and posted by James M. Kauffman, Ed.D. Professor Emeritus, Dept. of Curriculum, Instruction and Special Education, University of Virginia.

From the publisher

As publishers Joshua Books believe in freedom of speech and your right to have access to all points of view. The controversy created by Author Ian Ross Vayro will continue as more and more people seek the Truth.

Joshua Books is also the publisher for the internationally acclaimed author Tony Bushby.

If you have enjoyed reading *'Strange & Mysterious Anomalies'* then please take time to look at other titles by these authors, featured over the following pages.

We also invite you to log on to www.joshuabooks.com and subscribe to our **free newsletter.** That way you will be kept right up to date with all that is happening at Joshua Books.

Joshua Books

JoshuaBooks.com

ALSO FROM IAN ROSS VAYRO

To purchase visit www.joshuabooks.com

THEY LIED TO US IN SUNDAY SCHOOL

In this book Ian Ross Vayro has given us the facts in a way that is impossible to dispute. This book provides proof of the tampering that has altered the Word of God into the deception that we have today. Ian is trained in Archaeology and Ancient History and has spent a lifetime studying Theology.

GOD SAVE US FROM RELIGION

Read about the deception, tampering and conspiracy within the Roman Church. No stone is left unturned as Ian Ross Vayro walks us through various versions of the Bible, Sumerian tablets and early Egyptian papyrus records in a vigilant search for the truth.

TEARS IN HEAVEN

Despite a mandate of helping the people of this planet, the cleverly veneered assurances of world-wide Governments and Church Leaders under a guise of 'goodness' have served only to create distrust, disharmony and religious wars. There is a reason that conflict is occuring.

BOOKS BY TONY BUSHBY

To purchase visit www.joshuabooks.com

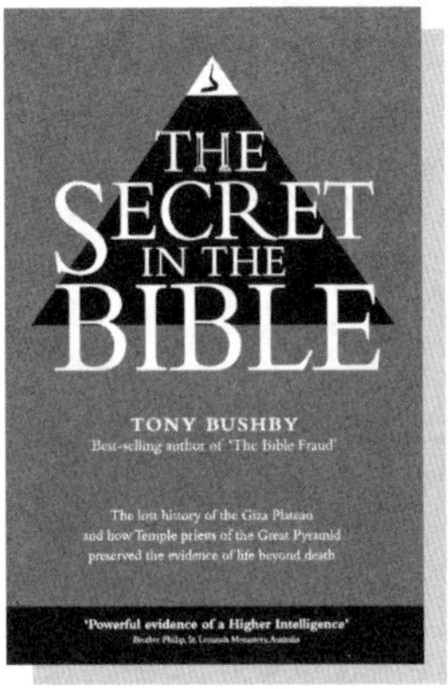

What others have said about Tony Bushby's books...

I thoroughly enjoyed Tony Bushby's ***The Bible Fraud****. Its tale ended my own research into the origins and source material of the Bible (not for a book! Just my own curious hunger to know!). This author has done in a careful and extremely well researched book, far better than most in this genre. The attention to detail, which I have confirmed myself over the past twenty years from various sources, is validated and more accurate than many academic papers found in our universities.*

It is undoubtedly the most important book on Christianity and the Roman legacy ever written, and most likely will have the least impact because it explodes the mythology and power basis for a religion which will be impossible for most to swallow. It opens eyes to the true wonders and we finally put away the destructive toy of over simplified pacification tripe that exists in political, commercial establishment religions.

MAE, Isle of Sanday, Orkney, Scotland

A real truth seeker will realise that a guy who brings his bedroll to a library so he can research night and day would be an infinitely more reliable source than a writer whose main focus is fame and ego enhancement.
Congratulations Tony Bushby.

Claudia, USA